CATALYST

CATALYST

In the Wake of the Great Bhola Cyclone

Cornelia Rohde

Silence. No crows cackled, no cows rumbled, no palm leaves rustled. It was as if all life had been snuffed out. Reeling from the oppressive odor, Jon, Viquar and Mahmoud force their way to shore through a surface floating with decaying flesh. The dead bob around in the water, or are strewn on the shore, washed up by the tide to bloat and rot in the sun. It is a scene they will never forget.

—landing on the island of Manpura after the cyclone,
November 23, 1970

Contents

Acknowledgments

Jon, for being my keystone

Father Timm, for his elucidations and his mighty spirit

Keith Miller, for his responsive editing

Judy Conway, for serving as my bell-metal sounding board

Emily and Ola d'Aulaire, for handing me secluded use of their top floor

Jane Gilman, for putting a half nelson around the neck of one adversarial chapter

My writing retreat-ants, for their kindred spirits

Bread for the World, for digging deep into their archives

Walter Schweppe, for his skillful translation

The mice in the barn, for their restraint

Author's Note

"Tell what is yours to tell . . . Because someone has to bear witness."

—Margaret Atwood, *Nine Beginnings*

"The 1970 cyclone is a legend in our family, but we only hear bits and pieces of it. We want to know the whole story. If you don't write it, Candy Aunty, no one will." So, Simone, here goes . . .

This is a telling of how a group of friends of many nationalities were able to establish an effective relief operation after the massive cyclone of November 1970 in the Bay of Bengal; an effort that moved within a few weeks into stages of rehabilitation and development, before civil war scattered most of us into different lives in different lands. Material for this account comes from cartons of original field notes saved for forty years in the loft of the Rohde family barn on Cape Cod. The mice must have known they would be of use some day and left them alone. Primary documentation gives this account an accuracy that would never have been possible by drawing only on shifting memories. While seen mostly through my eyes, in the spirit of making it a group memoir, I contacted a significant number of participants to ask for their reflections about their involvement with Manpura. I have attempted to include their comments wherever relevant.

This is a work of creative nonfiction, with the writing at all times solidly grounded in fact. At times, such as when I take the voice of the victims of the storm, I have reimagined or reconstructed the way things happened to reflect the essence of the scene and event in the minds and hearts of the people who lived through it. In any instance where I have reimagined an event or created a conversation, I have made every effort to hold to the profound truth of the experience. The point of view and any errors are mine, but I hope they are few and will be forgiven.

A Note on the Text Elements

Original communications to or from the field and letters are in a font resembling the old typewriter we had on Manpura: `like this`.

Passages about political situation are marked by a flag:

Voices of islanders are marked by a palm tree:

"Of the ten deadliest tropical storms in world history, eight have occurred in the Bay of Bengal, and all have over 100,000 fatalities attributed to them." www.island.net

Prologue

Ganges Delta, East Bengal, November 12, 1970

The dogs were nervous, alert and watchful. Abdul couldn't sleep. Bursts of wind and curtains of rain had been intensifying for several days. Then he heard a sound he had never heard before, like the roar of a maddened jinn. The air filled with a sharpening wind, and he knew something fierce was coming. He shouted to his wife, Fatima, to grab their infant Jarita. He scooped up his young son Fazil. Rain pummeled them. The wind raged, forcing them to bend over as they tried to run into it. Seawater was already swirling around their legs, rising rapidly, threatening to pull them into its churning depths as they struggled up the trunk of a tall palm tree in the dark. With a sound like a dozen locomotives, a churning wall of muddy water engulfed them. "Climb, climb as high as you can!" he yelled to Fatima. Six-foot waves topped with foam tore at them as they clung, chafing them against the rough bark, tearing at their grip. "Allah, Allah! Save us. Save our children," his wife sobbed, choking on the sea. They could barely climb ahead of the raging, wind-driven water.

Abdul shakes as he tells his story. "I am the only one left," he laments. "The world was black and the wind was wild; so wild that everything flew around us. I clung to the trunk as tightly as I could. My arms ached terribly. I could hardly feel them because the rain was cold and stung me. I tried to hold my son against my chest with my arm around him, but the wind became so fierce I couldn't hang on to him anymore and he slipped out of my grip. I could still see my wife and baby on the tree next to me, but the water kept rising around us. It grew higher than the palm tree she was clinging to. It crashed over the tree with dreadful force. She swept right past me. I could hear her shrieking and I could do nothing." He stops and stares blankly. He can't go on.*

* There was an above-average lunar high tide on November 12. Average winds were estimated at 225 km per hour (140 mph).

"A churning wall of muddy water engulfed them."

In Dacca, the First Day After the Cyclone
November 13, 1970

On a cool November morning, following a night of heavy wind and rain, I sit cross-legged on a low divan with two friends in a sparsely furnished study in Gulshan, a newly developed upper-class garden suburb of Dacca. We wear traditional bright cotton saris with soft woolen shawls across our shoulders, our long hair twisted at the napes of our necks. Jasmine scents the room; one unfinished wall is open to the garden, allowing the fragrance to float freely through the moist air.

Runi remarks, "Strange to have rain this time of year, isn't it? It's usually dry in Hemanto season." She offers a plate of crisp, spicy *dal puri*s (puffed lentil pastries), freshly made that morning. We explode with laughter as we recall how, the night before, a journalist friend momentarily stunned his opponent in their hot debate by categorically declaring, "How can you have a valid political opinion? You've never been in jail!" As we warm our hands around steaming cups of fragrant tea, Putul, her younger sister, unfolds the *Pakistan Observer*. She reads out the headline: "50 feared lost in coastal cyclone." The casualties will climb to ten thousand times that figure—more than five hundred thousand estimated deaths. Sitting in that jasmine-scented room, none of us imagine how deeply we will change in the wake of this unprecedented storm.

We are shocked to learn that on the previous night, November 12, full moon and high tide coincided to create a killer storm that built up a twenty-foot wall of water surging with deadly force across the low-lying islands in the Bay of Bengal. We are vaguely aware of the numerous islands lying in the mouth of the Megna River as it pours the waters of the Ganges and the Brahmaputra into the bay—islands recently formed from rich river silt and settled by farmers desperate for land. We are completely ignorant of Manpura, Faizuddin and Sakuchia, a chain of narrow chars, or mud bars, about twenty miles long, less than two miles wide and only a few feet above sea level. We cannot foresee how involved we will become with these three remote islands.

When the deadly storm hit, we were enjoying an evening under the full moon with our friends in Dacca, unaware of the havoc happening south of us. More than half the population of thirty thousand inhabiting these three tiny islands, along with their livestock, boats, possessions and any buildings not made of concrete, were flung into the raging wind and sea, where most of the women, children, sick and elderly perished. The survivors were those strong enough to climb high up the trunks of palm trees and cling for their lives. As the storm subsided, both land and sea were littered with the dead. The Great Bhola Cyclone will attain the unfortunate distinction of being ranked as the deadliest tropical cyclone in recorded history.

The motivation and commitment that we pull from somewhere inside us in the days ahead springs from the certainty that whoever has lived through this terrible storm must be desperate for help. What we do in the following months is a result of the deep friendship among us and our circle of friends, whose strong connections formed several years prior to the storm.

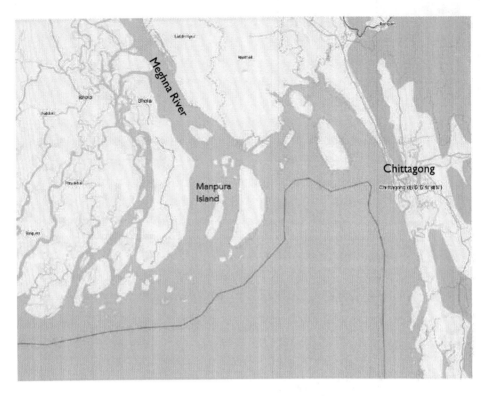

The Meghna estuary is famous for its funnel shape,
outlined on the map by the black line.

Like the rest of the Bangladesh coast, the Meghna estuary is famous for its funnel shape, which predisposes the estuary mouth to violent cyclones. The Meghna estuary is subject to cyclones and storm surges into both the easterly Sandwip and westerly Hatiya channels. About 41 per cent of cyclones in the Bay of Bengal travel through this funnel-shaped region each year. This environmental factor, coupled with the fact that rivers in Bengal are notorious for changing course almost overnight, makes the entire area highly vulnerable to violent storms.

—Wikipedia

A storm surge or wave is popularly but improperly called "tidal wave," because its main cause is not the tide. The surge is caused by high wind across the water surface, including the rise due to reduced atmospheric pressure. As the surge moves ahead into ever-shallower and more constricting channels, it builds up in height. The height of the surge is not only influenced by the daily tide at the time, whether it is high or low, but also by the phase of the moon, because at the full moon the highest tide of the month occurs.

—Fr. Richard Timm

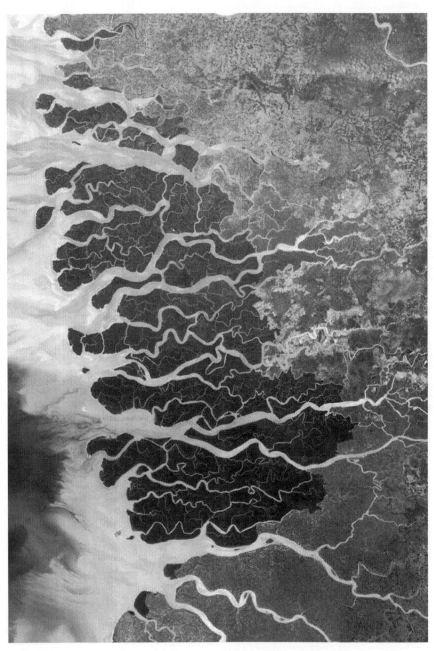

Tidal lands, Bay of Bengal

CHAPTER 1
Two Years Before the Cyclone

Boston, June 1968

A bomb explodes in our kitchen in Back Bay. My husband Jon, his scrubs spattered with blood, eyes sagging from another relentless thirty-six-hour shift at Boston City Hospital, detonates it. "I've been drafted," he announces. I feel our lives shatter.

It's almost impossible for America's doctors to escape being sent to Vietnam. We both decry our country's involvement in the war, but that won't help us. All medical personnel are vulnerable to military service.

Jon's professors at Harvard Medical School are horrified. They envision a different future for their top-ranking graduate. They coach Jon on how to fail the physical exam: "Tip over when they ask you to duck walk. Emphasize your congenital heart murmur." He follows their advice and fails to qualify. It is a brief reprieve. Conscription of doctors is relentless; many will serve on the front lines. By the time the second draft notice appears, he has explored options for alternate service. The most appealing is presented by his godparents' son-in-law, Bucky Greenough, who chose to fulfill his military duty at the Pakistan SEATO Cholera Research Laboratory (commonly called the CRL) in Dacca, East Pakistan.

When Jon is accepted, he learns he will undergo training in radio isotopes at Oak Ridge, Tennessee, to enable him to study the transport of electrolytes across intestinal membranes, the basic physiologic flaw causing cholera. "There goes my curriculum-writing career with the Newton Public Schools," flashes through my head, before I grab the atlas with excitement. We both agree cholera research is constructive work and, if we must go, the Ganges Delta is a better choice than the Mekong.

Most well-wishers send us off to Africa, saying, "Hope Dakar is a great experience." One thing is certain: Dacca is not on everyone's mental map. It clearly is not a sought-after travel destination. Arriving in the soggy heat of August, we wave at the hundreds gathered on the flat roof of the little airport and, to our amazement, they all wave back, as if they've been waiting only for us.

In the apartment temporarily assigned to us, the air conditioner keeps the humidity at bay. The cook rolls out a piecrust with a vinegar bottle while I read longed-for letters from home. Outside the window, skeletal women and children, under black umbrellas in the midday sun, pound bricks into small rocks on the stoneless alluvial plain.

Getting to know the neighbors

How to create building material on a stoneless delta:

hammer imported stones into small rocks . . .

. . . or turn bricks into rubble.

CHAPTER 2
1968–70: New Dimensions

Shortly after we arrive in the green, riverine world of Bengal, Jim Taylor, who has recently finished his service at the cholera lab, returns to Dacca from Boston to hand over his research project to Jon. We host a gathering of his friends, including a group of lively British-educated Bengalis who are close to Jim and his wife Anna.

"What brings you to Dacca?" Monowar Hussain asks me.

"Escaping the draft," I explain.

Monowar opposes the Vietnam War as vehemently as we do. Later, Viquar Choudhury joins me in a conversation about Shakespeare, and moves me on to the less-familiar ground of Tagore's poetry and an explanation of the ongoing Argatala Conspiracy trial of thirty-six Bengalis charged with planning secession of East from West Pakistan. As one of the barristers defending the accused, he is clearly sympathetic to the issues driving the conspiracy. His intelligent conversation is refreshing, especially after weeks of enduring expat-community gripers, who feel they have been exiled to a remote cow town. They wander the aisles of the commissary with outbursts such as: "Oh my God, where are the tins of mandarin oranges? Don't tell me they haven't arrived yet. How long can a shipment from the States possibly take?" At our official welcome, we are shocked when a consular briefing officer walks over to the window, looks out at the crowded streets and remarks, in what are intended to be reassuring words, "At the moment the natives are quiet."

Candy and Jon Rohde, 1968

I am equally weary of Bengali functions where I am segre-
gated from my husband and the other men, to sit with women
who treat me as a curiosity or ask, "How many children do you
have?", then sigh and look away. They have all borne children
when they were far younger than my twenty-seven years. I cover
my smile when they say they will pray for me at shrines. I feel if I
tell them we are deliberately planning when we want to have a
child, they will only be more confused.

Many women in the official expat community preside over
gatherings where bearers in starched white uniforms proffer
trays of cucumber sandwiches and whole grapefruit festooned
with skewered shrimp like tiny flags. Tea is politely dispensed
from silver services. I learn with relief that the spouses connected
to the cholera hospital are immersed in Bengali culture and embrace their environment with high spirits. My growing love of

Bengal is immediately enhanced by their enthusiasm and mentorship.

Rob and Quincy Northrup have been chosen as our cholera laboratory sponsors to help launch us into our new life. I marvel at how perfectly Quincy masters the intricate dance elements of *Bharat Natyam*, and I welcome being included in her yoga sessions with a pretzel-limbed teacher called Goshai, who confidently announces he can walk on water.

Yoga with Goshai

Quincy and Rob Northrup, 1969

Richard Cash is an old hand in Dacca. He tells us that when he first walked into his house, he thought he was sharing the place with the men dressed in starched white shirts and couldn't figure out why they refused to let him help with the housework. His travels in the region have already become legendary. Soon Jon finds himself on a trek with him into remote areas of the Chittagong Hill Tracts bordering Burma.

Richard Cash in the Chittagong Hill Tracts, 1969

At the CRL's field station in Matlab, we chuckle when George Curlin softly drawls "Hey shortstop" to the sick toddler he needs to examine. Richard's easygoing exploits and George's humorous comments give us a positive perspective on the challenges of living in Dacca. Jon is delighted to find that George will share a fourteen-foot sailboat with him and Pat Talmon, the administrator of the cholera hospital.

Our shared GP14 sailboat

Peggy Curlin's sunny laugh is infectious. She is happy to try out on her students the curriculum about Bengali culture the board of the small American school has asked me to develop, and amazes me with her skill as an actress in the local amateur theater.

Aysen Talmon, fluent in Bengali, is at ease bargaining in the markets, and is an unrivalled hostess, bringing people together with matchless flair.

Aysen Talmon, 1970

David Nalin is so comfortable in Bengali he can recite Tagore's poems by heart. He is also an avid connoisseur and collector of South Asian sculpture. Through them we are introduced to a wider circle of actively engaged expats, such as John and Myrtle Ratcliffe, who expose us to the world of fakirs and *Bauls*, the mystical folk singers of Bengal.

John Ratcliffe in 1968

When the cyclone strikes, many of the expats, including Richard, David, the Ratcliffes and the Northrups, will be gone from East Pakistan, their tour of duty complete, but their willingness to embrace new experiences creates a foundation that helps us reach out in the ensuing crisis. Although no longer living in Bengal, they respond to the relief effort from a distance in effective and heartfelt ways. While we thrive on the relationships we form within the lively expat community, friendship with our Bengali neighbors begins to establish new dimensions in our lives.

Expanding the Circle

It is easy to follow up on Jim's introduction to the Choudhurys, because Viquar and his wife Runi live only a few streets beyond the scrubby stretch of open land next to the house we have been issued in Gulshan. My cook warns, "Don't walk there, Mem-sahib. It's full of cobras, and jackals will surely attack you and tear you to pieces." Their howls often wake us up at night.

Where the jackals hang out

Ignoring his admonitions, I risk going on foot the short distance to their house. It is much easier to walk than to use the phone. Telephone communication is incredibly frustrating, with operators struggling to make connections. One day, when Jon becomes more and more furious after shouting "seven, eight, six, four" and having it repeated "three, seven, five, two" by the operator, he rips the wires out of the wall and smashes the heavy black instrument in frustration. We hardly miss it, because it is common custom to drop in on one another. We soon find ourselves welcomed by the Choudhurys and their circle of stimulating friends, who include newspaper editors, journalists, economists, barristers, writers, scientists and politicians.

Jim Taylor with Runi and Viquar Choudhury in the garden of the unfinished house at Road 113, Gulshan in 1967 (*photo courtesy of Jim Taylor*)

The unfinished house on Road 113 is their chosen meeting point, the epicenter of their intellectual debates. One defends communism, another democracy, another socialism and secularism. They are the first to admit that if you put three Bengalis together they will form two political parties and a literary magazine, but at heart they are all strongly Bengali, and unified in their resentment of Pakistan's perceived exploitation of their country. Discussions center on the tensions growing out of Mujib's controversial call for East Pakistan's provincial autonomy.

Mass civil disobedience in the form of general strikes, or *hartals*, begins. Jon walks in with a shocked face early one morning after his tennis game. He shakily tells me, "Someone smashed a brick through the windshield of our VW. It just missed my head." We quickly learn to stay off the streets during a general strike. Anyone who does not heed the warning risks being a target. Jackals in the park seem less of a threat than angry protestors.

Long evenings are filled with the animated discussions of our circle of friends, while during the day Runi and I often set out together. I plunge into our excursions with enthusiasm, fascinated by a world so radically different from my Ohio apple orchard. We schedule our time around school runs for her two young children, Chamoun and Simone, and around my field trips to document the myriad methods of fishing for my cultural-appreciation curriculum.

Fisherboys with scoop nets

35

We go at dawn to the crowded fish market near the Buri-ganga ghats (landing areas) for fresh *hilsa* or *rui* (large river fish) to make one of her delicious family recipes for that evening's gathering.

Fish market

"But where are the fish?" I ask, unable to see anything beyond the huge crowd of astonished, slack-jawed men staring at us. For a treat, we wend our way through a frenzy of bell-tingling rickshaws to the best sweet shop, Morand Chand, in Old Dacca.

On the way to the sweet shop

Piles of *jalebis* (pretzel-shaped sweets), *gulab jamun* (sweet doughy balls), *rashgulla* (milk-based sweet) and *pistash barfi* (pistachio fudge) topped with edible silver foil are on display.

"Which one would you like to try?" she asks.

It's a simple choice: "I'd like the one without a fly on it."

We jump into my beat-up VW Bug to deliver invitations to a wedding, only to find ourselves having to be hauled out of a stinking open sewer in the teeming narrow lanes of the old city. When straining men pulling a loaded *talagari* (two-wheeled pushcart) crush my fender, I wave them on. What's one more dent in our old car?

Typical *talagari*. This one is loaded with cholera vaccine.

The panel beaters

Runi coaches me how to hold a sari with grace. "Whatever you do, don't let your feet show," she explains. We experiment with the current hip-hugging fashion in sheer chiffons that reveals our slim waists.

Candy in chiffon sari

We weave jasmine and *champak* (frangipani) into our long hair. My sari collection expands each time we shop at Baitul Makarram or New Market. It is hard to resist the salesmen who remove with a flourish any number of saris I fancy from the cabinets behind them, unfurling six meters of pure Rajshai silk, *jamdani* (a hand-loomed sari with traditional motifs) or Tangail cottons. The most amusing part is the modeling act, when a man unfolds his crossed legs and rises, rapidly pleats the cloth, then drapes one end over his left shoulder, while his other hand deftly folds more of the bright fabric to hold at his narrow waist. He assumes a provocative stance to show how attractive the pattern will be when worn.

Packages in hand, we zigzag around rickshaws and baby taxis, desperate to outflank the terrifying beggar with no face who waits patiently for us to emerge from the shops so he can wiggle his tongue in the hollow where his nose and chin have rotted away.*

Unwinding over tea in the luxury of the Intercontinental Hotel, we escape into a discussion of Doris Lessing's *The Golden Notebook*, and gossip about the superficial flirtations of the previous night's gathering. After tea, if Viquar can escape his law chambers, he will join us for whatever overly emotional film is playing at the one cinema in Motijheel, or we'll go for simple Chinese fare at the only restaurant in town. Viquar has a number of clients he defends pro bono, including humble ones like our cook, Totomiah, who seeks compensation for his leg, badly crushed by a careening overloaded *talagari*.

"I'm going to arrange a concert for an accomplished sarod musician friend who will be coming from Calcutta next week to raise money for his relatives living in Comilla," Runi tells us ex-

---

* No Face suffered from "noma," a type of gangrene that destroys the mucous membranes of the mouth and other tissues; an acute and ravaging infection, exacerbated by extreme poverty and malnutrition. When cholera lab doctors offered him free reconstructive surgery, he refused, because it would take away his livelihood as a beggar.

citedly. She plans to ask him to perform in their unfinished living room open to the garden. I immediately imagine the sound of ragas floating in the heavy monsoon air, filled with the scent of jasmine and roses. The intimacy of the setting she creates will give us the rare pleasure of a performance without the distorting amplification common at public venues. Although there is often a paucity of cash in their house, it is never apparent in their generous hospitality. House 333, Road 113 sustains an intimate group of intellectuals in Dacca, whose friendships deepen in its welcoming setting. We feel carefree, filled with the natural high spirits of our youth.

Viquar Choudhury in his garden in Gulshan, 1967 (*photo courtesy of Jim Taylor*)

Abed-bhai Returns

One unfortunate day in 1969, Viquar is rushed to the emergency room with a bleeding ulcer. Runi is in a nearby ward, recuperating from crashing her car into a telephone pole to avoid a darting pedestrian.

A messenger appears at our gate with a note: "Candy, please stop on your way to visiting hours, and let our very close family friend, Abed-bhai, know we are in hospital. He has just returned after seventeen years in London." (*Bhai* means "brother.")

"What has drawn you home?" I ask this attractive bachelor. He leans back on a divan in his corduroy jacket, one elbow on a bolster, and lights his pipe.

"The sound of Brahmaputra gives me shivers," he replies with an easy humor. He has been warmly welcomed again by his longstanding circle of friends, particularly Viquar and Runi, her sister Putul and her mother Mrs. Ismail, whom he has called *cha-chi* (aunt) since he was a boy. We often find ourselves meeting again at family gatherings. We swap news, talk about literature or politics, or discuss art exhibits and performances, while enjoying Runi's brain curry or Mrs. Ismail's *chingri mach malai* (shrimp) curry accompanied by her legendary *achar* (spicy condiment).

Abed's balanced perspective and easygoing chuckle are infectious. He decides to take an accountant's position with Pakistan Shell Oil.

"Do come for an exhibition of my friend Rashid Choudhury's jute tapestries mounted in my house," he enthuses. "They are such striking abstracts in a unique medium. We can also drive out to see the fires in the Hill Tracts. They are set by the Chakma farmers' *jhuming* (slash-and-burn agriculture) after the harvest. The burning fields are splendid at night." I fly for a weekend to Chittagong in response to his invitation, but most weekends he returns to Dacca to be with our circle of friends.

Abed

Distant Thunder

Although tension mounts throughout the country, Jon and I are able to move around freely and deepen our experiences in the country and abroad. We stay at Dr. MacKay's bungalow at a tea plantation in Sylhet, ride the old paddle steamers into the Sundarbans, climb onto the *puja* (Hindu ceremony) boats in the dark of the moon to immerse the goddess Durga, fly kite competitions in Dhamrai, sail our small sloop on the Brahmaputra out of Narayanganj or set our tent up on the beach in Cox's Bazaar.

On the dock in Narayanganj, where our sailboat is moored

The Goddess Durga makes her way to immersion in the river

"The Rocket" Paddle Steamer churns toward the Sundarbans

I brave unfriendly border guard inspections when taking the land route to Calcutta, or light candles in the Buddhist temple near the Chakma *rajbari* (rajah's home) in Rangamati. I grab every opportunity to travel abroad: Kyoto, Hong Kong, Singapore, Indonesia's Pulau Seribu, Cambodia's Siem Riep, Bangkok, Burma, North and South India, the Maldives and Sri Lanka. We trek to the base camp of Mt. Everest and into Gilgit. We go on work-related trips to Iran, Afghanistan, Copenhagen, London and Belfast, as well as return to our family homes on Narragansett Bay, Ohio and the Bahamas. But more and more often we find ourselves landing at Tejgaon Airport in the middle of a *hartal*. We are pressured by the protestors to wear a black armband and shout slogans of solidarity with them. Luckily, they do not force us to walk home barefoot.

The turmoil of protest is escalating over what is widely perceived as ethnic discrimination and arbitrary control by the West wing under General Yahya Khan's martial law regime. Increasingly, we are confined to our houses by prolonged *hartals*. We invite friends to stay in our spacious house during these days of enforced leisure. The men consume stockpiled cases of beer, toss horseshoes in the yard, or play poker and dominoes. When the curfew is lifted for a few hours, Totomiah nimbly vaults over the back gate on his one good leg. Returning with a squawking chicken, he wrings, plucks and cooks it to serve with *sobji* (vegetables) and rice.

When the Apollo spaceship lands on the moon, Totomiah is appalled. Learning the astronauts breakfasted on eggs and bacon, he laments, "The pork eaters have landed on *our* Ramzan moon." I am relieved he is still willing to cook for us infidels who have violated outer space.

Totomiah

Sheik Mujipur Rahman Released

The government caves to mounting pressure and in 1969 uncon-
ditionally releases Sheik Mujib, who is a public hero. We all con-
gratulate Viquar for his part in the successful defense case. Our
talk turns to the elections scheduled for December 1970, unaware
that even more tumultuous events will engage our attention in
the year remaining before the election. As we make rounds in a
hired *tonga* (horse cart), singing Christmas carols outside our foreign colleagues' houses, Sheik Mujib announces to a mass of his
Awami League supporters at a public meeting: "There was a
time when all efforts were made to erase the word 'Bangla' from
this land and its map . . . today this land will be called Bangladesh instead of East Pakistan." Agitations for political autonomy
intensify. Mujib's rousing declarations "can mesmerize hundreds
of thousands in the pouring rain," though our friend George
Curlin quips, "I'm sure I attracted a far bigger audience by eating
a peanut butter sandwich in the Modipur Forest."

Richard Cash, Sue Woodward with children Billy and Lauren,
Candy and Jon Rohde in *tonga* doing rounds of caroling

47

Come

Come come to me
I've got the moon
for you to walk on
the star that sees only you
I've got the sun
orbiting you
come come

I have planted a plot
with saplings of hope
that will only grow
with you living on it
I have invented flowers
fragrant with you
and animals walking
and calling like you
come come

I've got a word for you
that never wears
my eyes make you beautiful
put your ear by my side
you'll hear my pulse
beating your name
come come

I want to adorn you
with a chain of freedom
a dress of kisses
the ring of my loneliness
and the floating shoes
you wear in my dream
come come

I've got the poverty
that enriches the fault
on which you will feast
I've got the disease
that only you
can cure in me
there is something ahead of you
bestowing upon you even today
the eloquent
dignity of the widow
come to me . . .

Walter Schweppe

Swimming in the Buriganga

I flip backwards
over the gunwale,
sink into the broad Buriganga,
to cool in waves
of sun-soaked laughter.

Hauled back
wet over the rail,
I leave drops of myself
frisking with
childlike dolphins in
the monsoon heavy river.

Cornelia Rohde

CHAPTER 3
The Ripples Expand

Leap, and the Net Will Be There!

Come back now into Runi's study in Gulshan where I sit with her and her sister Putul. It is November 13, 1970, more than two years after we arrived in Dacca. Our tea grows cold as we stare at the headline about the death and destruction caused by the cyclone. I blurt out, "Let's do something, anything that helps." These few words are like pebbles. Once cast, they cause ripples that expand and expand in ever-increasing circles; ripples that touch many lives and leave indelible memories. But on that morning, we have no idea where these impulsive words will lead us. I see Runi and Putul's eyes catch the spark in mine.

"I'll call Abed-bhai," Runi immediately offers. "I'm sure he will be willing to help us. You and Putul must go to Chittagong to find out what can be done. I'm sure you will find a way to help."

I continue with a simple suggestion, nothing particularly ambitious: "Maybe we can make contact with a village and try to give direct aid. That way we'll know that it reaches the people who need it.

"Yes, that's a good idea," Runi says, "because that way we will be sure where our money is going. I really want to go with you, but I have the children to look after. I will do whatever I can from this end."

She clearly longs to be with us, but because Kishan, her third child, is only three months old, there is no question of her join-

51

ing. Putul is ready to sacrifice the chance of a restful break from her studies in London. I suggest to Runi, "I think Marty Chen and Peggy Curlin might be willing to help you here in Dacca."

Marty arrived just three months prior to the cyclone, but as her CRL sponsor, I've had a chance to get to know her a bit, and feel confident she will be eager to be involved. She is at home in the subcontinent, having grown up in Uttar Pradesh, the daughter of a Christian missionary family. It turns out to be easy to interest her in our idea. I ask if she will contact Peggy Curlin, a dependable organizer, who is always willing to reach out. They agree to back us up from Dacca, where they can attend to their young children.

Peggy Curlin with Sheroo, 1968

Two Days After the Cyclone

Convincing Abed proves hard for Runi. He's concerned about his company-issued house being used for other business.

"Come on, Abed-bhai," she pleads. "Let Candy and Putul come to you to see if there's something we can all do about this tragedy. The headlines are saying the death toll could be in the thousands. Dead bodies are out there hanging from the trees, and you're right next to the worst-affected area." I know I will miss Runi's persuasiveness when I am in Chittagong.

I present the idea to Jon about pooling our resources to go to the coastal areas to see if we can help. "What can we do?" he asks skeptically, but scrolls open the sea chart of Bengal bought from a chandlery in Boston when we learned about our assignment. We look again at the many islands formed in the Bay of Bengal from silt deposited by the large river system pouring out of the Himalayas to create the massive delta of Bangladesh. As soon as the rich silt builds up enough to create islands barely above sea level, landless farmers from other parts of the delta move there with their families, desperate for land they can plant and claim as their own. Because the islands are low, shifting and vulnerable to storms, only the most courageous, the most driven for opportunity—primarily the landless poor—attempt to settle on them. These *char* islands are the ones that took the cyclone's direct hit.

"You might want the marine chart with you," Jon suggests. "At least you'll have some idea of the lay of the land."

We make rough paper tracings of the affected islands to help orient others.

"I can't see how you'll be able to make much impact. I have to go off to the hospital now to work. Try to get a message to me when you arrive. Good luck."

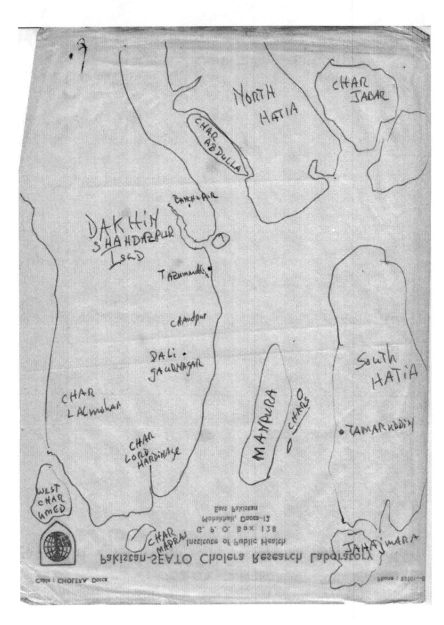

The only map we had of some of the affected islands, traced from a marine chart purchased in Boston. It was already out of date, the alluvial mud islands having changed nearly beyond recognition.

Four Days After the Cyclone

We draw up a list of thirty-five people we think will give monetary aid immediately. I fly to Chittagong on November 17 carrying the cash we've collected. Because it is the port closest to the affected area, I expect to see the airport and the city on war footing to launch a major relief effort, but the airport is deserted and the city appears exactly as it did when I came to Rashid Choudhury's art exhibit. "Where are the planes to ferry supplies?" I wonder. "Where are the trucks moving goods onto ships?"

Abed's driver is waiting. We set off on streets pulsing with their normal blaring, hectic congestion. Sweating laborers bend double to pull *talagaris* loaded high with jute bags of rice.

Talagari loaded with bags of rice.

Markets full of fresh vegetables

Crows, hovering over stalls with hanging strips of stinking offal, flap their wings hoping that a shop owner will be distracted, giving them a chance to dart in and snatch a bite. Baskets arrayed in street markets offer gourds, pumpkins, legumes, jackfruits, coconuts, bananas and custard apples.

The pungent smell of *shutki mach* (dried fish), a Chittagonian favorite, assails my nose. Stringy men strain to pedal their gaily decorated bicycle rickshaws overloaded with passengers, the air jangling with the constant ringing of their handlebar bells, warning the throngs of pedestrians to get out of the way.

Rickshaw puller

Conductors hang off the back steps of dilapidated buses calling out the destination. They inch along in traffic, sounding shrill air horns in an effort to force their way through the crowded streets. My driver joins the cacophony, honking at every bump in the road. We work our way through the congestion, moving slowly enough for threadbare children to run alongside us, and for beggars to shove beseeching hands in the window at stoplights, whining, "Memsahib, baksheeeeesh." I anticipate the restful quiet of Abed's leafy neighborhood, and wonder why I have not seen any mobilization to send help to the devastated islands in the bay.

"No national mobilization was visible and there was no Government commitment on the scale that was necessary. Even for an undeveloped country with limited human and technical resources, the effort seemed deficient" (Sydney Schanberg, *New York Times*, December 30, 1970, p. 2).

My letter from Chittagong to my parents on November 18, makes a similar observation: "There are so many supplies being flown in from all over the world, but they are stuck in Dacca. The problem is IMMEDIATE DISTRIBUTION."

"Though the Government is a military one, the army was not fully mobilized for ten days. Though airdrops were the only way to get relief supplies to most of the survivors . . . not a single one was made in the first few days" (Schanberg 1970, p. 2).

Five Days After the Cyclone:
From Quiet Refuge to Hectic Relief Hub

Abed's concern that his Pak Shell–issued house will be taken over is justified. Kick-off time starts when he invites members of Rotary and Lions Clubs to come tell us how we might get involved in relief work. He produces a gathering on November 18 of half a dozen leaders from both of these organizations, as well as executives of Pakistan-Shell.

Among them is Kaiser Zaman, employee relations officer, whose insight quickly surfaces. When the Rotarian offers me the option of handing a donation to a long-running, worthy project located on the mainland, an area largely unaffected by the storm, Kaiser says, "What I'm hearing her say is that they want to help people in a place that has been heavily devastated by the cyclone." I immediately feel that he and I are on the same wavelength. Iqbal Dada, president of Lions Club, explains, "We are ordering five thousand rupees worth of high-priority relief supplies at cost price to be loaded onto a coastal steamer bound for

Sandwip and Hatiya, two of the more accessible and larger islands in the *char* area that have been heavily affected."

I say, "Why don't we also use the five thousand rupees we've collected to send relief materials bought from the markets in Chittagong, and organize a team of volunteers to distribute them to victims of the storm?" If we have a team to supervise what is given, we can make sure that our donations reach the survivors directly.

As soon as I suggest this, Mr. Dada amiably agrees: "I will double our order to include your donation. It is difficult to get space for relief workers, but I will secure two places on the boat so that your volunteers can accompany your relief supplies." His offer seems to be the quickest and most reliable way of getting materials to nearby Sandwip Island, where we might contribute toward rehabilitating a village. My eyes brighten.

Six Days After the Cyclone

My first reports for Dacca are filled with information about what is needed and how we can give direct help:

```
Nov. 19, Thursday

Made contact with the Control Room at the Cir-
cuit House to reserve space on the next boat for
goods and volunteers. Mr. Anis Ahmed in charge.
General lack of coordination apparent. Relief
Commissioner lost 51 members of his family on
Sandwip and is in distressed state. Were in-
formed that from Friday, a boat is going every
day instead of every other day to Sandwip, the
northern end of South Hatiya Island, and to
Banchapur. The last ship that left Chittagong
had 100 tons of a 600 ton capacity filled. Sand-
wip is getting more relief than South Hatiya,
where the relief goods cannot be distributed to
the hardest hit areas (those at the southern
portion of the island, and the chars in the
```

channel between Hatiya and Manpura) (only 5% of the population of Manpura is left). The large boats cannot ply the shallow waters in this area, and what are needed are speedboats with outboards and drivers to distribute goods, plus doctors with medicines. They informed us that they did not have medicines to give medical personnel that we might supply, but were extremely eager for volunteer doctors. They also informed us that they can give us any amount of space for our goods, and that they can give us priorities for volunteers, on every ship leaving daily from Chittagong. Priorities in relief goods for Hatiya — medicines, water, water purification tablets, bleaching powder, foodstuffs, clothing, fuel, matches, oil lamps, milk, tinned foods with openers. Time is the crucial factor, and clearly it is an open field for those who can organize.

Circuit House where control room is located

First Team of Volunteers for Cyclone Relief

We plan to send Monowar Hossain, Rezaur Rahman, and Ranju Samad (who have arrived on the last flight from Dacca) with our relief goods to Sandwip Island for direct distribution, and also to locate Mr. Das (formerly a tutor in Sandwip known to Runi and Viquar Choudhury) to see if we could use his house as a base, what materials we should send, and if we could organize relief for a particular spot. Two of the volunteers would remain on Sandwip, while the third would continue on to Hatiya to determine if a camp could be set up there, and if we should send goods, as well as doctors, boats and medicines (the boats can be loaded directly onto the large ship and transported to the island), or if there are already materials there and we should concentrate instead on getting a means to transport them to the southern reaches of the island. Spent the evening drawing maps, trying to locate student volunteer workmen through Rashid Choudhury of Chittagong University (reliable students working independently), packing personal gear such as some foodstuffs, old curtains of Abed's which the volunteers would use for blankets and then leave for distribution, water, medicines (personal). The plan is to stay the night and return with the boat coming to Chittagong by Saturday evening. The relief boat will normally leave the jetty at 5 am every day, and goods should be at the dock by 7 pm the night before for loading.

Monowar Hossain and Habibus (Ranju) Samad, two of the volunteers in the first team (*photo courtesy of Ranju Samad*)

Peggy and Marty inform me they have sourced donations of crates of tea and maunds of rice, as well as bundles of saris and lunghis, and that bales of blankets have been stacked in Runi's living room. Everything will be loaded onto the truck they have persuaded the Commissary to release, along with a driver to transport the collected goods to Chittagong, where they will be added to our first shipment (author's letter to parents, November 18, 1970).

Seven Days After the Cyclone
Friday, November 20

The National Shipping Corporation (NSC) boat was to leave the dock across from the Burma Eastern depot today at 8:30 am. We went along with the volunteers to supervise the loading of goods and to assess what other relief goods were going, how crowded the ship was, and if there were other volunteers on board. Three members of the Lions Club were waiting for us, including the president, Iqbal Dada. They were wearing red badges saying Lions' Relief, which we thought was a very good idea, and decided to make some for ourselves saying "relief" in English lettering as well as Bengali. Most of the passengers were men whose families live on the islands, and they were taking some immediate supplies to contact directly with their relatives. Other men walked on with cartons of cigarettes or 2 dozen oil lamps to set up small stands to sell to the victims.(!!!) We looked in the hold and could see no goods, nor were any piled on the decks as expected for a relief ship. Our goods were at the moment being loaded by hook into the hold of the ship: cooking utensils, rice, saris and lunghis, cartons of milk, matches and fuels. We did not see any other goods being loaded, but are hoping that some may have gotten on the evening before. Monowar was to assess what the ship held after they started off, and he could have a chance to have a good look. At any rate we were satisfied that our goods made it directly to the dock, at cost price, and are going directly to the relief area to be distributed by our people. We are also aware of the immediate needs of the people who were affected by the cyclone, the lack of coordination of relief supplies, and the importance of our relief work.

The 600-ton ship churns across the broad sea for nearly two hours before pulling into Sandwip, the closest island to Chittagong. Monowar recalls that when his group lands and tries to distribute the materials in the first shipment, a huge crowd gathers, immediately overwhelming the three of them.

Monowar relates: "Recently having been immersed in the scholarly approach of the London School of Economics, I started methodically to make a list of the names of the survivors so we could be orderly and fair in the distribution. My effort was quickly overcome by their anxiety to get to the supplies."

With the crowd pushing and shoving to get to the offloaded goods, the three men have a tough time trying to achieve anything approaching an equitable handout. At one point, Monowar resorts to picking up a large stick and threatening the milling survivors. It is the first sobering lesson in how critical it is to have enough volunteers and supplies to organize a well-regulated distribution plan so that the strongest cannot dominate, taking an unfair share. The original idea that two of them would remain on Sandwip while one continued on to Hatiya is aborted.

Seven Days after the Cyclone:
Revving Up for Relief

The logistics of starting a relief operation from scratch are formidable. Kaiser makes a wish list of about twenty necessities for the initial shipment: lunghis, saris, vests, *gamcha* (small towel-like cloths), rice, *muri* (dried puffed rice), *cheera* (crushed puffed rice), salt, lentils, mustard oil, sugar, water drums for fresh water, matchboxes, cooking utensils, *dekshi*s (large, straight-sided aluminum pots), spoons, aluminum plates and mugs, ropes or string, bleaching powder, kerosene, kerosene lamps, diesel oil and petrol. Putul, who has flown down with Monowar's team, Kaiser and I move into overdrive to assemble vital supplies. Overnight, Abed's home has become a staging ground. He is bombarded with questions and ideas when he returns from office. Not only has his home been turned into a buzzing godown (warehouse), but he cannot escape even during working hours. On November 20, I brazenly breach his office protocol, whizzing straight past the shocked Pak Shell receptionist and into his office with my urgent request for two boats to allow our team mobility in the shallow coastal waters where big boats cannot go. I continue with my list of requests: dinghies, petrol, outboards, drivers . . . and why not throw in some water drums? And how about lining up some student laborers? Oh, and please don't forget to ask the night guard at Pak Shell to direct the truck to your house.

With an eyebrow raised only slightly at my invasion of his sanctum, and without missing a beat, he says, "Right. I'll order two boats to be sent here from the company's flotilla at the Kaptai dam." The twelve-foot aluminum dinghies appear two days later. He also radios the field supervisor: "Could you please send by next courier one of your two outboard engines for relief work in the offshore islands?" Two minutes later, the officer radios back: "Sending tonight by courier." Abed's enthusiasm for the operation seems to be growing.

"Jon!" I shout excitedly into the crackling connection. "Bring an outboard motor and ask everyone we know to give you at least a hundred dollars."

"You know I can't leave my work at the hospital. Why are you asking me to come?"

"We've organized a shipload of food, kerosene and clothing. Can you bring tetracycline, water purification tablets and some typhoid vaccine? The boat leaves day after tomorrow for Hatiya and you need to put together a team of doctors and be on board."

"I'm too involved in experiments and the hospital is full of cholera patients. I can't leave."

65

"But Jon, this is the work we are meant to be doing. I'm sure of it."

Immediate Goal: Rapid Aid

In order to raise money as rapidly as possible to buy more relief goods, we make an appeal to circulate among our friends and other concerned groups in Dacca who may be looking for a way to donate. At this time, we are considering trying to help just a small number of victims, possibly on Sandwip Island, where Runi and Viquar have a close family friend.

[Candy's] Message from Chittagong to Dacca:

Requisitioning through Iqbal Dada's business contacts another shipment of Rs. 5000* with the goal of leaving Sunday for Sandwip or Hatiya depending on the reports which will reach us from our three contacts that went with the first supply, as to which area we can most directly affect according to the severity of their condition.

We can get two aluminum speedboats through Pak Shell but we need outboard engines. Locate these. Drivers are available.

Set up a team of doctors and volunteer laborers with medicines which we hope to get through a contact in Dacca. (Tetracycline, water purification tablets, antibiotics, bleaching powder, typhoid vaccine.)

Make an effort to mobilize groups in Dacca who don't know how to get aid to the victims directly.

Raise immediate donations so we can send goods to the islands quickly, buying them at cost in Chittagong.

---

* The exchange rate in 1970 was 4.76 Pakistani rupees to $1 US, making Rs. 5,000 the equivalent of over $1,000.

The Dacca base responds immediately by launching the first appeal to generate startup funds:

Operation Sandwip

In an effort to circumvent time consuming organizational relief, and to gain the satisfaction of significantly aiding the destitute (even if a small number), several CRL families in cooperation with some Pakistanis are trying to initiate a relief program for a single village on Sandwip Island. It is absolutely crucial to obtain funds immediately as the first group hopes to set out from Chittagong by Thursday noon (Nov. 20). This group, consisting of one or two CRL wives and Pakistani business people, will try to establish a relief center to supply rice to 1000-2000 people for a couple of weeks. During the first few days they will speak with village elders and the like, trying to assess the most pressing needs of the community. Hopefully, over the next month or two we can help one small group of people to get on their feet again.

Please give generously to make this program a success. We will give you a regular progress report and perhaps ask you for specific things (old bed sheets, pots, etc.) if the program succeeds. If it is apparent to us that the money is not being well-utilized we will turn it over entirely to the government relief funds.

Please try to get your contribution to us today.

Marty and Lincoln Chen
Candy and Jon Rohde

The next appeal includes a map to Aysen Talmon's and Marty Chen's houses to drop off donations of used clothing (children's or adults'), used linen (towels, sheets, etc.), and used kitchen utensils (*dekshis*, spoons, etc.).

Cash-Rupee donations will be put in an account through Pat Talmon at the Cholera Research Laboratory and records will be kept of expenditures. Checks should be made payable to either Mrs. Martha Chen or Mrs. Cornelia Rohde. Also, please solicit funds from your relatives and friends back home.
Male volunteers are needed. Let us know if you are available.

The response is heartening. People want to donate after reading descriptions of the horror of the disaster in the newspaper, and feel an effort initiated by known friends is more likely to be able to reach the victims directly.

Nine Days After the Cyclone: Second Field Team

The phones work so poorly that I fly back to Dacca to make further arrangements. I board the PIA return flight to Chittagong with Jon, who carries a nine-horsepower outboard motor on his shoulder. He has persuaded Mark Tucker, the head of maintenance, to release it from the cholera lab's depot. In our pockets are pooled contributions from a dozen friends to provide our working budget to buy relief goods. Many others have also volunteered to come to the cyclone area to help, willing to take care of all their own costs.

Jon's shock at the extent of the tragedy has mounted along with ours. Each day's headline ratchets the estimated death toll up dramatically: one hundred thousand, then two hundred thousand.

On Nov 13th, Friday, by nightfall the papers reported 50 dead. By Saturday, the papers began to talk of tens of thousands dead, and by Sunday the 15th, hundreds of thousands, but the Government figure did not rise above 40,000 until 8 days after the storm (Schanberg 1970, p. 2).

Poor official reporting concerning the scale of the disaster confuses foreign governments and delays relief.

Deplaning on the nearly deserted airport tarmac in Chittagong, we spot two small single-engine crop-dusting planes loading sacks of food. Ignoring regulations, Jon strolls over to the area away from the terminal, where these planes are sitting.

"Hi, I'm Jon Rohde," he says to the young pilot. "I'd like to go up with you to recce the area for existing distribution and need."

Jon recalls: Although a bit cool at first because they had been approached by many reporters, they warmed up very rapidly to the idea that we might indeed be going out to the stricken areas where they had seen no effort of organized relief work.

"You're welcome on board," the pilot said. "I'm Noel Kinvig, and this is Bill Sharp." We listen to him recount: "Bill and I flew over the devastated area immediately after the cyclone, and decided to convince our company to let us abort dusting crops in the delta to make relief-supply drops onto the affected area. Our planes are still the only ones making runs out of Chittagong. We hope others will show up soon because there are so many remote areas where people are in serious distress."

The next morning, Jon appears early for his reconnaissance with Noel. "Hop on board. We're taking off right now," he says.

Jon describes the flight: The cockpit of the Porter Pilatus fills with noise as we labor off the airfield with a cargo-hold of rice. Not yet dawn: the cool air is positively frigid as it whistles into the open plane, its doors and hatches removed so that its life-giving cargo can be shoved out as we soar low over bedraggled groups of survivors. Noel knows the delta well by now, having ceased his normal crop-dusting work and initiated his market in the sky almost a week ago in the wake of the cyclone. Although land-based rescue teams have reached many coastal areas, most islands are still depending on a few tons of grain per day scattered from the sky, perhaps an average of an ounce per person. In reality, only a few eat, for only the strongest can run after the heavy burlap bags as they are pushed out at eighty knots, just a few yards over the flattened paddy fields. A crude game of winner-take-all; every man fights desperately for those sacks. Some burst on impact, spreading their precious contents for yards, but not a grain is lost, as a flock of women and children descend to scratch each kernel out of its muddy resting place.

We make long low runs down to twenty-foot levels over the polders, along the shores where survivors have congregated for the comfort of ten feet of elevation over the still-wet fields. Once an impressive ridge running the perimeter of many coastal islands, the dikes are now more like a perforated line running around the top edge of a cereal box. The real damage came not when the tide swept over these earthworks, but when the storm subsided, and the interior of each island became a virtual lake contained within its own embankment. What was not destroyed by the cyclone perished in the slower drowning of a huge man-and-god-made inland sea. The water poured out, taking the banks with it. Now, a week later, the remnants of the dikes are still the only inhabitable land, higher than the once-green fields. As we swoop out of the skies, scores of hopeful gaunt arms reach up toward the plane.

"Now!" shouts Noel, as he holds the course carefully aligned with the top of the dike. I kick and shove sack after sack into the hungry emptiness of the open doorway.

"Here comes a corner," Noel warns, and crams the stick to the left with full rudder. My belly floats up into my throat as we bank ninety degrees and the view at the door flips from clouds and sky to mud and hopeful upturned faces flashing past. The left wing tip almost touches the straw tops of makeshift huts.

"Any lower and they'll climb aboard," I yell. "That's the last sack."

Pulling into a steep climb, we arc back to see the results of our airborne catering service. In spite of a limited menu, we couldn't have a more appreciative clientele. We run back along our route. People wave, and even smile, thankful for a brief respite in the relentless course of hunger. It is my first look at the ravaged islands.

CHAPTER 4
An Island Beyond Help

The Ayes Have It

Our small base expands mid-afternoon Sunday, November 21, with recruited Bengali and foreign friends flying in from Dacca to join the relief effort. It feels like things are beginning to move when a dozen volunteers fill Abed's drawing room. Eight of them will go out in the morning on the ship *Sandwip*.

From my first report about the night before departure on the ship:

```
Evening conversation confirmed feasibility of
air supply with red cross on white sheet signal.
Needed goods to be letter coded on sheets to pi-
lot. Far into the night Putul and I ripped a red
sari and old white sheets into pieces to fashion
signal flags for the crew of volunteers to carry
with them. The plan is that they will lay them
on the ground to show Noel their location and to
indicate what is most needed. We hand-stitch a
red cross on a large white cloth to be used to
mark the drop zone. We cut and stitch smaller
signal flags with the letters:
P=people
W=water
M=medicines
 MB=bandages, antiseptics
 MO=eye ointment (tenacortin, etc.)
 MC=antibiotics (tetracycline, penicillin)
 MP=splints
C=clothes
F=food (non-cooked)
```

```
FO="our" food (canned, cooked rice)
FC=cooked foodstuffs
O=oil
OP=stoves
G=glucose
S=salts
L=land (so the pilot will know he can land
safely)
```

As Putul and I are feverishly cutting and sewing the flags, one of the newly arrived volunteers remarks, "This is crazy. It's never going to work. Nobody here knows anything about this sort of operation." I look up to see doubt spreading over several faces. I think, "He's right. We're clearly winging it, but it sure seems as if no one else is even in takeoff position. It's been days since the cyclone hit and there's almost no response."

I answer him: "We're doing this because no one else seems to be doing anything, so it's not as if we can link up with any more experienced group already in operation. The victims are going to need all the help they can get. Why not give it a try? What is there to lose? We might actually do some good, who knows? At the very least we will learn something." Heads nod. The ship *Sandwip* is loaded that night with the aluminum dinghies, engines, milk and emergency foodstuffs.

Ten Days After the Cyclone: Departure of Second Team

Putul and I, with eight of the twelve Dacca volunteers—Zakaria (Jack) Choudhury, a political activist; Viquar Choudhury, our barrister friend; Jon, Al Sommer, and Richard Guerrant, all doctors from the cholera hospital; along with a visiting CRL consultant from Harvard Medical School, Dr. Geoffery Sharp; Jon's CRL medical technician, Ahseque Rahman; and the Ford Foundation representative, Steve Baldwin—gather at the ghat at dawn to supervise the final loading of our cargo onto the long, battered Landing Craft Tank (LCT) boat with a drop bow: vintage World War II. A speedboat driver arranged by Abed also appears. (The other four volunteers, Lincoln Chen of CRL, CRL demographer John Stoekel, Zack Hahn of USAID and Dick Reynolds of Ford Foundation return to Dacca later that day.)

Typical LCT craft, WWII vintage, on which HELP's supplies are loaded

Although the wharf teems with people, many of whom are anxious to bring relief to relatives who live on the *char* islands, the amount of goods being loaded seems minor by comparison to the scale of the tragedy. The beat-up thirty-year-old LCT does not have any accommodation for passengers, yet it is the only cargo boat available, and we are happy to be given space on it. With no seats on board, the men will have to stand on deck or perch on bags of relief supplies. As we discuss plans to proceed with a medical survey and distribution after establishing a base in the stricken area, idle men surround us and stare, wondering what these foreigners, especially two young women, are doing. We are too busy planning, and stowing our shipment, to be distracted by the press of their unflinching curiosity, except by a fleeting thought that they could be more useful by focusing on the calamity.

Contact is made with the army officer in charge, Major Salamat,* who is keen to provide assistance. We assure him we will keep him well informed of our plans and needs. After the first reconnaissance team's input, we expect our work to be on the island of Hatiya because of its central location in the stricken area, so we come up with the name Hatiya Emergency Lifesaving Project. We like its catchy acronym, HELP. The volunteers look self-conscious in the large homemade red-and-yellow HELP badges Putul and I pin to their shirts to distinguish them as members of a relief team. An hour after departure, they spot Lincoln Chen making a reconnaissance run with Noel to help establish priorities.

Steve Baldwin on Chittagong dock with HELP's second field team about to board LTC, November 22, 1970
(*photo courtesy of Richard Guerrant*)

---

* *Salamat* means wishing peace to those you meet and wishing for them to be safe from any harm.

On the steamer dock in Chittagong before second HELP team departs. Left to right: Candy Rohde, Putul (Saroya) Ismail and Jon Rohde wearing "HELP Hatiya" badge (*photo courtesy of Richard Guerrant*)

Disembarking on mud bank
(*Rainer Kruse, photographer; photo courtesy of Bread for the World*)

Negotiating the Currents

When the ship churns into Sandwip, the local people at shore side assure the volunteers that relief is well established, so they continue with the plan to go on to the next island, Hatiya. The LCT departs under a ripping adverse current. Rivers in this area are notorious for changing course almost overnight. Land quickly disappears from sight as the boat heaves its way across the open ocean for almost another six hours before plowing into the mud bank that forms the shore of Hatiya. Located in the center of the Megna River's estuary, the island has no port. The large landing ramp drops down on the bank at the north end at 6:30 p.m. After so long on the open ocean, the distance from Chittagong feels vast, although it is only about fifty miles.

The HELP team scrambles up the slippery mud bank to find the shore crowded with a number of soldiers of the Pakistan Army giving orders to local men to haul piles of relief goods to the nearby IWTA warehouse. Looking inside, the team finds the space stacked to the ceiling with grain and kerosene. Viquar approaches a tall army officer who looks as if he's in charge, and explains: "We have shipped four tons of relief goods, which we plan to distribute to survivors. Would you be able to arrange for your workers to help us offload them from the LCT?"

The officer scowls. "I'm sorry. Can't you see that all the laborers are engaged with other work? Speak to the ADC over there."

Jon walks over to the harried ADC official: "We have a large load of goods we want to give to storm victims. Can you spare some men to take them off the landing craft? We would really appreciate your help."

"We are happy you have brought donations for the suffering people, but I can only help you if you are a government organization."

Jon can see there will be no action from the ADC. The sun is low on the horizon, and Jon is aware the ship's captain is impatient to be rid of the cargo.

While Jon is trying without luck to persuade the ADC, Viquar finds a Bengali army officer who is far more helpful. Speaking to the Relief Commissioner (ADC), the officer gives HELP the break they need: "Please arrange to have some workers bring this group's relief supplies off the landing craft." Prodded by the officer, the commissioner gives an order, and HELP's cargo of tins of kerosene, cooking utensils and foodstuffs are offloaded and piled at last on the mud bank.

Jon asks the commissioner, "Where would you advise us to begin our work? When I flew over the southern part of the island yesterday, it seemed as if there was no organized relief there. Would you suggest we go there?"

The ADC admits, "It is true that many areas in the south are still without food or adequate evaluation. We are trying our best to reach them, but we are lacking personnel. Perhaps you could set up a distribution point at Sonadia." When Jon and Viquar inform the other members of the team what the commissioner has suggested, they agree to head south in the morning to Sonadia with the supplies.

The team is relieved to see how many country boats have survived the storm and are clustered around the ghat. They make arrangements with the boatmen to transfer HELP's goods to their boats to be rowed or, preferably, towed by launch to Sonadia. Towing will be faster and will lessen the chance that the country boats will be swept off course by tidal changes and currents. The army officer suggests they secure a launch for this purpose, so Jon and Viquar walk up the dirt road at midnight to the town of Hatiya to see what they can arrange.

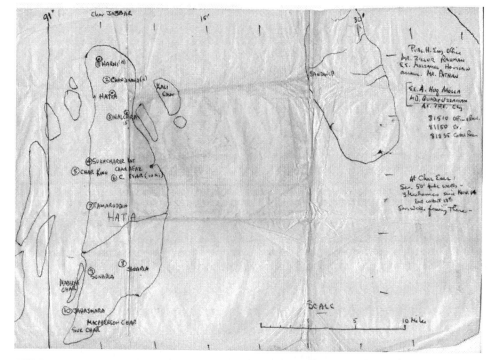

HELP team's hand-sketched scaled map showing ten locations on Hatiya. Sonadia in south Hatiya, where they are advised to go, is marked No. 9. Contacts on Sandwip are noted on the right of the drawing.

All the buildings in the town have survived the cyclone because Hatiya, an older island, is higher above the sea than newer *chars*, and is surrounded by a ten-foot earthwork polder for flood protection. The *thana* (county) headquarters of the police assures them everything is under control, although a crush of supplicants are milling around their station. The policemen refer them to an army camp a mile south, where they find a cooperative officer, another Major Salamat. When he finds out why they have come, he jolts his colleague, Major Rustom, awake, to apprise him of the HELP team's purpose. The major maintains that the army ships are short of diesel and there is no petrol for vehicles, but he promises to have a launch (equivalent to a small type of tugboat) tow the country boats to our proposed drop zone at Sonadia.

```
    Viquar and I walked and got a rickshaw back
to the water area (it was then about 2:30 am).
It was a lovely evening but the balmy air that
should have been there was replaced by the most
foul odor of decaying flesh that permeated the
area for the next several weeks. When our rick-
shaw driver brought us into camp, I gave out the
first of the relief goods in the form of two
tins of kerosene, which he promised to distrib-
ute in his village. They were very valuable to
him and I also gave him double fare for his
rickshaw and he was just elated. He had lost so
much — family, friends and all of his home had
been washed away, but not his rickshaw.
```

After Viquar and Jon return to the camp, the team decides one of their speed boats will leave at five a.m. with Sommer, Guerrant, Sharp, Jack and the speedboat driver in order to establish a distribution site. Viquar, Asheque and Rohde will stay behind to signal the CIBA* plane, break camp and coordinate the loading and departure of the country boat.

The Persuasion of a Plan

Back at Abed's house, after seeing the HELP team off, I wrap my red cotton sari, grab my sunglasses and clipboard, and set off to the Circuit House to meet Rob Choudhury, the Relief Commissioner. The Control Room is full of men, who stop talking as soon as they see me, jump up and move aside to open the way to the man in charge. One deferentially escorts me to the chair clos-

---

* CIBA-Pilatus Aerial Spraying Co. Ltd., Switzerland

est to the commissioner's large desk. The commissioner focuses his attention exclusively on me, as if he had nothing else occupying his mind. I lay out our plans and outline our needs. I specifically want to know what relief materials have entered the country, who is involved in their distribution, and how he can help us obtain supplies for our ground crew's operation.

"I will be happy to cooperate with you in any way I can," the commissioner assures me. "The Russians have sent a boatload of medicines, which should be docking soon. Just keep me informed about what you need."

Receiving preferred treatment in government offices becomes an established pattern over the next weeks. Doors open, queues are skirted, and I am ushered straight to the chief bureaucrat, who greets me with a gracious smile. If our agenda benefits from my being a confident young American woman wearing a sari, then the attention is welcome. Their slightly stunned, but traditional gentlemanly attitude, combined with my ability to hear *yes* and never *no*, makes it faster and far easier for me to get things done. Or perhaps they open their doors to someone with a sensible plan, because they don't appear to have one yet. Government response is still almost nonexistent.

Trying to Connect with HELP on Hatiya

Finding a way from our base in Chittagong to connect with the volunteers heading into the affected area is one of our primary concerns, since we are their supply line and information link. The plan is for the HELP team to establish their base on Hatiya, so I send a message with the relief commissioner to let our volunteers know they can communicate by radio with us in Chittagong by using Pak Shell frequencies, something Abed has arranged. We are hopeful that radios will be available on Hatiya, as satellite communication on the *char* islands is nonexistent.

Eleventh Day After the Cyclone: Change of Plan

At two a.m., the seed of a new plan sprouts in the minds of Viquar and Jon. Still walking around scouting the scene, they run into an industrious group of students from an engineering institute in Dacca, led by a Dr. Mahmoud. Their group has just returned to Hatiya after a day on a remote *char* called Manpura, which they say lies farther west. According to them, relief has yet to reach any of the survivors. Frustrated by the local bureaucracy, and finding the army has already taken over much of the relief operation on Hatiya, Jon and Viquar are drawn to the report of an island where others have not yet landed, and where their help could be crucial. They go back to the landing point where the team has settled down to try to rest before moving on the following day. For the next couple hours, they give up trying to catch any sleep on the mud embankment. Instead, they keep watch over the supplies while beating off hordes of mosquitoes. The plan is still to head south to Sonadia at dawn.

```
    Nov 23 0500 up as planned. Much work getting
boats and help. Got a little more when sahibs
started doing all the carrying. Set up red cross
and huge words spelled with kerosene tins SON-
ADIA for CIBA. We made a huge, huge word, Son-
adia, using 4 gallon tin cans laid out on the
ground, but he kept flying directly over the
letters so he couldn't see them.
    Army Lt. Rashid arrives with less enthusiasm
than Majors had had. Rohde to LCT finds that de-
lay may be indefinite for launch. Country boats
loading. Motor from Pak Shell won't run so
Rohde, Jack, Sommer take CRL 9.5 horse motor to
look south.
```

The composition of the members of the team who will set off before the country boats to find a distribution site changes, because the Pak Shell motor has broken down. Since Jon has been entrusted with the CRL motor, he takes the responsibility to skipper it. The three of them set off south along the coast to see what the launch delay is about. They get another offer instead, and the confirmation that Manpura is an island as yet largely ignored.

0900 Reach hospital ship off Marnia (off coast further south). Brief chat with Army Doc shows that Manpura worst need and he wastes no time in giving us his launch to send back and pick up boats. This is the most decisive man we met.

They return to the Hatiya ghat and finish loading the army launch, which has at last arrived. Jon proposes looking for Manpura. If it is actually as needy as has been reported, their supplies will be critical to keep the survivors alive. The group agrees to the new plan.

Several volunteer groups want to come along and after a lot of organizational rearranging, all get aboard Army launch finally impatient to leave. Meanwhile, launch from hospital ship arrives and I'm embarrassed to say we've gone on without it but deeply appreciate help. Engineering group [the ones Viquar and Jon had met late the previous night] were still making up minds as the launch took off and Rohde tried to ferry as many as possible out to rapidly disappearing boat.

The launch, filled with members of the HELP team and the other willing volunteers they met on Hatiya, head out the channel to open sea to avoid running onto the shallow mud bars that make navigation treacherous around the islands. They drag behind them the country boats HELP has hired to transport the supplies.

1000 Viquar arrives from Hatiya town wireless having sent message to Candy: Look SONADIA, if not there MANPURA. We take on Mahmoud and put rest of students into country boats.

The wire never reaches me in Chittagong. Meanwhile, Viquar and Jon rearrange the kerosene tins spelling "Sonadia" to form an arrow pointed due west. The decision is made to head over the horizon to find Manpura.

Looking for the Island Said to Be "Beyond Help"

With a five-gallon container of drinking water and a spare jerrican of petrol for the nine-horsepower motor from CRL, Jon takes the helm of the twelve-foot Pak Shell aluminum dinghy. He hopes Dr. Mahmoud will help direct them to Manpura. Mahmoud looks doubtful about committing himself to such a small boat, but steps into the bow where Jon asks him to sit. Jon then directs Viquar to take a place on the center thwart so their weight will be as evenly balanced as possible. Viquar moves onto the plank seat, although his face lacks its usual confidence. His unease deepens when he hears the outboard motor splutter when Jon yanks the cord. On the second try the engine kicks in assertively. They push off from the mud bank, navigating west toward a blank horizon, with the sun behind them. As soon as they move out into the waters of the vast bay, a salty sea breeze clears their heads of the noisome smell of the milling crowds at the landing ghat. Rather than going around the passage between the islands like the deeper draft launch and country boats must do, Jon takes a direct route westward, while hoping to avoid running up on a mud bank. Having grown up around boats, and used to his father's five-horsepower outboard, Jon calculates how much fuel they can expend before they have to turn around. He quickly pushes aside the thought that, without any oars, they are completely dependent on the reliability of the small outboard motor and would be in an extremely vulnerable position if it were to break down. The options for being rescued look rather slim.

Without navigational equipment, he feels very much at sea as the boat moves rapidly away from the shore. He figures if he can keep land in sight, it is less likely they will be pulled off course by the strong currents of the open channel. As Hatiya begins to disappear behind them over the horizon, Jon tells Viquar, "I'll stand up to make sure we keep the coastline behind us in view." He balances against the swell and roll of the sea by steadying himself with a hand on Viquar's shoulder. Looking frequently back over his own shoulder to be sure he can still see Hatiya, he maneuvers through the chop. Mahmoud, huddled in the bow, is doused by spray. Jon feels the tension in Viquar's shoulders. He can tell by his expression that he must be wondering why he ever agreed to set off across the Bay of Bengal in such a small and miserably frail boat.

Shoreline of Hatiya disappearing on horizon

Now that there are no other boats in sight, and the landmass being used to steady their bearings is out of sight, all of them feel a keen sense of isolation. Jon thinks, "This craft is far too flimsy for the open ocean." His next thought is whether there is enough petrol in the tank to make it back. As Jon reported later:

I ran up on a couple of *chars* and had to wade off dragging the boat hundreds of yards to get propeller clearance again. They'd been swept clean in the tidal wave — not a man, not a stick left, with only an occasional bloated carcass of a buffalo or a small child thrown up on the muck. I'd been assured Manpura was off there somewhere — almost twenty miles long and two wide, it couldn't have disappeared entirely in one night. The smell came first, then the tops of coconut palms, floating on tiny stalks above the placid bay — at last the low mud bank with its horrendous burden of decaying bodies. I had to run the dinghy down the coast for over a mile before I could find a spot to land without stepping on one of the luckless victims of the cyclone. I scrambled up the slippery bank, nearly retching, and stood on a dirt mound that only last week had been a home. There before me was a beautiful, golden, flattened and utterly desolate land.

Silence. No crows cackle, no cows rumble, no palm leaves rustle. It is as if all life has been snuffed out. Reeling from the oppressive odor filling their noses and throats, Jon, Viquar and Mahmoud force their way to shore through a surface floating with decaying flesh. The dead bob around in the water, or are strewn on the shore washed up by the tide to bloat and rot in the sun. It is a scene they will never forget. Surely, they think, someone of the thirty thousand must have survived.

CHAPTER 5
Aftermath of the Perfect Storm

Surendra managed to save his wife. Her scream "I don't want to live anymore!" fills his head. Neither can erase the vision of their sons and daughters being swept away by the receding tidal surge. He remembers how desperately he grabbed at her when she swirled by him after letting go of the palm tree she had been clutching. She was limp and her eyes were glazed, but she was still alive. He gripped her tightly in one arm and clung to the palm trunk with the other until the water receded. He still can't believe how he found the strength to slide down from the tree holding onto her limp body. Their clothes were shredded off them; their chests, arms and thighs ripped and bleeding from being pummeled against the rough palm bark. They stumbled in a daze, hoping to find a few rags to cover their nakedness. One of the hardest things he ever did in his life was to remove cloth strips from the corpses littering the ground around them. They slept on soggy ground, exhausted. Before he mercifully fell asleep, his last thought was, "How will we find anything to eat with everything gone?"

November 23: HELP Arrives on Manpura

At first no living beings appear when Jon, Viquar and Mahmood land the dinghy. Jon describes the scene: A breeze gently rustled the palms above my head and I gazed up to see an agglomeration of straw, bamboo, even strips of roofing tin interwoven in the tree tops by the crashing onslaught of the tidal wave. First inspection: island worse than Hatiya — not a standing *bari* [home]. Shelter entirely lacking.

Silent aftermath of the storm

The island appears totally devastated and without life, but that soon changes when survivors begin to assemble around the three men, staring at them with flat, suffering eyes sunk in their heads, looking as if they don't believe that rescue has truly arrived.

Many have only meager scraps cloth to cover themselves, or have been stripped bare. More and more people in desperately weak condition begin to move toward the mud bank where the dinghy has landed. Viquar and Jon are greatly relieved when the team in the country boats catches up with them, because now they will have food to offer the survivors. Everyone pitches in to offload the supplies they have brought. The stronger ones assist the team to carry the cartons to shore. Jon is aware that the locals are calm, helpful and anxious.

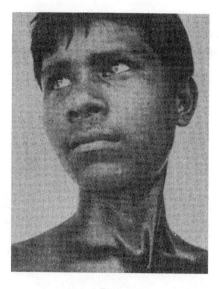

Dazed

The doctors on the team observe the physical condition of the survivors. Jon writes: The major problem we faced was "palm tree syndrome," the severe maceration of flesh on the chest, inner arms and thighs from clinging to the coarse tops of palms through hours of battering by the voracious sea. There were amazingly few health problems in the survivors, for the young and old, the weak and infirm were washed away first ... Sinewy men sobbed as they recounted the loss of entire families, one by one picked off the tree tops and swallowed in the maelstrom.

Hunger and stress among the victims are obvious. They have small amounts of food, but claim each day is uncertain. "They lived through that grim first week, drinking polluted water, clawing rice out of the mud, finding an occasional coconut, whose milk and white meat they carefully divided, and sometimes—when their bellies were so empty they were in pain—eating the roots of banana trees" (Schanberg 1970, p. 2).

The rice crop is devastated, with layers of rice straw hanging in the trees about fifteen or twenty feet up. Hunger has driven the survivors to eat their rice stock even though it is wet, at the same time fearing the future, knowing there will be nothing left to plant. More than medical care, the need is food and drinkable water uncontaminated by decaying bodies.

News spreads rapidly that help has reached the island. The hungry crowd swells. Pleading arms threaten to overwhelm the HELP team. Jon grabs a stick from the shore and sweeps a long line in the ground. "Form a queue behind the line," Viquar orders. "Anyone stepping over that mark will not be given any food." The team holds their collective breath, knowing how hard it would be to obey Viquar's order if they were the ones who had been deprived of food for over a week. A line forms.

Anxious survivors

Cyclone victims organized into lines (two of men and one with four
women survivors plus one child) waiting for relief distributions from
HELP volunteers

Jon has located the ropes that were included in the shipment, and he and Asheque cordon off an area to surround the goods. Geoff and Steve tear up pieces of paper for chits and number them, while Mahmoud, Jack and Viquar make certain that only persons who are in line receive one. Lines of distribution are set up in this order: clothes, *dekshis*, rice, *dal*, matches, mustard oil, kerosene and a tin lamp. Jack and Viquar make sure that chits are collected at beginning of the line and marked by pen at the end. Building a sense of orderliness calms the people, who realize that they will all be served in turn.

Relief distribution in roped-off area (*photo courtesy of Richard Guerrant*)

Children with milk distributed in first relief shipment

The engineering students, led by Mahmoud, take on the job of handing out clothes. All children get a quart of milk, delivered already-open by Baldwin.

Guerrant and Sommer take medical cases — about twenty, from compound fractures to "cyclone syndrome" — the latter have a greater or lesser degree by all survivors consisting of severe abrasions, often like a 3rd degree burn on volar forearm, biceps and inner thighs and less on chest. Invariably survivors had clung to a palm tree and been able to hug it for the hours of the maelstrom. Most were granulating in well and required topical cleaning, dressing and antibiotics.

Dick Guerrant conducting a medical examination
(*photo courtesy of Richard Guerrant*)

One of the few female
survivors

94

But there is one unexpected need that we had not included in the shipment: Not long after we fed long lines of dazed and glassy-eyed men, and few remaining wives and children, we were inundated with requests to import women, that the business of family rearing could go on.

At dark the team closes the distribution. Very little food is left, although there are still a thousand cans of milk, kerosene and plenty of clothes. Jon recounts:

The last item was our nemesis as people badly wanted clothes and were never satisfied with the article given them. The boys issuing them tried to please and as a result, as the best items were taken, it took progressively longer to get people through the lines.

In about four hours the team manages to distribute rations to more than 1,400 hungry persons.

"You will be the first to receive help in the morning," Jon promises to the last-comers who have walked from the farthest distance. "Show us this chit and you will be at the head of the line."

Viquar is approached by several men. "Sahib," they say, "we know others farther south have heard that help has arrived. We beg you to save enough supplies to give those who must still be trying to reach your camp."

Viquar, moved by their selflessness, thinks, "They are so desperate themselves, and yet they still want to lessen the suffering of others." Around nine p.m., interviews with the locals indicate deep appreciation for our fairness. They clearly recognize how limited in supplies we are.

Waiting for rations

Asheque seated next to HELP tent
after first day's distribution (*photo
courtesy of Richard Guerrant*)

The team holds a planning session:

"There are so many more people in need, and we really don't have enough," Steve says. "Even if they say they understand we have run out, there's no getting around their hunger, plus there will be others who have heard about us who will expect to have supplies."

"Yes, hopefully there will be an air drop in the morning, but what if there is not?" Al adds.

Viquar suggests: "Look, why don't Jack and I take the country boat and return to Hatiya to make a case for goods from their stocks of relief supplies?"

Jack agrees: "Yes, that's what we should do, because we saw plenty stacked in the godowns there. We can arrange with the government authorities for some of them to be used for victims on Manpura."

Viquar says, "We'll explain the dire condition of the survivors here, and they will surely respond positively."

Jon is not so optimistic: "We didn't find any officers there to be very cooperative, but it is probably worth a try, since the need here is so great, and we are not certain the plane will find us tomorrow."

"We should stall in the morning to see if any planes or boats arrive," Geoff suggests.

"I agree," Jon says. "It's obviously better if we are here to hand things out fairly, the way we did this afternoon."

"Right," Dick adds. "Anyway, there may be more victims who appear with cyclone syndrome, and we can treat their wounds, even though we can't give them relief supplies."

Jon writes: One group of students were deeply concerned because the Muslim women would not come out of purdah to receive goods and we were thereby "favoring" Hindus. We agreed reluctantly (as we needed every man to run our base) to have a group of them go to the baris and give chits there to be carried to us by men to receive saris and other women items (e.g., dekshis).

Cyclone victim with relief supplies from HELP

After the meeting, the HELP team slept by the depot and the students went north to a grove where the air was better. Dick Guerrant recalls: "Camping amidst corpses on the beach . . . a certain future Public Health Dean and ID [infectious disease] guy swore secrecy about [our taking] prophylactic antibiotics as we contemplated getting cholera from local water after there were only a few bottles of safe water available. In fact we stayed healthy" (unpublished cholera lab memoir, July 1970–March 1971).

The enormity of the misery affects Jon deeply:

The first night we cooked ourselves a large pot of stew and rice, but in spite of a daylong fast and backbreaking labor unloading supplies from our native country boats that had followed me to Manpura, the stench of death defied the strongest appetite. I carried the cooking pot into the inky night beyond the ring of our small lantern to find two naked boys huddled against the chest of their father, clad only in a tattered waistcloth. Placing the food before them, they looked at me with blank fear. "Here, it's for you. Go ahead. Eat," I implored. No response. "They've not eaten in twelve days, Sahib. They don't believe it's really for them." The father coaxed and they dug their hands into the pot. They ate in the frantic silence of those who have seen death. I slipped back into the wall of blackness, lay on my back looking at the riotous heavens above with the Milky Way coursing down the center, and wept.

At five a.m. the next morning, the people began to gather and quietly watched us arise guiltily from our warm blankets, damp with dew. A few good citizens pushed dead bodies into the rapid tidal current, hoping to clear the air in our area. The ensuing stench incapacitated some of the volunteers.

On waking, Jon contemplates the nature of the *char* islands:
I shivered as the wet chill moved back from the river, embracing me on the low mud bank as I gazed across the wide mouth of the Ganges. Eddies snatched at the crumbling bank in the never-ending process of tearing down what had only recently been built. Manpura is one of hundreds of islands throughout the delta, never more than six feet above the silent rushing river, evanes-

cent though fertile homes for those who prefer the menace of a capricious sea to the insidious onslaught of population on the more stable soil of Bengal.

Fast Food Drops

At the Chittagong base, we decide to package air drops of emergency rations in the form of a prepared meal, at least until supplies of fuel and cooking oil reach the devastated area. Abed's serene drawing room, decorated with old masters from Florence in brushed-gold frames, and a dramatic modernist Rashid Choudhury jute hanging, is transformed into a bustling food-production line. Kaiser has organized the purchase of foodstuffs from local bazaars with our pooled cash. As he explains: "What could we do? In those days there was no such thing as bottled water or packaged or canned food in the country. We decided that the best thing we could do was make as many 'care packages' as we could. . . . I went to the main produce market in town and bought large quantities of whatever was available to make our packets" (Zaman, Kaiser. *Nine Lives of the Cat That Keeps Going and Going*. Unpublished manuscript, last modified 2013).

Huge aluminum pots full of eggs hardboiled by Abed's overworked cook, sagging raffia baskets piled with *khirai* (a kind of cucumber), large plastic bags filled with *muri*, and jute bags with big chunks of dark-brown *gur* (unrefined sugar) are stacked around the carpet. We form an assembly line. Kaiser drops an egg into a strong plastic bag, and passes it to Putul, who puts in a *khirai* before handing it to Mohamed Ali, who breaks off a chunk of *gur* to add to it. We joke about "Abed's Fast Food" as I measure out *muri*. One of the drivers, Hasan Ali, volunteers to tie the packets firmly shut so they won't split open when dropped. These emergency rations will provide vital protein and energy to the survivors who are without cooking fuel. Although we work feverishly, the intensive process of packing plastic packets consumes most of the night. Toward dawn, we have hundreds ready to load on Noel's plane for the morning air drop. We also purchase one hundred tins of kerosene and five drums of petrol to load into space we've secured on the ship leaving November 24 from Chittagong to Hatiya.

Abed: The Eye of the Storm

As pressure to produce a supply line from Chittagong to the relief team on the island intensifies, those of us based at Abed's house catch only a few hours of sleep, running mainly on adrenalin, but in spite of eighteen- to twenty-hour workdays, we manage to stay focused and organized. Abed seems to resign himself to the whirlwind that has invaded his life. He turns up fresh every morning for breakfast, impeccably dressed in a suit and tie, and steps into his chauffeur-driven car to put in the day's accounting work. If he ever tires of us, it is not apparent, although sometimes I suspect he finds that eight hours of keeping accounts orderly at the office provide a welcome respite from the chaos that has overtaken his home. But he always appears engaged with the challenge we face. There is definitely a "can-do" spirit bouncing around, and more and more it seems to energize him as well. I sense his amazement at our energy and determination and a quiet admiration of how much we have been able to accomplish in a few days. In turn, I am as impressed with his thoughtful contributions and seemingly unflappable nature, as I am with Kaiser's cheerful attitude and ability as a facilitator. Abed sits in his easy chair, one leg crossed casually over the other, scotch in hand, drawing on his pipe, while contemplating the buzz around him or contributing his opinion and help. I envy his ability never to accumulate any paper. As soon as he finishes reading something, he gives a command or a comment, crumples the sheet into a ball, and hands it over his shoulder to Mohammed Ali, his bearer, who stands behind ready to serve him. I begin to think of Mohammed Ali as a devoted wastebasket.

Mohammed Ali

Locating the HELP Team

Greeting Noel Kinvig on the tarmac early in the morning of the 24th, I tell him, "Thanks for letting me come along with you. Our team set off for Hatiya two days ago. I really need you to help me locate them, so I can find out what supplies they need. You're our best hope of finding where their camp is."

"We'll look for them, but how will you know what they need?" he asks.

"By signal flags we sewed for them to spread out on the ground."

"That's a good idea," he says. "Glad to have you on board. The supplies you've brought have been loaded. Climb in. We're taking off."

We ease out smoothly over the vast expanse of ocean. After about twenty minutes, Noel shouts over the loud drone of the engine, "There's Hatiya."

The southernmost tip of an island appears on the horizon. The nose of the small plane takes a dive, and I taste papaya. I suck in a deep breath, swallow hard, and hope that the rest of my breakfast doesn't follow. I see small dots running toward the sound of the plane. As we skim just above the palm tops, weaving in and out, Noel's loader, Mike, kicks and shoves bundles out of the open door of the cargo hold whenever he sees anyone waving on the ground. My head spins woozily with every swoop, but I force myself to concentrate on locating the HELP team.

"Where are they? Where are they?" I ask myself anxiously as we approach the northern end of the island. No sight of flags, team or organized activity; just random people running for bundles dropped from the plane's belly. Noel yells over the roar of the engine that he is going to head back.

"Can't we look just a bit longer?" I shout back. "I *must* find them!"

I feel desperate. I can't bear failing to locate the team. Suddenly, my eye catches blinding sunlight flashing off metal. Kerosene tins! We swoop closer. The tins are arranged in the shape of an arrow pointing west.

"Noel! See those tins? They've left a signal!"

He looks skeptical.

"Oh *please*, Noel. *Please* fly in that direction to see if there could be another island," I plead.

The plane lifts sharply upward. My stomach lurches again as he heads out across the ocean. It seems to take forever until we spot land, although it must only have been a few minutes. I look down to see lines of people streaming northward along the bunds of the barren fields. They stare up as we fly low over them, before trudging on with determination.

Streams of survivors moving north to reach HELP

It is eight a.m. and the exhausted men of the HELP team, nearly out of supplies and besieged by a thousand hungry survivors, are ecstatic at the sound of the plane's engine.

"Look, Noel!" I shout over the roar of the engine, as I again spot flashes of sun on the metal of kerosene tins, and see the display of red crosses. "There's our team!"

We can't miss those men leaping up and down, wildly waving their arms over their heads. The lettered signal flags Putul and I sewed are spread out on the ground, clearly indicating they need more of everything except medicines and fuel. We swoop low over their camp searching for fields to drop bundles. While Noel's colleague dumps out the parcels of relief goods we have prepared, I wave as wildly as the men, and toss an old shuttlecock canister from my copilot's seat with a message rolled up inside that includes an assurance that the plane will make a run again tomorrow to provide the supplies they have signaled they need.

Noel yells, "Gotta go! Running low on fuel." He yanks the stick back, banking sharply east toward Chittagong. I am relieved that HELP has a base camp, although the ground reality looks horrific, full of desperate survivors and unburied corpses.

Later, Jon expresses the reaction of the team: I felt elated as Noel roared over our camp on Manpura and I saw my wife Candy waving frantically out of the cockpit. How we loved that plane and its jaunty cowboy pilot. We literally cried with happiness.

Noel Kinvig flying low over Manpura with relief supplies

Multiple Drops

Amazingly, we were able to collect most of Noel's drop over a ½ mile run with the help of quickly deputized locals. The crowd of about 1500 did pretty well. Not long thereafter a Pak Army bomber hit us with about 10 *maunds* [one *maund* equals eighty pounds] of much-needed rice, packaged in 25 lb. sacks. Now we could go, but within ten minutes a Pak Army chopper who had been called in by the plane dropped in with 15 *maunds* of rice and 15 *maunds* of *atta* [wheat flour].

The line for women and children

We decided to distribute from the other side of the field also, as one line would be too slow. A line for kerosene was established and dispensing and control of the line was done entirely by local recruits. Kajol, of the engineering school, and Rohde set up a line for rice that became also self-sufficient in labor. Kajol took four reliable-seeming chaps to check on people repeating, and each person was rapidly given about 3 seers [one seer equals one kilo] of grain. This was by far the fastest and best method of distribution, for we moved 30 maunds in two hours, distributing to about 1500 people. This, we decided, is important to remember in future areas — that if each line is policed by locals, and dispenses one type of goods, it will go quickly.

A dish filled with rice

At noon, CIBA dropped another load of needed grains, clothes and welcome messages from Candy Rohde that more would come. The line for women and children moved like a snail as some boys tried to satisfy each clothes request. Old clothes are of use but just cannot be distributed equitably. Should be done in a separate line or, perhaps, by the hand of reliable locals.

Engineering student giving out relief supplies

Swinging into High Gear

When Noel and I swoop over the base camp at noon our second flight of the day, I toss another shuttlecock tube out the window.

Dear wonderful HELP team!

Hooray, hooray! We know where you are and Noel will concentrate on anything you want. He's with us all the way. Try to get your code out in as big letters as possible. Hard to see the small stuff. That "P" was good.*

You have the message that Murphy and 6 volunteers from Eastern Refinery left on this morning's ship for Hatiya. I'm counting on your contact there to get in touch with them. (Saw only one speedboat so assume other is at Hatiya port.) Wednesday, 4 student volunteers are supposed to leave on the ship. They will have all info where to find you.

There is a *pukka* [brick] building in the center of the island — some sort of community center with lots of flags flying. You are probably better off where you are for sea mobility. Seem to be plenty of people (alive and dead) around you. Stench must be ghastly. Hope you can use nose masks.

I have made contact with the German Red Cross, who have 3 water distillation plants leaving for Ramgati today. They must locate there because they have to work with sweet water and need to get their microbuses by road. The man I spoke to, Peter Paulew, is going out with his unit today. They will give us the fullest cooperation in getting water supplies to you. They have helicopters coming and hopefully will drop to you other types of supplies. (I've had 2

---

* The code letter signal "P" is for "people", i.e., volunteers.

109

hours of sleep each night and still going break-neck so please disregard confused sentences.) Don't count on anything immediately from them because they have to get set up and get their copters down here. They're horribly frustrated by the red tape — were held up four days in Karachi for clearance. We hope their copters can take out our personnel for rapid transport. I've also asked them to get their transport plane to get tents and blankets to CIBA for immediate drop. They are getting goods from Dacca and can choose what they want. Also working now on Capt. Gilani for these items. They will contact me on return Thursday from Ramgati about water situation. Other goods (tents, etc.) will be loaded directly on CIBA if they come through.

George [Curlin] wants to come but can't be freed until you return. Other volunteers are being mobilized in shifts.

I have someone at airport now waiting for Swiss plane to try to get medicines off immediately and load them directly with Noel. Perhaps faster than Russian ship, which hasn't even unloaded yet. Try to signal your needs.

I'm working now on these things for you: people, tents, shovels, spray pump [for kerosene on bodies], blankets, more food, medicines, clothing.

Sandy [Baldwin, wife of Ford Foundation director] is working on helicopters in Dacca. Seems they only take high priority people on the US Army ones, so little chance of helping us. She is madly rounding up funds for us (as is Marty). Seems Steve's family is intimate with the head of relief operations in the States and she's talking in terms of a million dollars coming through us. ☺ I said ok as long as they send 7 administrators. Ford Foundation in Islamabad-Pindi is waiting for word from Steve about what to do and at present is giving us full cooperation if we want Pakistan staff from Dacca to

110

help with organizing and the two drivers and cars are now completely legitimate. Hasan Ali [one of the Ford Foundation drivers] is a golden one and is so happy to be involved. He was sitting last night till late helping with packaging. I've taken care of gas and per diem for them and kept records.

All voluntary organizations in Dacca are trying to channel through us and we have many funds coming in. We need to reassess situation. This is really snowballing. Right now we're concentrating on helping you, whom we love and adore most. We'll hope to get more information from you to help us in deciding what other directions to take.

We are going to drop water this afternoon in plastic cans — hoping they won't break. It is not boiled water because we're hurrying to get them to you today. Signal if you want more. If you use small letters, put them in an open space so they catch our eye and separate them. Also secure them so wind doesn't blow them. Did I love seeing your arms waving. Could see everyone so well. Happiness is knowing where you are.
♥♥♥♥♥

If you think you are capable of assessing if Noel could land, do so. He was trying to figure out if he could. There's space south of you, but need to know if it is hard-packed. Put an L out if you think he can land. Use G—glucose S—salts.

CHAPTER 6

Overwhelmed

Afternoon of November 24

News that aid has reached Manpura passes quickly by word of mouth down the island. Lines of starving villagers pour into the landing camp beginning early in the morning of the 24th. A hungry crowd swells. Tension fills the air as the victims become aware that the piles of relief goods are disappearing into the hands of those in line ahead of them. They also know that more and more people are approaching the distribution site. Panic swells with the fear that there might not be enough for everyone. Jon's line in the ground is smudged out when the orderliness of the distribution is shattered. Jostling hungry men try to get closer to the center where the rescuers are working. They press around the volunteers, stretching out their hands in supplication, before surging forward to try to grab whatever is left. The team has no solution to the desperation of the survivors, because they know that the supplies are nearly exhausted after feeding around 1,600 victims.

Nearly overwhelmed by the milling mob, the beleaguered volunteers ask each other, "How soon will we have more air drops? What if not enough supplies come to take care of all these people? What will happen if we can't satisfy this huge, hungry crowd? It's terrible to think we don't have enough for people who haven't eaten for over a week." It is agonizing to face the prospect of many helpless hours without food to distribute.

The crowd closes in

1300 As our stores dwindled, and more were sitting eating and hoping for more, the crowds closed in and made distribution difficult. We had fortunately set aside ample food and clothes to give the volunteers who had worked hard and well. We agreed to give them their share if they would first clear the area, asking people to go as no more would come.

It becomes harder for the volunteers to manage the ravenous crowd. Many have used whatever remaining strength they can muster to trudge up the chain of islands to reach the distribution point. After the expectation that their misery will be relieved, it is unbearable to be told they must go back to their stripped land and destroyed homes. Exhausted, they huddle weakly together, submitting to their fate.

Al Sommer walks back into a scene that is far less organized than when he left the distribution site to do a brief survey. Jon reports:

```
Sommer returned from a very useful epidemiol-
ogical tour. Found roughly 50% lost, not 90% as
Government estimates.* No significant disease.
Not a sign of shelter.
```

Unexpectedly, Al has found a solution to the HELP team's distribution problem: the local *zamindar* (landowner), Hafizullah Choudhury,** who turns out to be the patriarch of the largest landowning family on Manpura. Al reports, "I happened upon him at the school with medical students, distributing the few goods they have by a very well controlled system."

"Let's go together to meet him," Jon suggests to Al. "We can talk to him about ways we can cooperate with the relief work."

Hafuzullah's *pukka* house is the only structure still standing on the island other than the school. He invites Jon and Al in, where he recounts his story of the storm: "We had to keep crawling higher up the palm trees as the water rose. The wind lashed us so hard we were sure we would be swept away. Then everything went absolutely quiet, and the wind stopped. It was just like a TV screen when it loses the picture, all gray and fuzzy and crackly. We didn't dare come down from the trees, because we knew it was the eye of the storm, and sure enough, suddenly the wind returned to whip and slash us with the same horrible frenzy. A wall of water surged over us. It felt like it would never stop. We could barely hang on we were so exhausted." Realizing

---

* The major reason Manpura has higher mortality than nearby Hatiya is that, in contrast to Hatiya with its coastal embankments, Manpura is packed earth formed from silt deposited by the ebb and flow of the tide. With the island only as high as tidal level, the surge at high tide was devastating.

** Choudhury in Bengali means "landowner." There are a number of people mentioned in the account with this common surname.

how well organized Hafizullah is, Jon asks him, "Would you be willing to distribute the remaining HELP supplies?"

"My family will help you in any way we can," Hafizullah assures them.

Jon and Al are relieved to discover a local leader who knows the islanders and will be able to command respect and cooperation.

At two p.m., after talking to Hafizullah, Jon writes:

It appeared that a good organization was working for fair distribution through Choudhury. Each *bari* is surveyed and population counted. A list made and goods distributed by workers to the *bari* on a fair rotation basis. This delivers to all shut-ins, keeps the mobs off the airstrip, removes distribution problem from organizational persons like ourselves who are inundated with problems of procurement and delivery to the area.

Sommer and Rohde, with Murshed Choudhury, one of Hafizullah's sons, go to the primary school (around two and a half miles away) to hand over red cross markers and explain the airdrop system. As they walk to the school, they note that the center of the island has much good rice standing that will be ready for harvest within weeks. There is not one shelter standing and only one tube well is working. Al and Jon help the other volunteers shift the remaining HELP goods to the space where the Choudhurys are working. The discovery of local power marks the beginning of a long relationship between HELP and Manpura's most influential family, a connection that continues to grow and change over the course of the relief work.

Even concrete collapses

There is a more confident feeling among the HELP team after making the transfer. It seems to be a good transition, allowing them to make an orderly departure. They break camp. The base was closed out and personal gear moved into the waiting boat.* The volunteers feel confidence in the organized effort of the local leadership, although they have no assurance there will be

---

* Reflecting about why the team pulled out even after they spotted the plane returning with air drops, Jon recalls that because they had found "no significant disease" or medical problems among the survivors, the doctors among them believed that with no apparent need for trained medical services, they should get back to their patients and their scientific studies at the cholera hospital.

enough supplies to handle everyone's hunger. At least the situation is no longer out of control.

Just as the team is poised to leave on the army launch that came back for them, they spot Noel.

At 1500, old faithful CIBA came over with a load of blankets. Chaos broke and we did not try to control distribution. Gesticulation finally prompted the pilot to look towards the school and he found the new drop zone and finished his load there. We found on arriving in Chittagong that he has successfully continued dropping there all day today.

Trouble on Hatiya

Before the relief team returns to Hatiya from Manpura on the 24th, Viquar and Jack's expedition on the afternoon of the 23rd to plea for relief goods from the Hatiya authorities meets with denial, in spite of full stocks, because we are not working in their district. Manpura is the responsibility of the authorities on Bhola.* When they set off for the telegraph station to send a message to Chittagong, their expedition takes an unexpected twist. They encounter a group of agitated, hungry survivors marching to protest the chairman's alleged misappropriation of relief goods. They accuse him of taking them for his own benefit, instead of distributing them to the victims. "Join us!" they shout. "We are starving, yet the chairman steals what is rightfully ours. If you lead us, he will have to listen." Viquar, concerned with this violation of the government's obligation to distribute aid,

---

* When Viquar appraises us concerning the administrative setup of the islands, we learn that Manpura is a *thana* administered by Bhola, a larger island farther west. Hatiya on the east, where our team launched their mission, is not responsible for Manpura, so any launches from Hatiya would not drop on Manpura, which therefore fell in between the cracks of relief. Manpura was essentially ignored by the Bhola authorities, who could barely cope with the storm disaster on their much larger island.

and Jack, who is ready to take part in a protest, join the demonstration. Viquar's diplomatic explanation of why they did not have a chance to send any message to Chittagong reads:

Tuesday, 24th November

When we called on the Army Major in Hatiya for sending wireless message to Chittagong, we were urged by a large number of starving people to lead a deputation to the Chairman of Hatiya Basic Democracy for distribution of the relief goods which were stored in the godown for days and there was also allegation of the Chairman misappropriating the same. The crowd forcibly took away the relief goods from the Chairman so that they could distribute the goods amongst themselves. As we happened to be on the scene, on our way to the I.W.T.A. Terminal, police authority suspecting that we had instigated the agitation, asked us to get out of the island by the next morning. In the circumstances we decided to come to Chittagong and expedite supplies of goods to you. Viquar

Jack and Viquar do not wait until the next morning to leave Hatiya. Discovering that a boat returning to Chittagong is ready for boarding, and feeling unsafe, they leave immediately. Later, when Jon and Steve reconnect with Jack in Chittagong, he tells them gratefully, "It was your good relationship with the Hatiya authorities that protected us when we joined the protesters. Your contacts helped Viquar and me get off the island."

Steve Baldwin and Jon bring the dinghy back to Hatiya from Manpura. Steve reflects on their journey:

We stopped for a few minutes at a nearby *char*, lying inches above sea level, flat and barren-looking as a Scottish moor, although in fact more fertile than a riverbed—death-lonely and horrible in silence. The two of us stood for a moment in

118

all that emptiness, considering what it must have been like twelve days before, with crowds of harvesters shrieking panicked from their rolled blankets, to face the towering black wave and howling wind—then to die (C. Stephen Baldwin, *Shadows Over Sundials,* 2009, p. 224).

Steve Baldwin on Manpura (*photo courtesy of Steve Baldwin*)

When they land in Hatiya, Jon and Steve take a rickshaw into town, and wire Candy and Noel that they will return the next day to Chittagong, and that they should continue with the airdrops. Major Salamat, still in charge on Hatiya, has no news of Viquar and Jack, but responds supportively: "Call on me to help you at any time. Please let me know whatever I can do for you."

Upon returning to the steamship ghat, they are surprised and happy to find Bob Murphy, a teacher at the American School, who has come with more volunteers to join the operation. They consign one dinghy to him, and arrange for the three country boat pilots they brought from Manpura to return with the new group the next day (November 25), when Bob will take kerosene and volunteers over to Manpura. Jon and Steve sleep on the ship, planning to load the other Pak Shell dinghy on in the morning.

Steve recalls:

> There'd been little time to let the full scale and intensity of the horror really register, our minds and bodies having been protected, as in battle, by simply coping. Lying on top of my sleeping bag a while later, I finally had time to recall that first incredible sight of distant death, bodies clogging the island's shoreline as far as we could see, the close-up stench, awful swelling, the discolored disfiguration. I pored over stark images of horror-scarred survivors' faces, their struggles to eat for the first time in days, to break through dull resignation and regain their usual friendliness and warmth (Baldwin, p. 224).

When Jon arrives in Chittagong, I say, unsympathetically: "What are you doing here? You need to be on the island. We're ready to load the next airdrop. We have a guarantee from Noel of daily flights to give you regular supplies as well as communication with our base on the mainland."

I'm upset that the majority of Manpura's capable relief crew has melted away while we've been working at breakneck speed

120

to put together a full cargo of supplies. I'm also concerned about losing Jon's level head and problem-solving ability. With assurance of a reliable team on the ground, Noel is ready to devote his sorties almost exclusively to us. He knows Manpura's survivors are particularly desperate because of their extreme inaccessibility. He also appreciates the advantage of making safe airdrops that will be equitably dispersed. He has occasionally seen heavy bundles land on the heads of storm survivors, knocking them unconscious or killing them. He has witnessed the strongest men running first to grab the supplies from his airdrops, often leaving weaker victims with empty hands and bellies.

I appeal to Jon: "We don't want to risk losing his commitment to us. With him flying sorties to our camp, we have the capacity to expand our ground operation."

Although Jon feels he is overdue to return to the cholera lab, he realizes that at least one of us should have stayed to try to coordinate continued aid. As we had no communication we didn't know what to expect. Actually Candy had begun to drop notes as we left and we could have had good information.

Confronted by my determination, the assurance of air support, and because "it was the day before Thanksgiving and I knew nothing was going to get done at the lab," Jon decides to return to Manpura to stay until he is summoned back to work. Before setting off in the morning on the coastal steamer for his second journey to Manpura, Jon writes a detailed report about the HELP team's experience over the past two days, much of which is quoted in the preceding descriptions and observations made during the eventful hours they spent. His closing assessment is:

There are many excellent people working for relief, from the village level to the top of the Army. There are few or none who span the whole complex gamut of relief work from evaluation of needs, to procurement of goods, to bulk transport and distribution, to delivery to the needy. Godowns are too full in areas close to the needy; people are concerned about waiting for direction from the top, arbitrary governmental lines of geographic division retard distribution in areas that have received little. HELP has a key role to play in the Manpura Island area, perhaps extending to the inhabited *chars* and South Hatiya. These worst-affected areas need immediate stopgap measures to help the population until more substantial and long-lasting government programs can be established.

After finishing his report and taking a quick shower, Jon boards the battered cargo ship with more supplies, reaches the shores of Manpura on the 26th, and does not return to Chittagong for almost two weeks. By adding Moslem holidays to the Thanksgiving days off, he is able to stretch his time away from the hospital. He is heading back to try to create an effective relief operation on an isolated island with negligible government presence, no other doctors, without clinics, electricity, running water or sanitation facilities, roads or moving stock of any kind, and where the huts of flimsy bamboo thatch, with perhaps a bit of corrugated iron sheeting for a roof, have been swept away to become flotsam in the tidal wave, all water has been rendered undrinkable, and all food and recently harvested crops washed away. He takes on this enormous task, confident in our Chittagong supply line, Noel's air support and the assurance of plenty of willing volunteers to share the work. He knows Murphy will have reached Manpura, and he learns that a contingent from Notre Dame College is also on its way to Hatiya, heading to Manpura.

Pakistan's martial law president, Yahya Khan, was poised for travel to China when the cyclone struck. A low number of casualties had been reported, which may be why he bypassed East Bengal. When he returned from his diplomatic visit, the enormity of the destruction was more established.

Yahya Khan

Archer Blood writes in his 2004 memoirs:

President Yahya had stopped in Dacca on November 16 en route back from China where he had a very successful visit, winning a commitment for larger amounts of military assistance. It was reported, and widely believed in East Pakistan, that he had celebrated heavily on his flight back and had spent his one day in East Pakistan in something of an alcoholic daze. His aerial reconnaissance was not by helicopter but in a plane flying at 3,000 feet. Back at the Dacca airport before returning to Islamabad, Yahya made a few comments indicating his sorrow but, according to some press accounts, was heard to say, "It didn't look so bad." His seeming indifference to the plight of Bengali victims caused a great deal of animosity* (*The Cruel Birth of Bangladesh*, 2002, p. 77).

Opposition newspapers in Dacca accused the Pakistani government of impeding the efforts of international relief agencies and of "gross neglect, callous inattention, and bitter indifference." Mujib, who had been released from prison, lamented that "West Pakistan has a bumper wheat crop, but the first shipment of food grain to reach us is from abroad" and "that the textile merchants have not given a yard of cloth for our shrouds." "We have a large army," Mujib continued," but it is left to the British Marines to bury our dead." In an unveiled threat to the unity of Pakistan he added, "the feeling now pervades . . . every village, home, and slum that we must rule ourselves. We must make the decisions that matter. We will no longer suffer arbitrary rule by bureaucrats, capitalists, and feudal interests of West Pakistan" ("Emerging Discontent, 1966-70." Accessed September 20, 2013, http://countrystudies.us/bangladesh/16.htm).

---

* "Government of Pakistan was simply not in position either physically or psychologically to deal with disaster of scope of East Pakistan cyclone or to handle in-flow of large-scale foreign assistance. Initial reaction was to invoke traditional relief machinery which made for slow reaction, over-modest estimates of casualties, damage and relief needs. Pak military has clearly not made major effort of which it is capable and this fact, plus surprising failure of Yahya and cabinet to display more 'heart' has embittered East Pakistanis and fueled East Pak criticisms of GOP aid effort. Ironically, tremendous outpouring of foreign assistance and on spot relief efforts of U.S. and others have intensified East Pak resentment by putting West Pak concern and Government of Pakistan efforts in a poorer light" (Blood 2002, p. 99).

Third Note in the Shuttlecock Tube
(Dropped on morning of November 25)

Tuesday, Nov. 24

HI! How's the smell today?

I've been operating on two hours of sleep per night and no food today until 5:30 pm so I'm afraid what I have to say is not going to be too coherent. Please forgive.

1. Basically we have full cooperation from every possible organization and authority, and so does the team in Dacca. I was told tonight in the [government] Control Room that although they didn't feel really right about saying it to my face, they thought our group was doing the most the fastest. We literally have every connection, but we are depending on no one but ourselves to get things done, so we can be absolutely sure that things are accomplished.

2. Hope the goods we dropped today were useful. We have a huge operation going now, with Lions and Rotary donating food and clothing, etc. We should be fully mobilized soon so that we can drop on all of Noel's runs, or most of them. He is so exhausted that he stopped early today and we couldn't get the water cans to you in time. Will go out tomorrow morning. We also have access to the government's relief supplies, and I got half of Lincoln's list of medicines today by sitting on the medical control officer. Some will be airdropped Wed. and the rest are coming by boat with the nine volunteers from Dacca (6 Notre Dame students and three father-teachers) leaving in the morning on the

ship (Nov 25, 8 am). We also have authority to use the Russian ship's medical supplies and I will probably go to get them tomorrow afternoon.

3. Helicopter situation. We are contacting a Colonel Zillober tomorrow who is coming down from Dacca with the West German helicopters. They take one day to assemble and should be ready to go by Th. morning hopefully. We have been assured from several sources that these are available to us. We're really working on it from all angles, but it is still the most difficult thing to get. We realize how essential it is to your mobility. We're also trying to see what can be used from Barisal, since Manpura Char is under their jurisdiction and not Chittagong. We're mobilizing all the forces we can in your direction.

4. George arrives at 7 pm tomorrow night, and will be leaving on Thurs's boat along with 4 Bengali student volunteers and petrol and kerosene. We thought we should stop the petrol and kerosene after this for a while until we see how the groups can manage getting them off the boat. (We're giving them army names to contact.) (I hope we're not persona non grata after Jack's experience—however, he said that it was the army friends you made that saved him!) The boat is apparently under guard, but how awful not to have it running. Apparently the driver really cannot fix it. YUG. Lincoln is anxious to relieve you, but cannot leave the lab until someone gets back since he's the only one left. Can you possibly signal to us with your flags when you can leave? Initials and date is enough.

5. Situation at lab ok. Hare [Acting Director of CRL] not upset at all, just trying to plan for Eid [Muslim holy festival] and hoping some of you can get back to cover. (Some concern).

6. 12 tents are coming on a truck from Dacca tonight and we will air drop them to you as soon as possible.

7. Jack [Zakaria Choudhury] is going up in tomorrow's plane and I'm asking him to make a map of the population and *pukka* building, etc. on the island, but I think you are in a good spot, easy to recognize. I have marked you on every map in the Relief Control Room so they can't forget you. CBS is after you but has no real way to get to you easily— seems to be the basic problem.

8. Too tired to continue. Can send more as things develop. All things going well here, and we're trying to make you as happy as possible as soon as possible — no small job.

Love
Candy

Dick Guerrant (left) with Lincoln Chen at the cholera hospital

HELP Makes an Immediate Census

Al and Jon found the Choudhury family drawing up a list of survivors, making them the first persons to conduct a census in their immediate area. In order to have complete and reliable statistics on which to base relief and rehabilitation plans, Jon asks Fr. Timm and his Notre Dame students to conduct a house-to-house census of the whole of Manpura, counting every living person and recording the extent of losses. The relief commissioner, when I met him on November 19, estimated that only 5 percent of the population of Manpura remained alive.* However, we discover by careful tabulation that, although the loss of life is enormous,

---

* This shows the inaccuracy of initial casualty reports, which were probably derived from air reconnaissance.

more than 30 percent have survived. Most likely, the commissioner had flown over Manpura and, from aerial reconnaissance alone, thought nearly everyone had perished. The toll is indeed terrible: out of thirty thousand inhabitants, twelve thousand remain, but this is far more than an estimate taken by looking out of a plane window. With an accurate count of heads we are able to define the amount of food, clothing and shelter needed.

> Our main aim in the survey was to learn how many people had survived in each *bari* (family cluster) and what assets they still possessed: cows, buffaloes, chickens, ducks, farming implements, housing materials, etc. It was interesting to learn that the ducks had returned to their own *baris* (like cats), even several days after the storm surge. We also asked about the amount of land each one owned, since HELP was to carry out agricultural rehabilitation in the second phase of its program. About 75 *baris* could be covered in a single day, that is, if we stayed out all day without coming in to eat until dusk (Timm 1995, pp. 140–41).

Jon describes in a letter dated December 7 why accurate lists of survivors are necessary:

> I trekked to the center of the island where we had the first meeting of the Union Council and the few Union officials in the area. I told them that we were going to have airdrops, that we were going to have support in every way we could and that the only thing we asked of the people was honesty, and that we were going to give out one equal share of everything to every man, woman, and child across the island without regard to previous status or present status. It was quite clear to us that, with the exception of about four wealthy families who had had wooden, Burmese-type homes, everybody else's home had been washed away and with it all their possessions. All the people were starting out on a pretty even level. We insisted after the first day's distribution that all ward members must submit a complete list of

everyone in their ward by name—adult, male or female, or child—classification, and register all that we gave them. This seemed cumbersome at first, but provided the first basic data to come out of the cyclone area on what the survival rates were. It showed the tremendous loss of women as compared with men; and, in a country which has 50% of its population under 15 years of age, it showed children to account for less than 20% of the total population surviving. It was easy to see who had taken the brunt of the loss. . . . With these accurate lists, we began to make distributions. The distribution was handled through the ward chairmen and their volunteers who assembled in front of the schoolhouse. We would give them in front of their people how much each man in his ward was being allotted. Then they would go to an adjacent field, accompanied by one of our volunteers, where he gave out one blanket for every five people, one for every three, one for two and so on. Everyone knew where he should be. Also, it was known that if the lists were falsified and one man took ten items instead of the four he deserved, that was six less for the other people. So very quickly they got rid of dishonest people by and large. We have had a lot of problems with this right up to the present. I guess when people are destitute, a sense of moral rectitude is not important in life. But in several days, it became quite clear to the people of the island that we were going to be able to meet their needs and that we were honestly and sincerely interested in establishing a lasting distribution system and that we would somehow manage to keep it stocked.

Coordinating

Abed's dining table is littered with papers and accounts. I try not to stumble on the Petromaxes stacked near the table when I race for the insistently ringing telephone. It's another call from Dacca, this time asking me to inform the camp on Manpura about a large drop of blankets coming tomorrow. A truck appears at the gate delivering bundles of several thousand lunghis we ordered from the bazaar. I search for some money to pay the driver before I type out the message I will drop from the cockpit of the CIBA plane onto North camp in the afternoon. A reporter rings and is disappointed when I refuse an interview. I need to hurry to meet the captain of the Russian ship to ask him to give HELP medicines, before I connect with Noel for the flight. Rob Choudhury, the relief commissioner, says he's going to drop by for a drink early in the evening after Abed returns from work. The cook has been instructed to add nine more volunteers to the dinner list. They will also need breakfast and a briefing before they board the steamer for Hatiya. I must reserve space on the boat for them, as well as for more large bags of rice, and tins of kerosene and petrol for Manpura. I need to confirm with PIA about the return flight to Dacca for two volunteers who must return to work. In the back of my mind, I'm trying to figure out where to get more walkie-talkies. I'm not sure if I'll manage a shower before dinner.

CHAPTER 7
Sorting Out Priorities

A common understanding is that victims of disaster require the immediate attention of doctors. The day after HELP arrives on Manpura, a team of medical students landed at our camp and wanted to begin vaccinations for cholera. Not only had we seen no evidence of cholera, but also a team was vaccinating from Choudhury's center at the school. They were interested in little else so we let them go and get as many as they could.

Relief Commissioner Rob Choudhury's initial excitement about HELP is because the team is composed largely of trained personnel from the cholera hospital. He believes they will be able to provide much-needed expertise and medicines. Although not yet clear exactly what the team would require, Putul and I sewed a flag with the letter M to be spread out on the ground of the first base camp to signal the CIBA plane if medicine is needed. When Noel and I fly over Manpura, M is not laid out with the other flags. This disaster defies the common assumption that medical attention and supplies are a priority.

The realization that survivors have no pressing medical needs is revealed when the HELP team does an informal health survey while handing out initial relief supplies. They find survivors suffer primarily from "cyclone syndrome": flesh deeply torn from being buffeted when clinging to rough bark of palm trees. One of Jon's first observations is that their abrasive wounds are "granulating well," evidence that only a few basic medicines will be sufficient. There are also some broken bones, which can be set without need for medicine. Dispensaries will be able to handle most needs. Jon reports: It is quite evident to me (Rohde) that medically, these people have problems from the trauma suffered, and the next [need] is food and shelter.

Corpses are a public health hazard that can be controlled by burial and the use of lime disinfectant. For this work, shovels, not medicines, are required.

Demand for Field Hospitals

While our team is making the observation that medical needs are relatively insignificant and simple to treat, on November 23, Eric Griffel, the provincial USAID director, hears from the relief commissioner that "a crying need for foreign self-contained mobile field hospitals has developed." Apparently, without any information from the field, Kuwaitis, West Germans, and Japanese already have sent or are promising field hospitals. The United States is asked to provide three or four such units, but before they commit to this proposition, an evaluation is planned (Blood 2002, p. 78).

Lincoln Chen calls us in Chittagong with his message, which I relay in the next flight:

Apparently, Eric Griffel has requested that the epidemiology section of the laboratory take an active part evaluating the medical needs of the affected victims. Henry Mosley has been running all over Dacca trying to find out what he can. I have informed Marty that he should contact me regarding Al Sommer and Jon, who are now in perfect position to send back firsthand reports [from Manpura]. This has worked out ideally for all concerned and you all are in a perfect position to handle a vital need of the laboratory.

> The Relief Commissioner has sent the news to
> you by TELEX that Henry Mosley* along with Col.
> Davis of the Army Surgeon General's staff, is
> supposed to be in a US Army helicopter, flying
> over Hatiya all day to assess the situation. He
> knows to look for you. Try to establish a base
> camp and put out your white sheet to signal him
> your position. (If this reaches you by airdrop
> you should have already done so.) Relief Comm.
> is also carrying this same information in the
> letters I gave him to carry directly to you.

Neither the relief commissioner nor Henry locates the HELP team's doctors on Manpura, so they are unable to take advantage of their "perfect position" to transmit firsthand knowledge about the medical needs of the victims. Instead, Henry is flown to Char Chubia on Hatiya in a small Bell helicopter from USAID/Nepal on November 24, twelve days after the storm, to carry out a preliminary assessment of the situation on the ground.

The survey team's helicopter lands with its rotor blades going full speed. When hundreds of survivors run toward it, the relief commissioner on board orders the pilot to lift off to find a less-crowded area. The crowd surges forward in desperation, fearing they will miss out on the relief supplies. They grab hold of the landing gear, causing the tail rotor to strike the ground and shear off. When the copter crashes, the tail rotor blades slash three men, one of whom suffers a deep laceration in his leg. A U.S. Huey helicopter evacuates Henry, the relief commissioner and the pilot to the American base at Begamganj after receiving their "mayday" message. We learn later that PAF Air Commodore Masud advises U.S. officials not to try to evacuate the in-

---

* January 23, 2012 email message to author from Dr. Henry Mosley: "I was not directly involved in [the Manpura experiences] at all. Rather, I was leading our team of epidemiologists in working with the US Army on carrying out an initial survey of the cyclone affected areas [with helicopter support]."

jured Bengalis, most likely fearing mob fury against the Americans. The injured are treated locally, receiving very basic care.

All of us, along with the passengers on the helicopter, are sickened by this incident. We can't help but think that if USAID had linked up with our established ground operation's disciplined relief effort, the kind of injuries that storm victims suffered on Char Chubia would have been highly unlikely.

Henry recalls:

> Based on that assessment (of 24 Nov), I submitted to Col. Rex Davis a plan for a more extensive survey of the entire affected area over the next few days. Basically we mapped the entire area to determine locations for a field assessment, developed a rapid data collection instrument and then organized 4 epidemiological teams of 2 persons each. They were dropped by Huey helicopter early each morning at 4 specific designated locations. They spent the day gathering some quantitative and qualitative information regarding the local situation and then were picked up in the evening, before dark. Each night I consolidated the data into a comprehensive report (with a map of the visited localities), duplicated it, and it was distributed to all interested parties early the next morning. In the meantime, the teams were off to other areas. This way, in less than a week we had a basic epidemiological picture of destruction, the health conditions of survivors, and the acute needs for food, etc., covering the entire affected area (Mosley, email message to author, March 2, 2012).

Henry's report reflects what the HELP team doctors on Manpura discovered, and concludes that there is

> no need for the US to move hospitals to East Pakistan for surgical or medical patients. The survivors of the cyclone-tidal wave, that is, those who did not drown, were cold and hungry, and some suffered abrasions from clutching to palm trees, but virtually none suffered broken arms or legs.

They urged sending rice to those areas where 100% of the food had been washed away. It was only after we had this more "comprehensive" assessment that the decision was made not to send the field hospitals (Mosley, email message to author, March 2, 2012).

Other countries that send mobile hospitals at great expense find their doctors underutilized.

The cholera lab's opinion is that there will be no increase in cholera as a result of the cyclone, and it is also agreed that there is no need for typhoid vaccines. As the HELP team suspected, the cholera inoculations of victims by the medical students who first landed on Manpura were not a priority.

The news of Henry's expedition is accompanied by a request for Al Sommer to return to carry out additional surveys: The word from Marty is that Al Sommer should get back as soon as he can, since the lab has been told to assess the medical needs of the cyclone victims (i.e., epidemiology section) . . . you're probably more concerned with food, clothing, etc., right now for the people than a real field hospital.

Three months later, in February 1971, Al Sommer conducts an epidemiological survey concerning the extent of losses across the entire area affected by the cyclone: "Ten 2-man teams carried out a systematic survey of 2,973 families in 79 unions and in 9 thanas (the next larger local government unit than the union) in the cyclone area" (A. Sommer and W. H. Mosley, "East Bengal Cyclone of November, 1970: Epidemiological Approach to Disaster Assessment," 1972, *Lancet*).

The teams noted that, since only families were interviewed, the death rate did not take into account how many deaths occurred in families where everyone was wiped out. Neither did it include migrant laborers who made up a large part of the population in November, the harvest time. Their estimate of two hundred forty thousand dead is a minimum estimate. It may be twice as large if the deaths of migrants are considered. As HELP had already noted on Manpura, young children, the elderly, and women had the highest mortality.

The survey also indicated that 87% of the housing had been destroyed and, as of February, 52.4% were still living without adequate housing. 72.4% of the families had received some kind of food relief, and 73% some cash relief. The number of families unable to plant crops because of a lack of plows, bullock or seeds was 56.8%, while 35.1% of the families customarily engaged in fishing were unable to fish due to the loss of nets and boats (Sommer and Mosley 1972).

Only Mosley and Sommer are called to act in their official capacity by conducting epidemiological surveys. The majority of cholera hospital doctors continue to serve the emergency in their personal capacity as volunteers without any government orders, concentrating primarily on providing supplies of food and clothing for the cyclone victims. They do not act in their role as public health employees of the U.S. government.

Cold War Thaw

[My note to field] The Russian ship which has already landed contains over 9 tons of medical supplies, mostly oriented toward [cyclone] relief work. These supplies which we have not yet seen (just unloading Monday), should be perfect for our needs. We have been assured that we can have unlimited use of these supplies for our depot. One of us will review the inventory and acquire as much as possible. Please send information on our needs (specifically) as soon as possible.

With information from the field assessment, a list of medicines and equipment is drawn up by the CRL doctors on the HELP team:

```
Tetracycline tablets (20,000)
Penicillin tablets (10,000)
Antibiotic eye ointment (2 cases)
Vaccine and inoculation needles for cholera,
smallpox and diphtheria-tetanus
Needles (vaccine administration, intravenous
fluid)
Syringes
Bandages and gauze
Tape (all sizes)
Splints
Topical antibiotics
Blankets
Sterile alcohol pads
```

When the huge Russian freighter pulls into the Chittagong harbor loaded with medicines, I seek out the officer in charge. I am surprised by how cooperative he is with me, though he knows I am American.

"What medicines can you give us?" I ask.

"Anything you need. Give us a list," he offers without hesitation.

I hand him our list, and he gives the order to have it fulfilled. Though it is the height of the Cold War, the cyclone makes it possible for some rare personal encounters between citizens of otherwise antagonistic countries. We are pleased to have support from this unlikely source.

The Russians continue their active involvement in cyclone relief for many weeks, and HELP has a number of interactions with them. Their helicopters are based in Dacca, so my contact is limited to obtaining supplies from their ship in Chittagong harbor. At our Dacca base, it is Aysen Talmon's renowned entertaining skills that thaw the normally self-isolating Russians. They love being invited to her soirees to mingle and down vodka. At least in this corner of the world, a catastrophe is warming up the Cold War.

Jon examining a young boy's eyes. He treats him with antibiotic eye ointment sent by the Russians.

Dealing with the Casualties of the Storm

Bodies are still strewn on mud banks, in ponds and across the fields. The smell of decay continues to permeate the air. Jon writes that the team has tried to get farther south, but found coast shoals up and carcasses every few feet. The HELP team organizes the remaining islanders into burial details in a food-for-work scheme, but people are reluctant to participate because they want to honor the dead with dignified rites. They finally realize that there is no choice. The public health hazard is stronger than the need for traditional rituals. HELP ships shovels and spray pumps. The pumps are to douse the dead with kerosene to stall the spread of contamination. Over the next weeks shallow graves are dug for thousands of corpses. Some bodies are piled onto rafts hastily lashed together from storm debris. The grim floats are then pushed out to sea. Thousands of bloated cattle and goats are dragged into piles to be burned.

Murshed Choudhury becomes an enthusiastic participant in the HELP team's relief efforts. As one of the sons of the largest landowning family, he is able to command respect. The relief workers are impressed with how willing he is to take on responsibility. He has been energetic and effective in organizing distribution, and now they call on him to head a burial team for the victims of the cyclone. The grim task sits heavily on his young shoulders. Everywhere he looks there are bodies swelling as they rot; bodies of friends and neighbors who were alive only a week before. He breaks down when he finds Ali, who had played football with him, and Javed, who had kept everyone laughing. He nearly steps on his mother's close friend, Didi Aunty. She and his mother liked to gossip and tell stories as they stitched old saris into quilts. How terrible he feels to see her lying facedown in the stricken rice plants, her sari torn and twisted, her flesh distorted and discolored purple.

Never again will the elders wend their way along the bunds after a hard day's work to gather around his father in the cool evenings, talking about how to store their bumper rice harvest so they could sell it when the price rose. No longer will he hear them chatting companionably while they smoke bidis. Their bodies lie rotting in the stripped fields. Murshed is sure he hears the dreadful whoosh of vulture wings. He shakes his head, trying to bring the silence back. He would rather have no sound than the cackle of carrion birds. He struggles to remember. Weren't all the birds were blown away by the fierce wind?

He lifts a *kodal* [short-handled hoe] he has rescued from the tank near his house, and sets out to do the duty that has been assigned to him. As he picks his way gingerly through the salt-encrusted fields, terrified that he might stumble unexpectedly onto some wretched body, he feels lost in a maze without an end. Worse yet, he has let go of the string he was sure he tied to the door of the house. He is convinced that if he had been able to hold on to one end of the string as he walked, he could find his way home. His distress increases when he remembers that the door to the family house has been ripped off and swept away in the tidal wave. His string is lost forever. The hot breath of jackals is on his neck. He's sure their vicious teeth are about to grab his ankles. He shakes his head again, hoping they will go away. "Why are they here?" he thinks. "No animals have survived." A voice keeps asking him, "What is the reason for this horror that has come to our golden island?" His troubled mind works the question over and over again without an answer. His thoughts are as fierce and threatening as the Bengal tigers he knows live in the nearby coastal jungle of the Sundarbans.

His sense of duty gives him the strength to bury six hapless souls during what seem like interminable hours. "Why did they die and not me? Why did they have to die? It doesn't make any sense." The questions crashing around in his head are as complex as the pattern on an intricate piece of brain coral, but finding an answer seems as hopeless as expecting his friends to return to life. His eyes are glazed and dull when he returns to his *bari* in late afternoon. "Why did so many people have to die?" he asks his father in bewilderment. He feels the bottom has fallen out of his world.

Striding up and giving him an encouraging pat on the shoulder, the leader of the relief team tells him, "You're doing a great job, Murshed."

"How can this man always be positive, as if no task is too difficult?" Murshed wonders. "How he can have a face like a lotus bud, filled with possibilities?"

141

There is no way for him to know that the volunteer wept in the dark after witnessing the same terrible scenes of suffering and death, nor can he know he is grappling with many of the same questions. The relief worker knows there are no certain answers, even if he could reach deep into the teachings of all the great masters. He does know, though, that lotus flowers rise out of muck. He urges in an encouraging tone of voice, "Carry on, Murshed. We really need you to help finish this difficult job. I know it's hard, but it's necessary to do to protect the living from sickness. We have confidence in you." Murshed's heart sits heavy in his chest. He manages to stifle the groans that threaten to burst from it. After seventeen days consigning the remains of his community to the earth, he crumbles.

Unfortunately, Murshed Choudhury must be committed to the mental institution in Pabna.* The trauma of burying hundreds of his community members seems to be principally responsible for his collapse. The HELP team worries that they may also have played a part in his breakdown by laying too many responsibilities and expectations on his young shoulders.

Unlike Murshed, if a volunteer who comes to the island is overwhelmed by the dreadful task of burying bodies, he has an alternative. He can go home. With thousands of fatalities on Manpura alone, the need to bury corpses continues for weeks. Fr. Timm describes the Catholic brothers and their students who bravely volunteer to take on this onerous but necessary task:

> Bro. Nicholas had brought three students of St. Gregory's High School to Manpura on December 6, and several more student volunteers from Notre Dame College, together with Fr. Jim Banas and 11 seminarians from the Archbishop's House in Dhaka. Their main task was to bury bodies. Several

---

* His illness continues to plague his family for years. "Murshed Choudhury has gone out of his mind again and they want me to bring him back for sending to the mental hospital at Pabna, since he often shouts that he is the leader of the Mukti Bahini [freedom fighters]" (Letter from Fr. Timm to the author, November 2, 1971.)

stomachs revolted against the gruesome work and one school boy had to be sent home as being too squeamish for the job (Timm 1995, pp. 140–41).

Kaiser's memoir tells of his reaction to bodies he found weeks after the storm.

One day, two of my new colleagues and I went off on a macabre "treasure hunt", as I called it. Although we were helping only the living and not burying the dead, someone had reported to me that there were still bodies hidden under the brush and in ditches. We located four shriveled bodies. One was only a torso, apparently of a young boy. It was grisly work and I was surprised that I felt no particular emotion other than the practical need to bury them. Not until many years later I thought of the mummified remains as people who had once lived.

Sister Joseph Mary recalls philosophically the homecoming of a corpse: "On the last day of our stay, Sister Perpetua and I met at North Camp where we could catch a boat to take us off the island. There, we saw a body of a man perfectly intact that had just been washed ashore, after almost three months at sea, returning to his homeland for burial" (Sister Joseph Mary, email message to author, July 23, 2012).

CHAPTER 8
"It's Really Moving"

November 25: More Air Support

Twelve days after the cyclone strikes, international aid starts to pour in. Five huge German Search and Rescue helicopters, with their imposing chopper blades, whir down onto the airport tarmac, dwarfing Noel's little plane. It's my turn to stride purposefully over to announce myself: "Hi! I'm Candy Rohde. We have an organized relief effort of volunteer doctors working on a remote island that is very difficult to reach. We really need you to do airdrops for us. We'll provide the provisions for the sorties. Won't you help us?"

The young captain looks at me incredulously, and I think, "Oh no, I guess I'm not as good at this as Jon," but suddenly there it is: the broad smile I've become accustomed to seeing on every face I've approached.

Speaking perfect English, he says, "Sounds good to me. My name is Wilfred. Let's get started. When can you be ready to go?" My two aerial partners are now a daredevil Kiwi cowboy and a precision-trained Teuton.

I brag to Jon in a November 26 message about building a friendly relationship with the pilots: `We're pretty well in with the German pilots. Drank beer and banged the tables heartily with my fist at the hotel. A few more drinking songs and they'll never drop anywhere else except on those we most love and adore.`

German Search and Rescue Helicopter Transport Wing 64's
Flying Bell UH-1D

The efficient Germans are delighted to see how organized our operation is in an otherwise still-chaotic relief effort. My daily flight with Wilfred becomes a major lifeline in communicating with the HELP crew. It's useful to be able to disembark even briefly to exchange some words with those on the ground. I become accustomed to bounding out of the helicopter cockpit, ducking quickly into crouch position, and darting through the blast of whirling blades. Conserving fuel, we touch ground just long enough to unload supplies and exchange messages, even if we have to yell over the roar of the engines. Often Wilfred is willing to drop off or pick up HELP volunteers at our base camp at the site of the two-story primary school building that withstood the cyclone. This one standing building, crumbling and without shutters in the window openings, is transformed into the nerve center for HELP's work on Manpura. The ground floor is converted into a storage spot from which to distribute goods. On the first level, reports are banged out on the old typewriter, and volunteers spread their sleeping bags on the cement floor at night.

The two-story primary school is the only surviving building. Fr. Timm (center left) has his foot on one of the wooden plows the islanders are examining. *(Rainer Kruse, photographer; photo courtesy of Bread for the World)*

November 26: Practical Priests

"Father Peixotto wants to send a group of Notre Dame College students to Manpura," Marty informs me in our daily call.

"That's great," I reply. "Maybe they can take responsibility for those thousand Canadian tents you say are coming."

We are open to all offers of help, figuring the more hands the better, as long as volunteers are able to endure camping in the rough, assailed by the stench of bloated corpses. Innate problem-solving skills are preferred attributes.

When Fr. Joe Peixotto and Fr. Richard Timm, his fellow priest, first set foot on Manpura on November 26, along with their student team, they set up camp outside the school where the HELP team had moved their operation. Jon came back to

Manpura on the same day, so they are all in time for the Pakistan Air Force Hercules cargo planes (C-130s) to drop tents onto the field, their parts bouncing and scattering all over the place. George Curlin remembers that "Dick Guerrant was spotted in the cargo door of the Pakistani cargo plane kicking out bales of blankets as it flew overhead. A PHS Officer in a foreign military plane! And no seatbelt" (email message to author, January 28, 2010).

Dick Guerrant recalls: "Thanksgiving dinner back at home in Dacca was delayed until I returned from the Pakistan Air Force C-130 flight, assisting in pushing out 980 Canadian tents from the open cargo door over the now established drop site on Manpura Island. I have lots more stories about how to deliver banana sandwich bag messages from the sky to alert those below prior to the tents dropping from the sky."*

Timm recounts with characteristic humor that these Sears, Roebuck discards have exotic names like Swiss Chalet, Holiday Ranch, Family Lodge and Highwall Marquee. He quickly discovers parts are missing and assembly is nearly impossible, even for volunteers armed with a higher degree. He sets the students to the challenge, spending many hours alongside them wrestling with the tents, while "openly expressing our extreme exasperation," as he candidly puts it. After hours of gritted teeth and sheer persistence, bright canvas shelters go up all over Manpura. Jon remarks, "They add a colorful air as one flies over the island in a helicopter" (Jon Rohde, letter to Northrups, December 7, 1970).

---

* "I recall meeting that close new friend and C-130 Pakistani Air Force copilot again on our 1971 evacuation flight amidst the war with Pakistan only four months later. He was too anguished by the bloodshed to look me in the eye" (Guerrant, Richard. "Brief Cholera Lab Memoir: July 1970–March 1971," Smriti, ed. Amal Mitra, 2012).

Chittagong Supply Line

Detailed messages to the field such as this one illustrate how we keep in touch about the complex operation that develops.

Message from Candy, Thursday, Nov 26:

1. Steve — Do you want either Hanan or Farouk on the island? They are ready to come anytime. Farouk is available over Eid. Osmani says things are going so well here, he would be better off in Dacca helping through Ford: organizing drivers and cars for us, funds, contacting people.* We're working on earphones for Noel although it looks like helicopter service is going to be so good that we won't need any.

2. I have got you an in-board, out-board cabin cruiser — an Almarene, 25', with a draft of 3'-4'. Has a small capacity for fresh water. Runs with diesel, 40 gallon tank. We will now send diesel fuel by boat, not petrol. It will be ready by Sat.** They also have a walkie-talkie and we will give you the channel. The U.N. is giving it, through a Mr. Christen Eriksen and I really had to bat my eyelashes over my bloodshot eyes for it. Comes with master named Sultan.

3. Murph [Bob Murphy, teacher at the American School] — What are your return plans? Janice needs to know for travel reservations. Saturday, Geoff [Sharp], Dick [Guerrant] and Al [Sommer] are coming by helicopter from Dacca and you can go back with the copter then if you want. Helicopter service will be every other day to/from Dacca. Sat., Mon., Wed. etc, at 5:30 a.m. Can

---

* With the encouragement of Steve Baldwin, the representative, a number of personnel of the Ford Foundation assisted in the cyclone relief effort. Osmani, Hanan and Farouk, employees of the foundation, worked with HELP both in Chittagong and on Manpura.

** In my field note on November 28, I report: "25 foot Almerene boat scheme down the drain—couldn't get insurance, one engine bad, working on other possibilities."

148

take 3 people and a few small items. 5 Pak-Acres engineers arrive here by car tomorrow around 2:30 p.m. Sandy [Baldwin] says use wisely for responsible position because they are skilled.

4. Today, (FRI) will be 2 helicopter drops with foodstuffs. Also PAF-C130 dropping 3000 blankets, 990 tents. Starting hopefully from Dacca at noon. Set up a landing area for drops on the southern base camp. Friday's C-130 will drop on northern camp because not sure of drop site on South. They will also be dropping every other day.

5. More commissary supplies are arriving with Geoff [Sharp] et al. on Sat.

6. Let us know WHATEVER you need. It will be supplied.

7. Medical supplies ordered through German goods at Dacca airport will be delivered Saturday morning. What a laugh it was with Marty and I telling Lt. Col. Henry Winthrop the amounts of medicine we needed. We just pulled numbers from the sky, and he kept saying, "Ja, Ja!"

8. Walter Schweppe will try to get out by copter from Chittagong on Friday.

9. Trying for battery-powered loudhailers. Japanese don't have any here. Are working on Skanska now in Dacca and Chittagong. [In my field communication two days later I mention that loudhailers are being used in the election campaign and are tough to get.]

10. Friday morning we are sending by boat to Hatiya/Manpura 3 Lions' Club members plus Mr. Samuels from Dacca and 3 high school boys. HOPE-FULLY the latter will be useful. One is his son, very young, but he insisted he's going. If there's any trouble, get rid of them. No more are being sent of this nature. (They came unan-nounced.)

We love you. It's really moving.

German helicopters will send everything you need. Just request.

Candy

Mujib Meets the Press

Sheik Mujibur Rahman holds a packed press conference in Dacca on November 26, just after he returns from a nine-day tour of the cyclone area. He makes his speech in English, reading from a prepared text, so that the dozens of foreign journalists will understand him.

Archer Blood writes in his memoirs:

"He dwelt at length on what he termed the 'criminal negligence' of the government in failing to respond effectively to the disaster, citing 'failures and bottlenecks' which prevented relief from reaching the people. He declared that 'the people of Bangladesh (not East Pakistan) will be eternally indebted to those countries who have so generously come to their rescue in their hour of need.' He said that 'the generous assistance received from abroad only underlines the tardiness and callousness of our own rulers.' He castigated West Pakistani politicians who preached the integration of the two wings but failed to visit East Pakistan to 'extend sympathy and succor to the survivors.'"

He also warned that "if the elections were postponed once more, there would be civil war." The Chief Election Commissioner "decided to postpone elections only in nine or ten of the most seriously affected constituencies in the disaster area" (Blood 2002, pp. 116–17).

Yahya "declared he wanted to hand over power as soon as possible to representative government, since 'I am a soldier and want to return to the barracks.'" (This may have been to allay concerns about his political ambitions.) His response "concerning local criticism of Government relief efforts, in particular, allegations of 'criminal negligence' made by Sheikh Mujib—'people of East Pakistan were emotionally hurt because of disaster, which is only normal.' In response to another question concerning Awami League criticism, he replied, 'I hope they come to power and do better. I have tried to do my maximum.' [Yahya] "expressed gratitude to foreign press for focusing attention of the world on the calamity, but cited 'fantastic stories' that had appeared, exclaiming 'why cash in on human miseries for sensationalism.'" [He] "told reporters that he felt that Pakistan had responded to a huge disaster as well as any underdeveloped country could be expected" (Blood 2002, p. 118).

Yahya made it clear that unless the constitution preserved the "integrity" of Pakistan, martial law would remain in force.

Blood remarks that in hindsight he believes that the reason for the indifference of West Pakistan to the suffering the cyclone brought, "was that the rift between the two wings had grown so great that any display of real empathy between East and West Pakistan was no longer a possibility" (Blood 2002, p. 120).

Circle of HELP: Chittagong, Dacca, Manpura

Jon, seated on an empty kerosene tin in front of the primary school, hunches over the battered typewriter I have managed to scrounge for him. His mind races with all the ideas he wants to write down to send with the chopper when it lands in the morning. The machine, propped on another kerosene tin, hiccups and its keys stick, but it is better than having to scratch out hasty messages in his nearly illegible handwriting. He has become used to wearing the same khaki shorts and old cotton *kurta* (long collarless shirt) day after day. There is no *dhobi* to wash, iron and fold his clothes before returning them neatly to his closet, as he is used to at home. Washing in the many tanks on the island is not an option. They are fetid, filled with storm debris, farm tools and the occasional rotting corpse. The islanders are more concerned about receiving food rations than following their normal twice-a-day bathing routine. Drinking water is airlifted, or sent on the coastal steamer.

Jon bats out detailed, specific instructions of what is immediately needed, and proactive plans to move swiftly into rehabilitation work as soon as the relief operation, already largely in the hands of local volunteers, is under control. His daily missives become the focus of my planning. With no remaining animals, crops, seeds, fishing nets or boats, and a dearth of shelter, we need to source experts to help us move into rehabilitation.

"We must find professionals trained in agriculture, in fishing cooperatives, in the best types of cyclone shelters. See if you can find skilled water and soil engineers as well," I urge Marty and Peggy in our daily conversation. They have set up a home-based control center in Dacca, where friends donate hours of their time to find a way to fulfill every request we send them from Chittagong, as well as being proactive networkers themselves. Volunteers offer to assist in the ground operation as the magnitude of destruction from the storm begins to be more accurately reported. Estimates of the dead are well over three hundred thousand, and continue to rise.

"I'm flying down to Chittagong for a few days so I can see what's happening from your end," Marty calls to say. She arrives on November 27th to find out how the supply line from Chittagong works, and to get a better understanding of what we do at the base we've set up at Abed's house. I immediately introduce her to the helicopter pilots, who are delighted to have us for another round of beer. We also arrange a social evening for her to meet HELP volunteers and various authorities assigned to the relief operation who are facilitating our work. After the intensity of eighteen-hour workdays, it is wonderful to dance again, reaffirming our youthful joy in the face of all the chaos and death we've seen. As Alice Walker maintains, "Hard times require furious dancing." It isn't until weeks later that the music goes off-key and the rounds of beer go flat.

Another member of the Dacca support team flies to Chittagong after Marty and Peggy call me with a demand: "You've got to take her. She's driving us nuts. We need a break from her." I agree to have her come, although we are not sure we can provide a calm atmosphere because we are bounding around like mad hares, rarely sleeping more than a couple of hours, but by the time the volunteer spouse arrives on the morning's flight from Dacca, Putul and I have quickly tidied Abed's otherwise hectic living room, and we greet her calmly and cheerfully. We don't want to feed into her hysteria by revealing that we are actually on war footing.

When Abed returns we pull off a leisurely dinner before sending her home to Dacca on the last flight. She seems to have calmed down. But not for long. Word comes that she is continually in a state of distress, so I am asked to send a message to Manpura requesting her husband to return on the next helicopter flight. He is less than sympathetic at the time, but comes up with a good plan: he takes her and their children on an extended holiday.

November 27: Expanding to Three Base Camps

Our first camp is settled inside the primary school, two miles south of where the team landed first at the northern end of the twenty-mile-long island of Manpura. In order to service the entire population more easily, we establish another relief site in the middle of the island, which we initially call South Camp, although its name is Faizuddin. A third, which we dub Char, is started on Sakuchia Char, a smaller island still considered part of Manpura, even though it is split off by a narrow channel at the southernmost end.

Logistics are even more complicated now that three camps are running. Different supplies are necessary for each camp. The number of details to keep track of is evident in this example from my notebook:

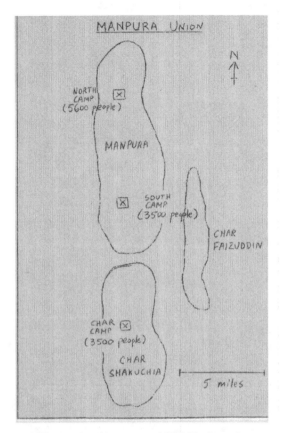

MANPURA UNION

NORTH CAMP
(5600 people)

MANPURA

SOUTH CAMP
(3500 people)

CHAR FAIZUDDIN

CHAR CAMP
(3500 people)

CHAR SHAKUCHIA

5 miles

1970 sketch of location of HELP's three base
camps. (Note: The placement of the three
islands is inaccurate.)

North and South need rice

Check Control Room — What has come on RAF plane
today?

Sunday — CIBA drop food and clothing on South 2

Buy 3000 *kachis* (sickles) in Chittagong

Tents: (drop directly) 400 North, 350 South, 250
Char

154

Receiving relief food

Jerry water containers: North 800, South 1160, Char 1100

2–3000 lunghis: North (Do not drop on center!)

Pick up walkie-talkie from South to recharge

For the twelve thousand survivors on Manpura we provide the following amount of relief food for daily consumption:

6 tons rice, 15 *maunds dal*, 25 *maunds* potatoes* to be shipped directly to Manpura for one month before the rice harvest, plus 50–100 drums cooking oil and 1000 *dekshis*.

---

* This was the amount of food needed daily until the remaining rice was ready for harvest in about a month's time.

155

These supplies are in addition to what the government is providing by ship of 25 tons of rice per week.

Keeping track of how many volunteers are needed at which camp and arranging their travel schedules is a challenge. At one point there are over thirty volunteers to coordinate:

North Camp
6 Notre Dame students
2 Fathers from Notre Dame
2 Acres engineers
3 American students from Dacca International School
Sadeq and 3 volunteers
2 Pakistani doctors
George [Curlin]
Jon [Rohde]
Mr. Samuels
Physics Teacher from Notre Dame
Sheroo's son and one other

South Camp

Lincoln [Chen]
Dick [Guerrant]
2 Acres engineers

Char Camp

Steve [Baldwin]
Gert [Pierot]
Walter [Schweppe]
K Choudhury

Dealing with the Daily Dispatches

Coordination between Dacca, Chittagong and Manpura is a constant necessity, whether for movement of personnel or supplies. For example, the Germans eventually base at least one of their helicopters at Hatiya to ferry HELP's orders of bulk supplies, which are transported by boat from Chittagong. We also need to coordinate airport pickups, cars and drivers. On top of this, we must seek contacts to facilitate our work. One of my cryptic jottings is to Marty: "contact Brigade air level, top army muscle." This note most likely refers to our effort, when the army finally lands on the island, to reach the top commanders to gain assurance they will not interfere with our work.

Other notes from me to the Dacca support team are more obvious:

```
C-130 drops — are they continuing?
Call German woman to engage as secretary
Find mature boys for volunteers from DASS
(American School — should stay at least 3 days
plus 2 for boat trip)
Ask Owen Boyle, Camp Dresser, McKee for water
expert (see Nov 30 report)
Register HELP Manpura telegraphic Dacca address
at Marty's
Long range plans — review Jon's report.
```

November 28: The Vagaries of Relief

Weaving house walls from bamboo

Nazir and Surendra are carefully weaving new walls for their houses when they hear the drone of the same huge cargo plane that had come to drop blankets a few days ago. Their eyes search the sky. Neither wonders where the plane comes from. They think only that things they need rain out of its belly as it flies over the island. They hurry along the well-worn path to the HELP distribution center. Others have heard the sound of the plane and are heading there too. They join the separate line for men, which is much longer than the line for women and children.

Young volunteers are opening large burlap-covered bundles of clothes. Surendra wrinkles his brow when he sees dainty pointed-toe shoes with long thin heels emerge. The volunteers laugh and toss them aside. Next out is a red miniskirt. "What could that be?" thinks Abdul. He hears the team leader remark, "Look at all these short dresses no women here will wear. What a waste of space on a relief flight." It is difficult to find culturally appropriate clothing in the well-meaning donations from abroad. Nazir and Surendra are about to give up when Nazir is handed a bright-yellow jacket and Surendra a pair of handsome purple bellbottom trousers. Their faith in good things appearing from the sky is restored.

Splitting bamboo to weave into house walls

Even when only women are allowed to come to collect items, they usually end up in the hands of men, because women are at the bottom of the social scale. Some men turn up in feminine sweaters, looking like cross-dressers. Sari blouses are the only clothing they don't appropriate, although there is no competition from anyone for the miniskirts and high heels the Italians send. Women's legs hide under layers of cloth on the subcontinent, and high heels would only sink into the mud of the delta.

From the outset HELP set up orderly lines for equal distribution of relief supplies. As goods flow to Manpura, local leaders of the Union Council are asked to organize the people and to check the master rolls to be sure everyone gets their fair share. It isn't long before news spreads that the Union Council chairman has taken seventeen blankets for himself and his family. The probability of a few well-placed people taking more goods than they are allotted is queried by Bob Murphy in a November 28 message for North Camp. He suggests that the Choudhury family are committing acts of favoritism, asserting their privileged position. Over the ensuing months, Fr. Timm will uncover more corrupt behavior by the powerful landowners.*

[Bob] Murphy feels the following points should be checked:

—is Choudhury [local landowner] handling distribution fairly? Do you think he's favoring certain people — that is, the volunteers? —should you tighten up the organization of local volunteers, perhaps with fewer? Are any putting supplies aside for themselves? -

---

* The team gravitates to these local leaders initially because there has not been time or opportunity to find any other reliable people among the survivors. As work continues, they learn that relying on the authority of the powerful landowning families may backfire, because they often have a stranglehold on the poor, who are dependent on them for loans at high interest rates. Moreover, the landless must sell their labor as sharecroppers to landowners, who give them minimal compensation for their work.

As Fr. Timm points out, "Such are the difficulties of even the simplest relief work, even in situations where the greatest cooperation could be expected" (Timm 1995, p. 141).

Union Council Leader checking master roll
to be sure relief distribution is fair

Data sheet of relief distribution on South Char

CHAPTER 9
Supplying Demands

November 29: Chittagong's Link with Ground Reality
Our procurement and shipping base in Chittagong depends on detailed reports from the field. Digesting the daily dispatches and summarizing them is critical. Here is a partial list of field demands found in my notebook:

From North and South Camp Field Reports Received 11/27:

```
Long-term needs: dekki [rice pounder] for South
In 3 weeks: (shipped directly to Manpura if
   possible)
20 tons rice
14 tons dal
Per month: 50-100 drums cooking oil
Short-term (3 day plan) by ship:
1000 dekshis [cooking pots]
tools: daos [machetes](fewer axes, hammers,
   mallets)
Food by PAF:
maunds of rice, large sacks to deliver at cen-
ters
Within week:
500-1000 tents
Several dozen stove wicks
For George Curlin:
stethoscope
injectable antibiotics
```

Personnel:
more administrative Bengali-speakers
need medical students to run dispensary in North
get extension for Eastern Refinery Chittagong volunteer
get Cholera Lab to extend as long as possible

Very long term:
experts to advise on —
    water salinity
    soil salinity
    forming cooperatives
    engineers to plan cyclone shelters for people and animals (probably elevated concrete structures down center of island)

Relief supplies delivered by PAF (Pakistan Air Force) helicopter

163

Jon continues to thump away, writing detailed messages on the cranky typewriter, struggling with carbon paper to make copies. Communication is limited to paper messages or walkie-talkie between HELP camps, although there is hope for a wireless hook-up. Jon's field dispatches are specific, logical and dense with operational details. We grow to rely on his suggestions and analyses. I pore through them underlining his requests. I learn to expect casual asides to pop up in the middle of a paragraph, such as: "by the way, several thousand lunghis could be used." I find that he gives daily shape to our work. Without this contact we would be guessing what is needed on the ground, and be far less effective. More significantly, he has his eye on the future, recommending we look for a full-time administrator.

Jon's report from Manpura North, November 29

This is the original typewriter.

Please invest the appropriate money to get several Petromax lanterns. I'm going blind trying to do my work at night. At least three would be well utilized.

John Smith arrived today and demonstrated his famous organizational ability by virtually planning out the short- and long-run priorities. A very detailed plan is established, including the reality of providing food for up to six months, building homes, construction of a road which has never been here before, cleaning tanks, irrigation, new crops, fishermen. A more detailed report will follow.

CIBA must stop dropping on Center. ["Center" is Kauartek, where the army is based. It is not a HELP camp.] They are invaluable but it takes us hours to try and recover the stuff and we never do. [This is because it has been picked up randomly by survivors.] Assure them that every man, woman, and child is covered by us. This is really important.

There is a telegraph here set up today. We will register as HELP MANPURA. You should go to Tel and Tel and register Abed's address and telephone as HELP CHITTAGONG. Tell them to call you on all messages. See if there is any way we can get use of this for free. We will post two men at the office which is at Center to receive messages. I must admit, we have not tried this yet. Try to wire us. Also set up HELP DACCA and inform us.

Walkie-talkies essential. Last time not charged correctly. Plug in and turn left-hand knob all the way counter-clockwise to off position. Six hours should do. When finished, switch to on and push position. See that little meter at bottom right inside on blue area.

We badly require carbon paper, more notebooks, pens, etc.

NORTH is self-running camp now— all goods must be bulk here. No more relief packs containing multiple things. We need only food, as does SOUTH. Every person on the island has a blanket. *Dekshis*, if over 1000 available, can be used. Fewer are impossible to give out fairly. Any chance of sugar? Deliver all in bulk. NORTH has 5600 population, SOUTH 3600 (both accurate figures), Char estimated at 3500. All camps are now in a phase 2 where we are sustaining. By the way, several thousand lunghis could be used. South and Char need collapsible water containers.

Army Brigadier Shafi came today and seems pleased with the organization. Has sent medical men and says we can use his launch and will have cooperation. We will see. Wireless may be set up.

Personal. I hope to stay to Sunday, as does Smith. George coming on Wednesday with two boys: reserve PIA. We need booze, bread, soap, HELP armbands, Gold Leaf cigarettes. I would like a few clothes if Candy goes home but not crucial. I just smell a little bad.

Volunteers: We need tent setters to go to Char and South if they get tents. We need agricultural expert and water expert for about one week. Acres engineers working on road budget, plan already drawn up.

Replacement for existing operations obviously needed. Can HELP hire a full-time administrator for Manpura? Will a company like Pak Shell donate a man like Kaiser for two months? This is very key to any kind of rehabilitation success.

I must sleep now. Will try to write more in morning.

In the next few weeks, HELP is well on the way to activating the "very long term" goals on his lists.

November 29: The Heart of the Islands

I continue to cheerlead from Chittagong: We think you're fabulous. Looks like we're really on the way, and entering phase two. Exciting possibilities. We're trying to follow through on all your messages.

Only six days have passed since we began work on Manpura, but in that short time we have become well established on the island. The German helicopters and Noel's crop-dusting plane now have us firmly logged into their flight schedules. Messages flying back and forth from island to mainland continue to contain information about supplies, volunteers, or equipment but also increasingly include plans for Phase Two of the Manpura Plan.

We nickname the three bases in the islands HELPland, and the operation in Chittagong HELPgong. Since we are based on Manpura, we drop Hatiya from our acronym. HELP becomes Heartland Emergency Lifesaving Project because Manpura is exactly in the center of the islands affected by the cyclone.

We proactively discuss and inform those in government positions of responsibility about our current work and future plans. We see transparency as a natural part of our effort. I mention our relationships with the authorities in one of the notes to North Camp:

```
Sunday, Nov. 29
We are making arrangements for long-term and
short-term priorities, and it's going very well.
The relief commissioner is responsive as is the
army represented by Capt. Gilani.
```

Captain Gilani of the Pakistan Army stands out in my mind as one who did everything in his power to facilitate our work, smoothing the way for us at every turn. Impeccable and ramrod straight in his army uniform, he frequently turns up at Abed's house to keep in touch with us and see what he can do to help. He even engages, reservedly, in the evening social gathering we organize for HELP supporters when Marty arrives to learn about the ground reality in Chittagong. He is an officer from West Pakistan who understands what injustices and hardships the Bengalis face. Unfortunately, Captain Gilani does not survive the 1971 war.

Effort to Increase Mobility Between Camps

"I really need to get over to Bhola to the OXFAM field camp. I want to see if we can borrow one of their speedboats. Will you drop me there?" I ask my captain friend, Wilfred, who has been generously devoting his country's Search and Rescue helicopters to HELP.

"Why not?" he smiles. "I'm sure I can fit it into the flight plan. When do you want to go?"

"How about tomorrow morning?" I suggest.

"Right. We'll take off at eight."

The Germans' schedules are exact, so I know he will indeed lift off precisely at eight. "Thanks. I'll be there on the dot," I promise him. I'm delighted he's willing to go out of his way to take me. We desperately need to secure reliable speedboats to facilitate movement of personnel and goods between the three HELP camps. Reportedly, OXFAM has a large fleet that is underutilized.

The next morning Wilfred neatly touches his helicopter down in an open area on Bhola near OXFAM's base camp. The swirling chopper blades create a storm of dust, causing tent awnings to flap. "I'll come back for you in an hour," he assures me, "Hope you get what you want." I throw open the passenger door with a practiced hand, slide out of the cockpit, then automatically double over and race to avoid the slashing blades. "Good luck!" I hear him shout behind me. I look around at the huge cartons of relief supplies piled up on the bare ground of a flat field next to the brown canvas tents of the headquarters.

The helicopter has attracted attention and a man strides toward me. Smiling, I say brightly, "Hi, I'm Candy Rohde. I need your help." A voice in my head whispers, "Here goes the brash young American act again. Will it work this time?" I carry on with enthusiasm: "We have a volunteer relief operation called HELP working on Manpura, the closest island east of here, where there are twelve thousand survivors. We're finding it difficult to move supplies and personnel between our three base camps because we only have one reliable boat. We're hoping you might be willing to let us borrow one from your fleet."

The dour, crusty Englishman looks at me as if I am asking him for the British crown jewels. "We cannot possibly lend you anything," he states abruptly.

I try again: "But we have drivers and mechanics who will keep your boat in good shape. You can send a message whenever you need to have us return it. It will make a huge impact on our relief operation if we can have greater coastal mobility."

"Every piece of equipment we have is going to stay right here on Bhola," the field coordinator counters in an unyielding voice.

Not used to refusals, I try once more: "It would only be a loan, and if you are not utilizing all your boats, I can't see how it would affect any of your work."

"No. I definitely will not authorize it," he says with finality. It is quite a shock to have such a curt rejection of my request. Obviously I have become too accustomed to everyone's willingness to facilitate our work. At least he offers me a camp table set up in the open where I can sit on a simple wooden chair to write notes while I'm waiting for the familiar whir of Wilfred's helicopter. I miss the quick positive decision-making of Abed, who met my request for boats in less time than it takes me to jump out of a chopper. My field note begins: "Still working on a boat . . ."

Candy at Oxfam's field camp on Bhola

Not until mid-December will we receive a major donation of speedboats from the German Red Cross, providing us much-needed mobility between camps.

Note to field from Sadek, 17.12.70:

```
4 speed boats with Johnson engines donated
by the German Red Cross to HELP at Manpura are
handed over to Mr. Walter Schweppe and Mr. Han-
nan. The following equipment for all the boats
are:

Petrol tank 4, Oars 4, Life-jackets 12, Pro-
peller 4, Plugs 8, Tools, Jerry-cans 8, Petrol
20 gallons

NOTE: The engines and a petrol tank of boat
no.1 are out of order. To be taken to Chittagong
today by chopper if possible for repair. Boats
should be washed every week.
```

The donation of boats is very welcome and immensely useful, even though they require constant maintenance and often need replacement parts. At last our three camps are connected by sea, largely overcoming the problem of no vehicles and no roads on the island.

November 30: A Brief but Demanding Initiative

After spending a couple of days volunteering on Manpura, Moudud Ahmed,* who is a close acquaintance of Runi and Viquar Choudhury, decides to bring relief to a small island south of Hatiya. He and his friend Jahangir ask HELP to arrange transport and airdrops for his expedition.

---

* Moudud Ahmed later went on to become, successively, vice-president, president, prime minister and minister of justice in the Bangladeshi government.

30 Nov Field Note from Jon at North Camp

Moudud and Jahangir are going by German chopper to the char south of Hatiya on Tuesday to set up a relief operation. They must be picked up Thursday afternoon. Reserve Dacca flight Thursday night for them. We will supply this camp with one load and we hope that Germans will be able to hit them with food at least once a day. We want them to phase themselves out by Thursday. They will organize and leave. We cannot continue direct control but rely on it being carried out under local leadership.

Moudud and Jahangir's report:

Dec 1, 1970 report on CHAR OSMAN (BALUA) (Point 10 for German helicopter). The Germans have a chart of the cyclone area with drop points numbered.

IMMEDIATE REQUIREMENTS

    Tents — 25 (no habitable house exists)
    Kerosene oil — 10 tins
    Hurricane (lantern) — 50
    Utensils, including 100 dekshis
    Salt — 2 bags
    Sugar — 4 bags
    Water — 20 Gerrycans (no tube well exists)
    Rice —

Approximately 100 persons alive out of 2000. Expecting these items by 2nd morning, if possible this evening.

Moudud
Jahangir

Note from Chittagong base to field:
The *char* island where Moudud and Jahangir are/
were is receiving help from many sources. A doctor (Yasin, head of medical control) and [Capt.]
Gilani went there with two helis yesterday and
reported 45 original inhabitants. The rest have
come by barge or boat because they hear that the
pickin's are good on the island. The original
settlers were asked to come to Hatiya for complete maintenance, but refused. Do you want them
as your responsibility? We are planning a rice
and water drop on them, and will await further
instruction.

With opportunists flocking from nearby islands for hand-
outs, the population suddenly swells. The few Char Osman survivors would have been better served by coming for help on
Hatiya. Moudud and Jahangir's effort has a brief lifespan. The
island they chose was small and well serviced by the time they
got there eighteen days after the storm.

Chittagong Base Continues to Deal with Supply, Personnel and Logistics

MESSAGES FOR HELPLAND Nov 30

> Does South Two [known as Char] have medi-
> cines — dressings, Phisohex, gauze, white
> tape, sponges? (Can be transferred from
> South one).

> David Stockley of the Rangunia Cooperative
> Society will be placed in Char [South Two]
> this morning. His advice should be very
> valuable.

Lincoln Chen suggested emphasizing the following:

a) self-help management for the islanders
b) the volunteers love military protocol. Stress that they are working for their people not as paid workers. Food is given because of their hard labor not as pay for their work in distribution.

Happy Eid
LOVE

Nov 30 evening

A truck from Dacca is reported arriving on Thursday with clothing, a table and chairs (where do you want it?) and 600 *dekshis*. We have asked the relief commissioner for 400 more and he says we can have them when they come in the market — one or two days. We'll sit on him.

Tents are extremely difficult to obtain. Marty says none in Dacca, and my only possible source is the British through Comm. Bain. Will keep trying. Do you think it's worth a purchase? (Very costly)

Thursday is requested by Dacca for a strategy session for long-term planning. Jon would be a valuable contribution to this, and Lincoln is dying to come down and replace. Abed and I will be going up for the evening, returning AM on Friday. You decide and I will report to them.

Viquar hopes to be in Chittagong on Thurs.

We're purchasing 4 Petromax at 300 rupees a shot.

CIBA will drop water containers today. Also lunghis if we can get them. No more drops on center. Walkie-talkie returned. Only Noel staying for a few days with one loader (Mike).

Pooh, hopefully your personals are on the way. Love.

Choudhury (the Relief Commissioner) says the gov't allotment of rice per head is ½ lb. and has therefore cut our figures in half. He can supply through Dacca 25 tons per week by ship. He also has access to mustard oil and salt, but not the other goods, so we'll have to spend our funds. We'll keep working with him.

Long-range plans sound very thorough and cogent. We're impressed with the whole operation. Hope the army is too.

Working on tel and tel today.

Did someone go to Hatiya to retrieve goods?

Notre Dame boys must come out by boat. 12 replacements coming very soon.

All those in Helpgong send love to all those in Helpland.

We could use an administrator

Luckily, the perfect person arrives to take over the Chittagong logistics. She is Lynn Bickley, the competent and engaging partner of Terry Myers, who is posted in Dhaka with USAID. "Having finished a family planning project for USAID, I was free to join HELP," she recalls (email to the author, March 4, 2013). She eagerly volunteers to take over the administration of HELP at Abed's house, allowing me to leave Chittagong after the first week in December to join Jon in Dacca, who will be returning at that time from Manpura.

Lynn Bickley

Bangladesh Haikus

Under peaceful palms
on the isle of Manpura
fears of floods again rise.

The helpless gestures
of begging hands pursue and
threaten me always.

You fill these hands
at your peril:
their taking from you
knows no pity.

Does red still glisten
the herb of hope that grows in
the swamp of despair?

Walter Schweppe

CHAPTER 10

Gearing Up for the Long Haul

After consultations with field staff on Manpura, Jon outlines three broad operational goals for HELP.

Goal 1: Immediate relief for the survivors of the disaster. This is fulfilled within the first few days of landing on the island.

Goal 2: Help in the restoration of normal life and rehabilitation of the affected people. This requires sustained effort, but much has already been accomplished in the one week the HELP team has been on the island:

The ward census is complete for eleven of sixteen wards. Knowing exactly how many survivors there are and what they will need to rehabilitate their lives facilitates planning for quick short-term needs proceeding to long-term projects.

Daily food needs will be covered in weekly blocks of procurement, delivery, inventory and distribution. This leaves the rest of the week for the people to work on projects.

A. Agricultural expert to assess present crop and land capability. Clean water including tank purification and cleaning, tube well repair, and distribution. Need plastic bags and water expert, plus availability of pumps and disinfectants.

B. Shelter: completion of tent program requires tents in each site. Slow process must
be speeded. Army may be of some help here if
delivery arranged. Phase two will involve
building with locally salvaged materials.
Requires *mistris* (skilled laborers) and
tools. CI and house timber will be needed as
this moves along.

C. Food: Long range suggests that food requirement will extend up to a year. Much had
been harvested and washed away. Estimated
left is 10,000 *maunds* which if distributed
entirely equally would be 2½ months' supply
for Manpura. However, crop is owned by very
few who may choose to sell outside. Farming
will require animals, plow and other tools.
Should have expert from Comilla cooperative
to assess feasibility of power tools and
more crops.

D. Public works: Construction of North-South
road plus *ghat*.* Estimate is already in our
hands, including drawings, culverts,
bridges. Road cost 17 *lakh*s, *ghat* 12 *lakh*s.
Feasibility for barrage connecting to Char
needed as this would give us distribution to
Char from our central ghat by road plus provide estimated 1500 acres of new cultivat-
able land within a year.

E. Buildings: 25 *pukka* buildings including
schools, and few others. N-S road will make

---

* "ROAD BUILDING
I feel a deep canal along N-S road will be very useful as sweetwater res-
ervoir and transport channel for boats. Could be by-product of road
building if planned. View land acquisition requirements. Government
must do all that. We could only supply labour for earth work. Contact
Mr. WR Khan, Engineering Advisor, Agricultural Department. He is my
brother-in-law" (Kaiser Zaman, "Fifty-Five Days After the Cyclone,"
January 6, 1971).

177

```
natural canal that could be filled by 10-
inch tube well in north for irrigation.

Goal 3. Promotion of self-sustaining devel-
opment programs on an aided self-help basis.
```

From the beginning, self-reliance is promoted and the islanders are encouraged to be involved in their own rehabilitation. Right when we need a person who knows how to cheerlead
people into helping themselves, T. Ali shows up spontaneously
from Noakhali Thana, where he was a trainer in a cooperative
society. His experience in the field of community motivation is
vitally needed on Manpura. He becomes so important to the
HELP effort that he ends up spending many months living on
Sakuchia donating his skills as a "self-help motivator."

Jon ends his field note with some ideas about how to sustain
the administration of HELP:

```
You need Chittagong organization. Will try
for full-time field director here. Abed could
work towards long-term, informing agencies, Re-
lief Commissioner, Government and Army of plans
and needs. Immediate operations as you've been
doing for supply and communications. If Candy
can handle it she must be director and have
tightest structure possible. You're doing won-
ders at present. How long can you continue?
    Dacca Director: Director of whole show whose
principle function is long range operation.
    Suggest Smith after next weekend. Supply as
now.

    Jon
```

Building with locally salvaged materials

On the old typewriter in North Camp, Jon continues to peck out the vision for Manpura he and John Smith have been discussing.

With Smith here, a highly detailed plan for immediate operations, plans over two weeks and a six month program has been drawn up, exact food and equipment estimates, specific public works projects with engineering plans and cost analysis.

He then lists suggestions of organizations to approach for long-term funding for the plan:

If you have any dealing with higher authorities tell them that a 6 month Manpura Plan will be submitted by the end of next week. Hit following to report our plans and tell them we'll have proposals in their hands soon: Education Dept. Social Welfare Dept., ADC and Agriculture Depts., Postal, Tel and Tel, EPWAPDA (East Pakistan Water and Power Development Authority.) Also foreign, like USAID, World Bank, Ford, and any others. Maybe Oxfam can continue early needs. Also UN. Promotion line should be development of Manpura Plan.

USAID should be hit hard. Get Eric to visit here if you can. Give us advance notice and fly him to North. Smith and I will lay it on. Our thoughts are that dollar costs will be quite small. Rupee large as program oriented to Pak availability.

November 30: Dropping on a Dime to Donate

U.S. helicopters make a surprise landing on Manpura from their base in Begamganj near Noakhali. According to Archer Blood's account, they were the first helicopters to arrive in the cyclone area.* Jon remarks after meeting the pilots: "These guys say they're straight from Nam. They look like teenagers and fly just as crazy." He warns one of the pilots about how small the open space close to his camp is: "The German helicopter pilots say they can't land here. It's too tight." His comment is like a challenge to arm wrestle. To his amazement, on their next sortie, all three U.S. helicopters descend in close formation with perfect synchronization precisely on the tiny piece of ground where the Germans say it is impossible to set down even one chopper.

"Anything we can bring you, Doc?" one of the grinning pilots shouts through the roaring whirr of the blades.

"A bottle of whiskey would really be great!" Jon replies.

---

* Actually, the helicopters had not been sent from Vietnam, but from Pope Air Force Base in North Carolina, where they were dismantled, loaded into C-141s and flown to Dacca.

"Gotcha!" the pilot yells.

On their next landing, Jon is greeted by Johnny Walker and someone from USAID. Jon had been waiting for Eric Griffel, the regional USAID director, to pay a visit to Manpura, and is disappointed to see a different official on board. Although delighted to see Johnny Walker, Jon asks the pilot who hands him the whiskey: "Why has that guy come?"

"I've been flying him around the cyclone area. I told him I met a cool American doctor on Manpura and he wants to meet you."

The passenger, Maurice Williams, introduces himself as the worldwide Deputy Administrator of USAID. Jon, the man with a plan, explains that HELP has already put the relief effort in the hands of local volunteers, and has drafted and begun to implement long-term goals for rehabilitation and development. Impressed with the vision of the typed Manpura Plan Jon shows him, and amazed it has been produced in less than a week since HELP began working, he says he will authorize a matching fund: USAID will give two dollars for every dollar HELP raises in donations.* We are pleased USAID is giving us a chance to double any donations we can solicit. It's a much better option than struggling to operate by digging into our own pockets.

---

* Jon will not be so pleased with Williams when they encounter each other again, giving opposing testimony about the Bangladesh liberation war in Senator Fulbright's congressional hearings in DC.

USAID Deputy Administrator Maurice Williams (left) at Base Camp with Jon, who is thinking, "$2 for every $1? Sounds like a good deal!"

Working to Assure a Harvest One Year Ahead: November 29–December 31

In our effort to plan for future food security, HELP recruits technical help from Comilla, Rangunia and Noakhali cooperative training centers. John Smith, the first one to arrive, is followed by David Stockley of Rangunia,* who is a pioneer of agricultural innovation. His initial effort is to organize survivors to harvest and store the remaining crop, but he is also an expert in developing more productive farming methods, and in modern methods of rice cultivation.

---

* Stockley received the OBE (Order of Merit of the British Empire) in 1976 for "outstanding service to agricultural development in Bangladesh." I have not been able to trace John Smith .

David Stockley doing field work in Rangunia

Stockley spends many days on Manpura, giving HELP expert advice and assistance about cooperatives, soil analysis, brickmaking machines and rice cultivation. Jon pays close attention and tries to follow his example. When Stockley leaves, he spends the afternoon trying to emulate his hands-on approach of assessing houses, road needs, farming prospects and people's attitudes. He recalls some of his interactions with the islanders as he walked that day through the northern end of the island:

"Assalam aleikum!" I called. No answer. Just as I began to think no one survived there, I heard a weak voice from under a stripped palm tree.

"Salam, Sahib. When is more food coming? I'm hungry." I saw his wife bent over in the mud of the paddy field using a trowel-like scrap of metal to scrape up grains into a broken clay pot.

"How fortunate you are that your wife survived," I offered, as he continued to slump against the palm. "Aren't you rebuilding your hut? Good palm leaves are left on that tree over there for roofing, and the bamboo floating in your tank is enough to make a frame. Come now, I just found your neighbor already rebuilding and he lost everything."

"Sahib, I'm too tired and hungry."

I tried to appeal to his sense of duty. "Your wife needs you to help. You must lash a shelter together and make a fireplace for her to cook the rice she finds. More food and tools are arriving tomorrow so you can start planting, but we'll only give them to people who have made a hut. We will help you if you work."

I tried to be sympathetic, but at the same time I needed to prod him to make an effort. "I'll be back in two days to see how you are coming along." I watched him slowly get to his feet and walk over to pull a couple of pieces of bamboo out of the tank. I felt like a cross between a cheerleader and an overseer, but I carried on, persuading and cajoling, hoping my presence alone might act as a catalyst.

As I walked further, I came upon a pile of bamboo sticks, sodden cloth and a few battered pots and tools. "*Assalam aleikum.* How's it going?" I said to a man leaning on his *kodal*. "Looks like you are making some progress! Did you salvage all that from your tank?"

"*Ji, Sahib,*" came the respectful reply. But then his lament followed: "*Sahib,* I have nothing. My two cows, chickens, all my tools are gone. What can I do?"

I encouraged him: "Looks like you are coming along well. I see your garden is ready to plant. Soon we'll have a power pump to empty your tank to find what other useful things landed in there. Then bamboos will come and soon you'll be able to build a new house."

"But what for, *Sahib*? My wife and two children are gone. What do I have to live for?"

"Ah, but you know if you rebuild and start to plant, you will have something to offer your new wife. Her family will see you as a man able to provide for her!"

"I will try, *Sahib*, but it is hard because I have nothing."

"We are with you, *petani bhai* (farmer brother). We will be here as you rebuild. Be sure to come two days from now to the meeting at the school, when we will talk about what is needed most."

"I will come, *Sahib*. As long as you bring a woman for me to marry, I will do the rest."

"Wonder how we deliver on that order?" I thought to myself as I padded on, barefoot, across the soft earth towards the next mound that used to be a home.

Jon makes an important discovery as he does his walkabout:
A most interesting observation was made in a number of *baris*. All houses are built on elevated ground taken from diggings in the immediate area. A virtual moat is created, and these are invariably black and foul. The reason is that all the goods in each house were washed into these, including the rice and tools. Thus rapid emptying of the tanks not only will remove this health menace, but provide many plows, hand tools, etc., which have to be there as they couldn't have floated away. Thus the pumps should be put on top priority along with men to run them. In general I was quite impressed with the work these people had done for themselves, especially by comparison with the survey I made on Nov. 24. *Kutcha* huts have been built to give shelter. The area is cleaned, and rice, picked from the fields and mud, is washed and drying. Small garden areas are being prepared for planting and every salvageable artifact is carefully stacked waiting for use (December 4, 1970).

We are also eager to involve the charismatic Mahbubal Alam Chashi in our work on Manpura. He heads the Shesagram

Service Centre at Char Alexander in Noakhali District, a training center for village cooperatives, based on the examples of Comilla and Rangunia. Rob Choudhury, the relief commissioner, drops by Abed's house one evening. He tells me: "I am going to visit Mahbub at his place near Noakhali. He is a charismatic organizer of cooperatives. Why don't you come along with me to meet him? I think you will be fascinated to see how he motivates villagers. You can try to get him involved with your work on Manpura."

When we attend one of Mahbub's gatherings, I am struck by his passionate exhortation, accented by hand gestures to show his audience what he means: "We must turn the hand of a beggar [he turns his palm up] into the hand of a worker [he turns his palm down]."

It is not difficult to persuade him to bring his message to Manpura. He becomes one of our most inspiring and involved cooperative experts, and a good friend, often staying with us when he comes to Dacca.*

Storing Seeds for the Next Harvest

Fr. Timm writes in his memoirs: "One big question on everyone's mind was: 'Is the soil too saline for cultivation?' A layer of white could be seen everywhere on the surface of the ground. Soil samples were sent out for expert analysis." Although there is some consideration of planting an experimental plot with the Irri-20 variety, it is decided local rice seeds are the best because they are adapted to Manpura's saline soil conditions.

---

* Mahbub Alam Chashi . . . wasn't a *chashi* (farmer) but a former member of the elite government service, called by the initials CSP. A Chittagonian from Rangunia with rural roots, he was a firm believer in the cooperative movement, women's emancipation and rural development. He was very keen to see village people live in brick homes rather than mud huts" (Zaman, email message to author, October 16, 2012). From April 1971, he served as Foreign Secretary for the Bangladesh government in exile. His contributions to the national life were recognized when he received the Independence Day Award in 1977, the highest civilian award in the country. He died in 1983 at the age of fifty-six.

HELP tells the farmers, "We will buy your seeds at a fair market price, and put them in safe, dry storage where they won't be destroyed by mold or rats. Bring your bags of seeds to be weighed. We will label them with your name. When it is time to plant again, you will have the option to buy them back at the same price." The plan is designed to guarantee food security and fair compensation, but some islanders, such as Abdul, try to figure out how they can gain unfairly from it.

Abdul is keen to store his seeds in the storage area being constructed with HELP funds. He thinks, "If I mix clay rubble with my seeds, the bag will be heavier and I will be given more money for it. They'll never know the difference."

He is surprised when the HELP volunteer simply puts a tag marked with his name on his bag without weighing it. David Stockley has alerted HELP that adulteration of the amount of seeds might happen, so instead of weighing them, the volunteers decide to give a set price for the same-size bags.

"This means I'm going to have to buy back all that rubble I put in with my seeds. I should never have done that," Abdul thinks.

Nazir listens to what the HELP volunteers announce. He understands how important it will be to have seeds for next year's planting, even though he only has a few because he has so little land to cultivate. "I know my seeds will be safe and dry if I store them with HELP," he thinks. "And I won't have to worry if the price of seeds goes up, because I will be able to buy them back for the same price I sold them."

Kaiser's note to the field volunteers on January 1, 1971, describes what is to be done about rice seed storage:

Rice should be purchased by Cooperative Societies. The manager should issue a receipt to the individual members stating that so many *maunds* of paddy has been sold by the member at Rs. 15 (or whatever is the current market price) per *maund* in exchange for promise to supply rehabilitation materials. The value of the rehabilitation materials will be fixed by the Coop Societies as instructed by HELP. When more permanent godowns are ready (one for each camp) seed will be centrally stored. Thus the seed will become the property of the co-op and the farmer can't take it back any time he pleases. Will have one rice seed store of a farmer's co-op in South ready before the weekend. If it goes well others will follow. Will send picture when ready.

HELP will supply empty gunny sacks, plastic sheets, and tarpaulin. Will give specifications later. Where are the moisture meters?*

It should be made clear to the members that if they were to make cash sale and buy their goods individually from Tajuddin or Bhola there would be a loss. If, instead, they receive goods from HELP in exchange, they will get more for the same quantity of rice sold because HELP has good contacts, can buy at concession prices and will have all the advantages of bulk purchase and shipping.

Not everyone on the island is concerned about working toward storing sufficient seeds for the next planting season. From the outset, HELP is aware that the crop is owned by very few, who may choose to sell outside. Walter Schweppe expresses concern about landowners selling their rice harvest to profit from the rising prices resulting from destruction of crops in the cyclone. If they sell their seeds, there will be not be enough to plant on Manpura.

---

* Moisture meters test the dryness of paddy before it is stored, to prevent mold.

Walter warns:

Received word from Char Sakuchia that rice
is sold and shipped off to Hatiya and Sandwip.
Suggest we buy up the harvest. For seeds about
200 *maunds* needed for Char Sakuchia. Rs. 40 per
maund = Rs. 8000. Need this money soon. Please
consult experts to arrange for rice storage. Are
reporting situation to Major Asif and ADC.

Kaiser urges everyone to watch out for the sale of rice off the
island:

Under no circumstances should paddy be allowed to go out of Manpura. If this happens
there will be a shortage of seed in the coming
sowing season. If necessary, cash purchase may
be made through cooperatives under exceptional
circumstances.

HELP's vigilance assures that stored rice seeds will be available in sufficient quantities to plant the next season, and that
they will be offered back to the farmer at the same price at which
he sold them to put into storage.

Fr. Timm summarizes the work that HELP accomplished
three weeks after the cyclone:

Two Pakistani engineers surveyed all the *pukurs* (excavated
ponds) with a view to cleaning out the ones containing pu-
trid water. Vegetable seeds for winter cultivation in the *baris*
were procured and distributed. *Kodals* (short-handled hoes)
were provided for doing earthwork. As a result, the people
began living in hope.

By mid-December they all had a sari or lunghi, a blanket
each and a week's supply of food, with an assurance of a
boatload of food every week. Feeding had to be arranged for
almost a year, since only about 35% of the rice had been harvested before the cyclone and the rest was more than 50%
destroyed" (Timm 1995, p. 145).

CHAPTER 11
Pathans on Manpura

November 29: The Army Lands on Manpura

It is seventeen days after the cyclone. Nazir stares at the tall men in clean uniforms with smart army turbans and polished brass belt buckles.

"They don't look like Bengalis. Must be Punjabis," he thinks. "At last they have come to help us, but if we had to wait for them to land after the storm, we would all be dead by now. What took them so long?"

Watching the soldiers set up their large dun army tents in an open area near the one remaining *pukka* building that used to be the island headquarters, he turns to his friend Surendra.

"Look how many of them have come," he marvels. They are used to the handful of HELP volunteers, and here are eighty men, under a Colonel Shahpur. They are Urdu-speaking Pathans from the Frontier Force Regiment, but the islanders can't distinguish Pathans from Punjabis. They call all West Pakistanis Punjabis.

This is the first time a large Pakistan Army contingent has landed on Manpura. Before that, there were just a few army personnel assigned to relief work, and they quickly leave when they discover how organized HELP is.

"I don't trust them," Surendra says quietly. "They have come to order us around and make us work for them. They won't understand us because they don't speak our language. We can talk with the HELP volunteers; even most of the foreigners know how to speak Bangla."

"Yes," agrees Nazir, "they listen to our problems and talk to us about what we need to help us improve our lives."

Fr. Timm walks over and offers a welcome to the colonel, who looks at him with an appraising eye. They are both over six feet tall, and if Timm had been in uniform, everyone would have thought he was part of their unit.

The colonel informs him: "The army is responsible from now on for the relief operations here."

Timm replies, "If that's the case, may I offer our services to help you figure out how the many tents sent for the islanders actually work? The instructions did not come with them, and they are very tricky to assemble. We've been struggling with them for the past two days, but we think we've got them sorted out now. We would be happy to explain what we've learned if you would be willing to assign one of your men to this duty."

"The army knows how to erect tents," the colonel snaps, puffing out his chest.

Timm thinks, "Suit yourself. We'll see what happens." Out loud, he says, "Okay. We'll leave you to it. Good luck."

"The army is in charge on this island from now on. I order your group to turn the distribution of all relief food, clothing and tents over to us."

The HELP team feels threatened by the non-negotiable terms the colonel lays out.

Jon's November 29 field note shows how he was initially optimistic that the army would want to liaise with the HELP team and even take up the work of island volunteers:

North will remain the direction point for now as the Army under Colonel Shahpur has moved in with 80 men. So far they are working on their

191

camp (at Kauartek) but we hope they will fit
into the system where before we've used volunteers. It seems likely that they will be happy
to work with us. Smith and I will sit with them
regarding master plan today and try to get some
of their men deputed to other two camps.

Others, as soon as they learn the army is coming, speculate
that they might take over all relief activities, ignore the Manpura
Plan and promote their own agenda. From the remarks of the
colonel, it appears that the worst-case scenario is becoming real.
HELP learns it will not be easy to rely on the army's cooperation.

West Pakistani soldier

Fear of Army Punishment

In the evening, Hafizullah Choudhury shows up at the HELP
camp. A fearful look has replaced the usual confidence on the
powerful man's face. He is trembling. "You have to protect us
from the army," he pleads.

"What has happened?" they ask.

"We're all afraid of them," is all he will mumble.

"Why? Have they hurt you?"

Although he is visibly scared, it is hard to get him to say what is troubling him. Finally he explains, "We're afraid they will hear about what happened on that new island, Dal Char. We told those land-grabbing Hatiya farmers that we have rights to it because it is closer to Manpura than to them. We will never share it with them. We are claiming it for ourselves."

The HELP team listens, and then asks, "Why should that be the army's concern?"

Hafizullah won't meet anyone's eyes. "We decided we would attack them if they landed on our *char*," he says, "so we took weapons with us when we went there. They showed up with guns, but after we killed several of them, they fled."

"No wonder he's worried about the army," everyone thinks. "He knows they are more powerful than he is and will punish wealthy landowners such as him if they hear about their murderous gun battle to gain land."

Luckily for Hafizullah, the army does not become involved in land disputes. For HELP, it clarifies why the Choudhury family is feared by the landless and other less-powerful islanders. Future development initiatives, such as BRAC, will find ways to circumvent the power bases in communities after experiencing the difficulties of helping the less fortunate improve their lives when they are under the stranglehold of the wealthier elements.

Pulling Strings

After Hafizullah leaves, HELP discusses Colonel Shahpur's order for them to cease their work. Steve Baldwin, director of the Ford Foundation, says, "I know General Wasiuddin personally. I'll grab the next helicopter and ask him to replace this colonel. The general is the highest-ranking Bengali officer in the Pakistan Army, and a friend. I'm sure he'll take care of it for us." Steve leaves on the next flight.

Those of us in Dacca and Chittagong also begin to ask our contacts to take action in support of HELP's work. Our response to the field from Chittagong on November 30 asks them to identify the particular soldiers in the unit that has just landed so that we can give their names to the authorities: "What NEW army personnel (not in the first group) are in N. Manpura? Can you give us their names and brigade numbers?"

We also continue with our efforts to reassure the field staff that we have been cultivating contacts with the army.

```
ARMY PROBLEM:
Shouldn't be one. The Army and Relief Commis-
sioner have been contacted both here and in
Dacca. Looks like HELP has the go ahead. Stave
'em off until official word reaches Capt. Rah-
man.
     Marty's contact in Dacca: Colonel Safat
     Candy's in Chittagong: Major Nasir (can go
higher if needed).
     AR Choudhury, Chittagong Relief Commissioner
is so sold on HELP, he actually called me today
and asked me to come for a private conference to
see if (very seriously) we would take over the
Ramgati area, which he thinks is being ne-
glected. He can give us the go-ahead on Manpura
control. Returns Eid afternoon and we will see.
Marty's contact will write letter. Hold them off
out there.
```

The field volunteers ask me to get formal sanction from the relief commissioner for them to continue working there.

November 30: The Army Is Jumpy
I try to reassure the field workers of the relief commissioner's continued support.

We have complete sanction, support, and con-
gratulations from the Relief Commissioner. He
even stops by the house for drinks. His opinion
about an official written sanction to the army
is that it might do more harm than good. His
suggestion is to wait 96 hours and see what happens in the elections. The army is a bit jumpy
now, he feels. What do you think we should do?
How's the cooperation?

We do not have to rely on written orders because our success in persuading high-level officials in Dacca and Chittagong
results in a more cooperative officer taking Colonel Shahpur's
place.

Setting a Personal Example

Shortly after the army lands, a wooden freight carrier waits
alongshore, loaded with over a hundred huge bundles of relief
blankets.

"Come on, everyone," Jon urges. "We need to get them off
before the tide changes or the captain will give the signal to clear
out."

Many islanders have gathered near the ship, but look sulkily
at Jon, unwilling to do any more volunteering that day.

"Come on, it's only a quarter mile to the camp. If everybody
pitches in it won't take long."

No one steps forward. Jon, becoming annoyed, cajoles them:
"Look, these blankets are for you. I have a blanket. It's you who
don't. It's your job to get them off the boat." No response. Jon
remembers:

"I angrily said I'd carry all hundred bales or so, one at a
time. I didn't think I could make it with the one bale I had managed to get on my head. (Someone helped me lift it.) I staggered
down the swaying gangplank onto the muddy path, sure I
would collapse or slip into the paddy field. Swearing under my
breath, I stumbled into camp at the school totally bushed and

195

deflated. Then I looked back . . ." George describes the rest of the story: "Jon singlehandedly started wobbling his way from the ship with the blankets on his head. After he got several hundred yards down the path, one, then two, then many men loaded bundles and followed Jon. The last sight was a long line of porters getting the blankets off the ship. Words didn't work. Personal example and action did. I'll never forget it."

The army uses a different approach. When Russian and American cargo helicopters fly in bags of rice to the camp at the southern end of Manpura, the soldiers order the islanders to move all the bags into a storage area located there. Each one weighs a staggering hundred pounds. It takes two large army men to lift it onto the head of a Bengali man half their size, who trots off with it on stick-thin legs, his neck looking like it might snap.

"Get moving. You're next. Yes! You over there. Step up!" orders one of the army men. Not understanding because the soldier is speaking to him in Urdu, the man he barks at hesitates. The soldier strides over and roughly shoves him, knocking him down. The crowd of bystanders is immediately hostile. They surge toward the soldiers, raising their fists and shouting in protest. Attempting to diffuse the tension, the new commanding officer tells his men to withdraw to their camp. After that incident, the islanders never expect help from the soldiers, nor do they offer any. Syd Schanberg noted in his article in the *New York Times* that tension rose among the islanders. The "warm, relaxed chats with the H.E.L.P. volunteers, most of whom spoke passable Bengali" stopped, and so did "the pep talks, about rebuilding bridges and repairing wells, so important to a community whose morale was shattered.

"'Our job,' said a young lieutenant, 'is to keep law and order and distribute relief goods fairly—nothing more'" (Schanberg 1971, p. 8).

Heavy head load

December 6: Trying to Please the Army

In the days following the army's arrival on Manpura, HELP makes every effort to be as friendly as possible with them, putting speedboats and helicopters at their service, and keeping the lines of communication with the new major open.

```
To: Major Asif and Mr. Anwar Mahmud
From: Dr. Jon Rohde, HELP
Re: Boat transportation today
December 6, 1970
As per our conversation last evening I have sent
a country boat to your area to pick up your men
for transport to Char Sarkuchia. The boat will
```

197

return on this afternoon's tide and I will pay the boatman for his work then.

I am sending the speedboat at 8:30 am to pick up you both and transport you to Char Sarkuchia. Unfortunately, due to weight limitations, the boat can only carry the two of you. I have asked the driver to have the boat back to us here at Manpura North camp by 12:30 midday. This should give you 2½ hours in the Char camp to establish things. If you wish to stay longer, the Germans can probably arrange for a chopper to bring you to Kauartek on its way to get me. If you decide to do that please send the boat back immediately.

I have written to our Chittagong headquarters last night with a request for a boat or barge to put at Mr. Anwar Mahmud's disposal. Please let us know where it will ply, if we are able to rent one for you.

I hope this will be of some help today. The speedboat will be kept here at the North camp and if HELP people are not in need of it on any particular day, you may borrow it for a few hours.

Regards,
Jon E. Rohde

However, cooperation with the army has its frustrations, as Jon indicates in this note to HELP in Chittagong:

Please give profuse apologies to the Germans for the SNAFU here regarding helicopter usage. They landed a total of 4 times this afternoon offering to take blankets to CHAR, and each time, the only army chaps here would not allow a single blanket to budge without orders from the major. As far as I'm concerned, we should be sure to never ask the Germans again. Only ask them to do what we need for our own program. A copy of my

noon letter to Asif is enclosed. No reply yet
(December 6, 1970).

Because the major must give direct orders to his men concerning any action they are allowed to take, the efficiency of our efforts is hampered, and our relationship with the German pilots, who count on HELP's dependability, is in danger of becoming strained.

Panning the Army

When a BBC *Panorama* film crew arrives in North Camp, they explain to Jon, "We want to shoot our first scene by starting out over the sea, then swoop toward land, roaring in over the island like a tidal wave."

"Can you take these guys up to film?" Jon asks the U.S. helicopter pilot who is on one of his runs to Manpura.

"Sure. You hop on with them too, Doc."

Jon thinks, "I knew these young Nam vets would be happy to make low-flying loops over the island. They're doing it all the time anyway." He and the *Panorama* crew jump on board the helicopter and the pilot does several daredevil runs close to the sea so they can shoot all the footage they want. It becomes the opening scene for their one-hour documentary.

After the soldiers withdraw following the bullying incident, they no longer take part in any relief work. In any case, they have brought no supplies with them for the survivors: no tools to help with building, no shovels to bury the dead, no blankets to distribute, no tents to donate. With nothing to do, they lounge around on the veranda of the former school at North Camp, sleeping or idly watching Fr. Peixotto, Fr. Timm and the Notre Dame students struggle to assemble the vexing holiday tents, while the cholera hospital doctors organize the distribution of relief food and blankets.

Watching the U.S. helicopter with the BBC *Panorama* team swoop in filming over the island

The director, Alan Hart, grabs the opportunity. His cameraman slowly pans along the long orderly line of ragged, hungry, but patient islanders waiting for HELP relief, then focuses on Jon taking charge of the distribution. The camera swings and pans again, this time over the smartly outfitted Pathan soldiers at ease, not lifting a finger of assistance. Finally, it swivels to film the group of island men in their prayer hats bowing toward Mecca, saying their *namaz* (prayers).

Hart talks to Jon about HELP's beginnings, motivation and what they hope to accomplish on the island. After the BBC film crew pulls out, the HELP team discusses the various scenes that were shot. Fr. Timm frets: "I hope they didn't record what we were calling those tents. We were totally exasperated trying to deal with them when they have so many missing parts, and we sure showed our annoyance." George is worried that they will broadcast his comments about how culturally inappropriate the donation of toddlers' training pants is. But everyone's real concern is the footage Hart captured of the army.

"If he shows them lying around while we're working, we're going to be cooked. The martial law authorities are going to be furious," Jon says.

"That's for sure," Lincoln agrees. "It might actually cause enough trouble to get us kicked off the island."

They all decide that Jon should return to Dacca immediately to try to locate Alan Hart before he flies back to London.

"If I can't catch him, I'll fire off an urgent cable asking him to cut the footage he took of the army. I hope he listens," Jon says anxiously.

December 4, 1970 Message to Candy in Chittagong from Jon on Manpura:

I'm going to enclose a letter to Alan Hart of BBC, to assure him that the army has worked well with us and he should not pursue the negative theme he was considering. This letter should be kept with a copy. I think that if the show he has planned is seen by Pakistani officials, there will be trouble for us. We should try and divorce ourselves from any criticism of the government or army. I sure hope he didn't film or record any of my less happy moments.

I cannot think of any way to force Hart not to use whatever he has, but I sure hope he realizes the importance of extreme discretion.

Please post letter immediately. (SEE TELEGRAMS BELOW) This has me worried. The final form was written along with George and Lincoln. We decided to get it off to Hart only in two copies. Book a telephone call from 312645 to Hart at BBC 6:30-7:30 Tuesday evening.

Urgent telegram to Mr. Alan Hart, BBC Panorama, Lime Grove Studio, London W-12, England:

URGENT HOLD FINAL CUT PANORAMA STOP IMPORTANT NEW DEVELOPMENTS STOP NEED YOUR HELP LETTER FOLLOWS

ROHDE HELP
2nd telegram:

PAY BET 100 DOLLARS. STOP. ARMY AND CIVIL IN CLOSE CO-OPERATION ENABLING HELP REHABILITATION PROGRAM IN PROGRESS. STOP. CO-OPERATIVES FORMED ISLAND REBUILDING DEVELOPING GREAT SET FOR YOUR SEQUEL. STOP. EXCEEDS ASPIRATIONS. STOP HEAVY FUNDING COMMITTED AWAITS FINAL PAKISTANI APPROVAL STOP CURRENT CRITICAL TREATMENT OF RELIEF SITUATION BY WORLD PRESS COULD SERIOUSLY HAMPER PROSPECT LONG TERM SUCCESS STOP HOPING RESPONSE TO PANORAMA NOT BACKFIRE HARMING HELP AND MANPURA STOP

ROHDE

"Extreme discretion" is not Hart's brief. The *Panorama* film, released on December 16, highlights the military lying around the field while the HELP team works, as the survivors line up for food looking hungry and weary. We learn to our consternation that it is nearly impossible to win retractions from the press. They will put whatever slant they choose to a story. You might as well stand in a rice field and shout at the moon as importune the press.

A London-based staff correspondent for the *Morning News** watches the *Panorama* film on BBC, along with millions of other viewers. He sends this dispatch to Dacca:

---

* A now-defunct English-language newspaper published weekly in Dacca. It consistently supported right-wing elements in politics.

Monday night's BBC TV topical program Panorama was devoted to East Pakistan disaster.

In film report by Alan Hart devoted exclusively to Manpura Island not one British or any foreign soldier was shown operating on island where out of 28,000 only half are alive today including just 100 children.

Certain charges were made by Hart which, if proved false, must be refuted at the earliest.

BBC Commentator Alan Hart for example said first person to reach Manpura with relief was American doctor John Rhodes [sic]—who works at cholera unit in Dacca and who formed relief organization called "Help". Pakistani troops, Hart said, landed on the island after full 19 days and then also empty-handed.

Hart said that Pakistani soldiers who finally came to Manpura Island came without shovels to bury dead, without much-needed tents, blankets, food or any relief supplies. He even accused Pakistani officers of trying to take over Doctor Rhodes' [sic] organization which, he said, John Rhodes [sic] refused to hand over (*Morning News*, December 17, 1970).

Efforts to Coordinate Civil and Military

In spite of these concerns, HELP continues to make an effort to promote smooth relations between the military and civil authorities. Jon writes to Dr. Quassam, who left his medical practice in Karachi to volunteer when the cyclone hit, and will take over from Jon as field coordinator:

```
December 5, 1970
Dr. Quassam — Projected activities in HELP

1. Liaison with army regarding any problems that
arise between local people regarding relief dis-
tribution
2. Acceptance  and  storage  of  rehabilitation
items sent by HELP for cooperative use in area
of Wards #1-6.  Be  sure  other  wards  are  ade-
```

quately supplied through other three centers we
have established. Try and keep contact by speedboat and travel to Hajirhat and Char when necessary to assess needs and distribute rehab materials.
3. Collection of data on population, present
needs, abilities and resources.
4. Checking of cooperative organization and actual dispersing of tools, seeds, and other items
supplied by Help. You should use your own judgment as to how much each group should receive,
etc.
5. Orientation for any consultants sent by Help
to Manpura - assistance to them regarding inter-
preters, food, housing and meeting the people.
6. Please keep army and civil officials informed
of our activities. Report any problems to us in
Chittagong.
7. Report as often as possible your needs and
progress and include personal things you want
like food, or other things. Send reports by German helicopter — not American or French.
    On final departure, if you do not have anyone
to turn over to, deposit HELP goods in the home
of Hafizullah Choudhury along with a list. Include outboard motor and boat, office supplies,
Petromax, bedding, containers, and our tents.

He also writes diplomatic letters to Major Asif of the Pakistan Army, and to Mr. Anwar Houssain, CSP, additional district
commissioner at Kauartek on Manpura. Houssain, deputed from
Mymensingh, is a young Punjabi who speaks no Bengali. He is
sent to take over the organization of public works. Unfortunately
for the islanders, he will only be able to communicate with the
Punjabi soldiers, and not with the survivors he has been assigned
to serve. This will not endear him to the Bengalis, who are increasingly disparaging about how the government has managed
relief. International readers will soon learn from Syd Schanberg

what an angry survivor on Sakuchia told him: "Government did nothing. After seven days two Government officers came in a launch and gave out a few pounds of rice and a tin of kerosene oil for 4000 survivors. They told us to be patient, that more supplies were coming, then they slipped away at night without telling us" (Schanberg 1970, p. 2).

Although HELP is still wary of army intervention in the rehabilitation effort, Jon writes a highly accommodating letter to Major Asif in an effort to keep on good terms, because we will have to work with or around them for the foreseeable future.

Dear Major Asif,

I am writing to thank you most sincerely for all the help you and your men have given the HELP organization over the past week. Under your guidance and that of the local government officials, it is clear that distribution of relief goods to every man, woman and child is proceeding rapidly, efficiently and with complete fairness. Having been here to know the problems, I realize that is an accomplishment in and of itself.

Most of all I wish to thank you for the close cooperation that we have shared on a personal basis. It has been an education for me to see how voluntary relief groups and government agencies can work hand in hand towards a common goal. I consider it a privilege to have worked with you and Mr. Anower Houssain.

HELP organization is now working entirely in trying to satisfy the long term rehabilitation needs of Manpura. We will at all times keep you appraised of our activities and welcome suggestions from you. As always, we fully recognize the jurisdiction of the Government and we will work entirely within that framework.

I will be leaving the island on Sunday, December 6, but representatives from HELP will be here trying to continue the programs of house building, road repair and a start on winter agriculture. I have asked them to keep you fully informed of their activities and hope that you will call on them if they can be of any help to you.

Khuda-Hafiz

Sincerely yours,

Jon E Rohde
HELP

CHAPTER 12
A Jostle of Reporters

As soon as the magnitude of the disaster begins to reach the ears of the world, volunteers, aid organizations and international journalists flood the airports. Most correspondents are seasoned, veteran reporters of war and disaster, but some are disoriented by the broken-down buildings, overcrowded slums and teeming, potholed streets. Upon landing in Dacca, one purportedly remarks with shock, "This is far worse than I thought. The destruction is terrible." His translator explains, "Oh no, none of Dacca was affected. The cyclone struck in the coastal areas far south of here."

Most reporters clamor and jostle for seats on relief helicopters and aircraft flying to the islands in the delta, although some of them (including Arnaud de Borchgrave, one of *Newsweek's* senior writers) never trouble to make the arduous journey to the cyclone region, relying instead on sources far from the disaster. The only two to reach Manpura are Alan Hart of BBC's *Panorama* and Sydney Schanberg of the *New York Times*, both of whom arrive on November 29, at the same time the army under Colonel Shahpur lands on the island.

Turning a Cold Shoulder to the New York Times
One-eyed veteran reporter Syd Schanberg* arrives unannounced at Abed's house one afternoon, expecting us to drop everything

---

* Schanberg would later win accolades for his coverage of Cambodia during the Khmer Rouge's takeover. The film *The Killing Fields* was based on his reporting.

to be interviewed about our work on Manpura. We rebuff him, saying we are not interested in publicity. If he wants to collect information, we tell him, he should talk to the survivors, not to us. "Go to the affected islands and see for yourself," we urge him.

We know he is clever at sourcing ways to investigate his story. He's proven that by finding his way to Abed's house. We have too much on our plate to be helpful or concerned about him and how he gets to Manpura, but he is indeed resourceful, and when I climb in next to Wilfred in the morning for my scheduled sortie to the island, Schanberg smiles triumphantly at me from his seat in the rear of the helicopter. He turns out to be the only reporter to spend several days on Manpura attentively listening to and documenting stories of victims. On December 30, 1970, his gripping interviews, combined with photographs of survivors, are given top billing, filling the first two pages of the *New York Times*. It is the only account we are aware of that describes with remarkable sensitivity the tragedy of the storm and its aftermath from the point of view of those who lived through it.

Fr. Timm, who is on Manpura when Schanberg arrives to interview victims, says in his memoirs:

"I was particularly annoyed by Sydney Schanberg of the *New York Times*. . . . One night in our tent at Hazirhat he was telling Drs. Lincoln Chen and George Curlin at length how the cyclone had broken the spirit of the people. They were still completely demoralized and all had broken down and cried when they spoke to him. I was sitting in the back of the tent writing up some survey results by lantern light. After listening for a half hour or so to the results of his interviews with the survivors I again could not contain myself. I exclaimed: "You do not know Bengali. You scare people with your aggressiveness. People tell you what they think you want to know through your leading questions. If you expect them to cry they will cry." I told him that I had visited over 500 *baris* myself and interviewed hundreds of people but only two persons had cried: one woman who was completely out of her mind and one of the richest men of the island. None of the others had showed signs of apathy or despair. In fact, they were rebounding rapidly, gathering scraps of materials for a shelter and already making plans for trips to the mainland to seek out new wives and repopulate the island as soon as possible.* To his credit as an outstanding journalist, Sydney listened attentively. Most reporters were much more superficial" (Timm 1995, pp. 144–45).

Trying to keep a low profile, so as not to have our work contrasted with the lack of organization of the authorities and indifference of the army, we are initially relieved that Schanberg has not publicized HELP's work specifically, but has focused on a portrayal of the storm and the survivors. Our relief is short-lived. He doesn't spare putting us in the spotlight. While on Manpura, he closely observes the ground operation of HELP, and on January 3, 1971, a column on page eight of the *New York Times* appears with the title: "A Western Group Aided Pakistanis; Doctors at SEATO Hospital Led Smooth Relief Effort." In the article, Schanberg calls HELP "the only life-sustaining presence" on Manpura and attributes our success to never allowing ourselves to be tied up in government red tape. He cites primarily the Americans, led by Jon working with George, Lincoln, Dick, and David Stockley, as well as the leaders on the mainland, "especially Dr. Rohde's wife, Cornelia, and F.H. Abed," assisted by Peggy Curlin and Martha Chen. He calls our effort an efficient and rapid "two-pronged campaign," and notes that our work is "greatly admired by the villagers."

In spite of our concern at the exposure, particularly because his spotlight is on Americans, we are grateful that his facts are accurate. We hope that most officials will not be aware of the ar-

---

* With the import of new wives, the age difference between married couples was often significant. "Several old men had very young wives and a few of them had teen-aged wives" (*Manpura: A Socio-Economic Survey*. Dacca University: Institute of Social Welfare and Research, 1973, p. 14).

ticle, with its reference to the choking effect of government red tape, our group's exclusive use of the German helicopters, and the islanders' fear of the army.

Schanberg's message is essentially the same as that of the BBC *Panorama* film:

> "The army does not care for us," a farmer said. "Where were they in our time of need? Now they come—after 21 days."
>
> As a Westerner was about to depart a villager whispered: "Please don't leave us alone with the army" (Schanberg 1971, pp. 1–2).

"Wheedling" and Dancing with Pilots

In stark contrast to Schanberg's accurate, sensitive, straight-from-the-field reporting is the work of Arnaud de Borchgrave, head of *Newsweek*'s international news bureau, who publishes his article "Pakistan: HELP for Manpura" on January 4, 1971. His information is secondhand, based on his conversations in Dacca with U.S. officials and HELP volunteers not directly involved with ground reality on the island. Consequently, his article is full of inaccuracies. One example of careless error is his statement that the Manpura Plan will provide "a cyclone-proof dike that would increase the amount of arable land by some 3000 acres." A dike takes up arable land, not increases it, and building a dike had never been in the plan. Instead, our plan includes houses, schools, roads, cyclone shelters and the introduction of more efficient agricultural methods.

We are also concerned that our work will be jeopardized by his dig at the unorganized response of Pakistani authorities, and his portrayal of HELP as outsiders: "Despite these admirable goals, some observers feel that HELP may run into trouble because it is predominantly a foreign group doing a job that should really be done by Pakistanis themselves." If he had come to Manpura, he would have recognized that HELP was a joint humanitarian response by concerned people of diverse nationalities, with a strong working partnership between Bengalis and foreigners.

His take on the women involved in the effort is insulting. Perhaps hoping to make his article appeal to more readers, he mentions that we are "attractive women" in our mid-twenties, before quoting Martha Chen's remark: "Since we were girls, the officials were generally receptive." He pounces on another remark made about our good relationship with the pilots, leading him to write that we use "such unabashed techniques of persuasion as dancing with aviators in the evening." And here we were thinking we had persuaded them because of our competent plans and impressive organizational abilities. De Borchgrave must have believed women can only count on their wiles to get things done. We wondered if he would consider it wily behavior for male volunteers to drink a beer in the evening in Chittagong with the aviators, or have a party in Dacca for them. He would most likely consider it normal social interaction, not "unabashed techniques of persuasion." HELP's women volunteers feel he belittles us with his choice of the word "wheedling" to describe our work.

Newsweek's wide circulation means that most educated Pakistanis read the article, leading them to focus not on what HELP is accomplishing on Manpura, but on de Borchgrave's stereotypical portrayal of Western women as being loose. His comments certainly have a negative impact on my carefully nurtured relationships in Chittagong with important government officials. I begin to have the feeling I am perceived as leading a sixties love-in, involving tricks in the relief blankets, instead of a well-organized relief operation. He does admit that we have "enthusiastic local support," but overall it appears to most of us that what he has written can only damage HELP.

Piggybacking on HELP

Negative reaction is not uniform. The U.S. government is pleased to have what they see as good publicity at last:

> *Newsweek* did subsequently run a flattering report of a voluntary relief organization called HELP formed by Cornelia (Candy) Rohde and Martha (Marty) Chen, wives of Drs. Jon Rohde and Lincoln Chen of the Cholera Lab. The January 4, 1971 *Newsweek* story told of the genesis of the HELP effort on Manpura Island, and included a picture of my wife, Meg, and Marty Chen loading relief supplies on to a plane. Meg really was piggybacking onto the story, because she had not been directly involved in HELP. Given that she was the mother of three children in college, Meg was tickled at being described by *Newsweek* as one of a trio of 'attractive women in their mid-20's.' . . .
>
> A week later *Newsweek* printed a letter from Benjamin Oehlert, a former Ambassador to Pakistan (1967–69) praising the work of "these young American women." Oehlert was indisputably the most ferociously pro-West Pakistan of any of our ambassadors to Pakistan. He had removed a Consul General from Dacca for warning that Bengali unhappiness with West Pakistan could lead to the breakup of Pakistan, and had even forbidden any Consulate General contacts with the Awami League. Would he have been so kind in his demands if he had known that the three women mentioned would later in the year be so supportive of an independent Bangladesh? (Blood 2002, pp. 104–05).

Until the *Newsweek* article, the U.S. embassy has not had one favorable piece written about U.S. cyclone response. With the photograph of the American Consul General's wife involved in loading relief goods, and the information that the U.S. government has offered a two-for-one dollar matching grant to what the journalist portrays as a largely American volunteer group, U.S. officials are able to gain their first good press.

However, Americans involved with HELP are not a part of the official U.S. cyclone response. As employees of the Pakistan-SEATO Cholera Research Lab, the cholera doctors are official Americans making a personal response to the cyclone. The director of the cholera hospital never openly endorses staff involvement on Manpura. He only turns a blind eye. From others, the reaction is stronger. Jon records: "Some of our severest critics say that we are wasting our talents as physicians to be going out to provide relief." None of us are doing the cyclone work to build a positive profile for the United States. We are there because of the human tragedy. To the extent we are concerned about the political situation, our desire is for Bengalis to achieve a democratic political outcome for their country.

Archer Blood's well-written account in *The Cruel Birth of Bangladesh*, published decades later, makes clear how we were used as part of the effort to gain good press for the United States. He calls disaster reporting "grossly unfair and self-serving." He writes that Ambassador Farland was furious about the misreporting of the unfortunate helicopter incident on Hatiya in which a journalist involved him, even though he had not been on board. Farland (unsuccessfully) "embarked upon a lengthy and mostly frustrating effort to win a retraction" (Blood 2002, p. 103).

We have no luck with retractions either. Just as we did with *Panorama*, HELP contacts de Borchgrave to urge him to correct his comments damaging the character of our effort, and meets with a similar rebuff. When the Chens manage to catch up with him, he unashamedly confesses to writing the article when he was drunk in Beirut. He seems to think it a reasonable excuse, and dismisses their request to publish a correction. We are left feeling that the way *our* involvement is portrayed is grossly unfair, but at least we are grateful for the reports of Syd Schanberg, whose journalism is Pulitzer quality.

Blood recalls that Secretary of State Henry Kissinger was going to make a trip to Dacca to find out why U.S. officials were unsuccessful in projecting a good image, but he stops him by writing a cable saying: "We have nothing to apologize for or cover up. We can show positive success. I, for one, am proud of what the U.S. has done and is doing in this great humanitarian effort." The "positive success" is largely a result of association with HELP. The *Newsweek* article has given the U.S. mission a boost.

As a result of our *Newsweek* publicity, an accusation of our being U.S. agents appears in a Dacca newspaper, *Express*, on January 29, 1971. With the embassy using HELP and *Newsweek* to look good, we appear linked to them, making us vulnerable to attacks from the local press. *Express* paints us as intelligence gatherers. The Bengali journalist who writes the piece claims that Americans are planning to stage a landing on Manpura in the "heartland" of Bengal, its soft underbelly. All we have seen are empty bellies. There is no mention that Manpura is a devastated half-submerged island in the path of frequent cyclones, hardly making it a desirable place to establish any kind of base.

Hot Potato

Repercussions from the *Newsweek* piece are long-lasting.* Linking HELP to the U.S. government turns us into a "hot potato," according to Kaiser's report in late January.

From Kaiser's 22 Jan., 1971 Fieldcord Report:

```
Toufiq is superintendent. Had frank discus-
sions. Said Government upset because we are so
secretive. What are our plans, what will we do,
what can we do, how much money we have, where
from and so on. Strong reaction due to Newsweek
```

---

* Months later, the news spotlight on HELP continues to generate negative reactions, linking our work to geopolitical issues and viewing us as tools of our government's policies. When Abed reconnects with Lynn Bickley in Karachi after he flees Chittagong to escape the war, she writes to us about the rumor he brings with him: "HELP, apparently, is again on thin ice. Manpura is now believed to be the supply point for Bangladesh arms from India."

article. Have explained how we feel about it. Government only interested in our bonafide.

Anything that has foreigners in it, they are cautious, especially the way foreign press has been attacking government. Foreigners or foreign agencies attract press attention.

However, the Government has not told anyone to quit except Salvation Army. Nor has it created obstacles or told any agency not to give things. Says attitude is not against volunteer organizations. Haven't had problems with so many others working in Bhola sub-division. HELP is a hot potato because of adverse publicity.

He advised, keep the Government informed about activities, get green signal before any big move (e.g., cluster housing, aerial anti-fly spraying) and send whatever you please. Bamboos: OK, C.I. sheet: OK, Food: he doesn't consider necessary. Told him about inadequate distribution in North. Things have improved since then. Assures no one will starve (agree, but remain half fed). Overall impression, need government approval only for major efforts (e.g., housing, model farming). Keep sending smaller things quietly and feed information to Government. Important: keep record of goods distributed.

Jon's letter to Rob Northrup on December 8 describes our concern about the press creating problems for us by calling us more effective than the military or civil authorities:

As you realize, this has been a largely private venture pushed by the persons you yourself know in Dacca. Although the government has supported us heavily and the military have been virtually working according to our plans, it is indeed embarrassing to be called by the press more effective than any local agency. We are a predominately Pakistani organization and our PR should be for fund raising, not glory of USA. We are stressing our close coordination with the civil and military and hope you will. You understand the problems of working here and can appreciate the touchy situation we face. With Pak approval we can go very far indeed. If they think we are showing them up we are quite naturally cooked . . .

No report of the disaster could have portrayed its ferocity and the desert left behind, but this area is Bengal's most fertile and it will come back. A never again chance to rebuild on new social and economic lines is here. . . . It's a long vision, but possible.

CHAPTER 13
Money, Politics and Rehab

HELPGONG TO HELPLAND

On December 5, twenty days after I first flew to the cyclone area and two days before the national election, I write to Helpland before I travel back to Dacca with Jon to establish headquarters in our home in Gulshan, where we will continue to spearhead planning and supply. My message includes notes about German wireless contact at South Char, about locating gear left by volunteers, about more Notre Dame students coming with Brother Nicholas, more supplies arriving, including 3,200 pounds of tents (for which a drop area equivalent to two football fields is required) and goods collected by Notre Dame arriving by boat: *dekhshis*, hurricane lamps, tools (including hammers, sickles and *daos*) and twelve bales of clothing. It indicates that we are trying to get Mahbub Alam Chassi to come to the island to give development advice. There is a schedule for transport of volunteers off Manpura and asks if there are any other requests for personnel to come and go. It concludes on a note of hope: We're all hoping USAID will come through with a big fat check in Dacca. No word yet.
Love from HELP-GONG

In a personal letter to Rob Northrup dated December 8, Jon writes of his disappointment at being expected to return from his work on Manpura to his assignment at the cholera lab. He has invested his energy and conviction in the rehabilitation of the island, and would prefer to carry on, but his studies and his cholera patients at the lab are waiting.

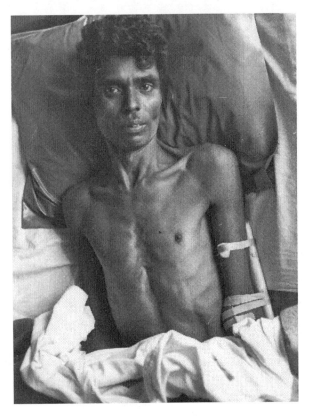

Has anyone seen my doctor?

Cyclonic Commuting

Although now based primarily in Dacca, I continue to plane-hop frequently back and forth from Chittagong to source people trained in various areas of development, or to procure supplies necessary for our rehabilitation efforts. The flight attendants and airport personnel greet me familiarly. At social gatherings I find myself initiating scintillating conversation: "Do you have any idea where we can get a two-cusec pump?" or "Would you be willing to volunteer for a while on a mud bar?" The small suitcase I take on flights is regularly lost by the airlines, but I find by the time I land either in Chittagong or Dacca, the ground crew triumphantly greets me with the bag from the previous flight, so I always have one in hand. Train is the most relaxing option for the commute. When I take the overnight express to Chittagong with Viquar and five-year-old Simone, she's the only one who sleeps. Viquar distracts me willingly from our relentless work on the cyclone. Peacefully cocooned in the bogie, we chat through the night about books and films we like, as the train wheels rhythmically *clack-clack* over the rails.

Sheik Mujipur Rahman's Awami League, has been hotly campaigning for elections set for December 7. They steamroller the other parties, who are underfunded and badly divided. Thirty-six candidates from minor parties withdraw from the campaign in the final week, offering the late excuse that it is not proper to hold an election so soon after the cyclone. Actually, they know they don't have a chance against the Awami League. Elections in the areas affected by the cyclone have already been postponed.

It is an historic election—the first held on a one-person, one-vote basis, and the first nationwide election on the basis of universal adult suffrage, which means another first: all women can vote. For the first time on the subcontinent, leaders of political parties are invited to present their parties' views over TV and radio. Sheik Mujib advocates nationalizing banking and insurance, as well as the cotton and jute trade. He wants land reform, including getting rid of landholding systems in West Pakistan. What appeals most to Bengalis is his call for a social revolution to eliminate the inequalities and injustices of Pakistani society. West Pakistani voters adamantly oppose his political platform.

Excitement in the electorate mounts. They believe in a chance to return to civilian rule after long years of being ruled by the military. Archer Blood in his memoirs includes a passage from the Bengali political historian Kazi Ahmed Kamal, which poignantly illuminates the situation of the majority of Bengalis and why the vote is so important to them:

> An East Pakistani does not expect much from his life. He does not know beyond his land, flood and storm — and poverty. To him death is normal, survival is odd. So long as he lives he wants a little rice and fish, a little of conjugal life and an unhurried death.
>
> The only exhilarating moment of his life was during an election in the time of parliamentary democracy when the candidates came to him, pampered his self-respect and promised to form a government with his consent . . .
>
> That little self-respect which hallowed his being had been snatched away by Ayub* and he was told day after day, year after year for the last eleven years that he does not know what is good for him and he does not know how to vote and elect a representative (Blood 2002, p. 126).

> Yahya . . . urged voters to elect candidates who were committed to the integrity and unity of Pakistan. The elections were the first in the history of Pakistan in which voters were able to elect members of the National Assembly directly. In a convincing demonstration of Bengali dissatisfaction with the West Pakistani regime, the Awami League won all but 2 of the 162 seats allotted East Pakistan in the National Assembly. Bhutto's Pakistan People's Party came in a poor second nationally, winning 81 out of the 138 West Pakistani seats in the National Assembly. The Awami League's electoral victory promised it control of the government, with Mujib as the country's prime minister, but the inaugural assembly never met ("Emerging Discontent, 1966-70").

The reaction of the Pakistani military to the overwhelming victory Bengali voters give the Awami League will affect millions of lives, including many of us involved with HELP.

---

* Field Marshal Ayub Khan became the second president of Pakistan and first chief martial law administrator in 1958. In 1969 he was forced to resign to be replaced by Yahya Khan.

December 9: Two-for-One Funds

The matching grant from USAID promised by Maurice Williams is now formalized. On December 9, Eric Griffel, provincial director of USAID, hands HELP the signed documents. Two weeks later, Jon writes a letter to Rob and Quincy Northrup to use for fundraising purposes. The terms are that every dollar donated from private sources will be matched by two from USAID.

> We have now distributed over 200,000 rupees ($40,000) worth of goods and supplies, and are well started on rehabilitation efforts. The Chittagong office is running 22 hours a day, and our operation now seems to be the only one still operating in the Manpura area. The local inhabitants have responded superbly, and we are now seeing a level of community cooperation and interaction which I would previously not have thought possible in Pakistan. Most of the on-the-scene work is in fact being run locally, which we have encouraged, while we have continued to provide materials and direction where needed. We are continually on the verge of running out of funds . . .

In our effort to widen the base of personal donations in order to get the matching funds, Jon writes on January 6, 1971, to Bob Gordon, a clinical director at the National Institutes of Health in Washington, and a founder of the cholera research laboratory in Dacca.*

> It is truly impossible to give an accurate portrayal of the work going on here. You well know the daily problem of communication, transportation, purchase, personnel, government liaison, planning and fieldwork in the most inaccessible area of Bengal. To date it is consuming every waking hour of dedicated wives as well as nights and weekends of those with jobs. Though clearly the most efficient project in the field, we are not happy for the type of publicity given by

---

* In November, Bob collected $700 in donations from members of St. Luke's Church in Bethesda.   221

Newsweek, for it draws the natural envy of larger and official groups who have a much bigger job. Our contacts with the government are good at the highest levels and we are busy channeling efforts through such sanctioned activities as the Cooperative Office. Nonetheless, our operation is entirely directed and run by volunteers, with the exception of a hired field coordinator and purchaser. You can well imagine the problems of recruiting good full time staff but we have some excellent men currently interested in the job of Executive Secretary. By this time next month, HELP should be running with a small full-time staff allowing the Governing Board and volunteers like me to settle into more of a policy making and advisory role . . .

We hope this project will get the long-term support it needs to make a significant change in one small area of the cyclone region.

Farewell Noel

In mid-December Noel is told by relief officials that sorties to the cyclone area are no longer necessary because there are enough agencies involved. Everyone appreciates that his planes were the first ones offered for relief airdropping on the worst-hit islands. For the past month we have witnessed him tirelessly flying several times a day. Not only did he provide the mobility we needed to contact our first base camp on Manpura, but his daily runs were our lifeline.

"We're really grateful to you, Noel," we tell him. "You were the guy who made it possible for us to launch our work. If you hadn't been so willing to take us on board, we never would have been able to get off the ground." We tell him how much we all admire his willing, spontaneous response to the disaster. His career in the country is not over, however. His planes will be enlisted by the UN, and he will find himself evacuating their personnel from Jessore, Bhola and Barisal just prior to the Indian Army's intervention in the Liberation War in December 1971.

The German Search and Rescue Team continue to book us on their sorties out of Chittagong. HELP uses them principally for transfer of personnel and emergency supplies: for example, to bring enough petrol for the boats until a lost shipment is recovered, as indicated in this request from Walter Schweppe from Manpura's South Camp on December 18, 1970:

    Kaiser and T. Ali went to Hatiya this morning on our last petrol to assist army boat in search for lost shipment. No results yet. Send emergency petrol by helicopter if possible.

    P.S. Have innumerable other requests not worth mentioning at this time (except our Christmas eggnog).

Walter Schweppe with Aysen Talmon
in background on Manpura
(*photo courtesy of
Aysen and Pat Talmon*)

CHAPTER 14
Reaching Out to Women

The first day the HELP team brings relief to Manpura, men who have lost their wives in the cyclone beg the volunteers to replace them. Schanberg observes:

> A man began quarrelling with local officials because they would not add some saris to his relief bundle of food and blankets. "What do you need saris for? Your wife was killed."
>
> "Yes," the man replied, "but I want to get married again, and I need them for a dowry" (Schanberg 1970, p. 2).

Winnowing

Women's work is taken for granted, but when men find themselves bereft of their wives, their role suddenly becomes recognized. The men depend on women's maintenance of the home, preparation of food, the tasks of husking, parboiling and drying rice, planting and weeding kitchen gardens, caring for cattle, ducks, chickens and goats, collecting manure for fuel and fertilizer, gathering firewood, fetching water, weaving mats and baskets, sewing blankets and clothes, and the very important task of producing and rearing offspring. Men are completely unaccustomed to doing any household work, and children are essential both for the joy they bring and, as soon as they are old enough to work, the contribution they make to the family welfare. Syd Schanberg remarks on what Manpura is like without children: "For days, and even weeks, there was a terrible silence where children by the dozen used to chatter and play, except for one persistent sound, the deep, rasping cough that can be heard across the fields as the respiratory legacy of the storm" (Schanberg 1970, p. 2).

Cleaning rice to cook

On our initial flights with Noel, we witness the desperation of women survivors clawing grains of rice out of the mud when, as occasionally happens, bags shoved from the cargo hold burst open upon impact. The few who appear in public to collect relief goods are almost exclusively from the minority Hindu population. Once organized relief arrives, Moslem women return to seclusion, hidden in shelters their husbands hastily patch together. The conservative social and religious norms of the island require them to stay in purdah, out of public view. After the storm, their men often find it difficult to provide for their needs.

Nazir's wife weeps constantly. She sits alone in the makeshift hut he has built of storm debris: withered palm leaves, a few strips of bamboo from ruined houses, broken pieces of wood from a doorframe. Her mind swirls like the waters of the tidal surge. She can't erase the moment her children were swept away by the sea, lost to her forever. When she rises from the dirt floor, she feels dizzy and feverish. She can't remember when she last bathed. With her baby no longer there to nurse, her breasts become engorged with milk, swollen and sore. Now they ooze, reddened from inflammation from the sores she got hanging to the trunk of a palm tree. She doesn't even have a rag to wipe them, because she's wearing whatever torn pieces of cloth Nazir could rescue from the flotsam. The wounds on her arms and legs from clinging to the rough bark are also festering. Nazir's abrasions were treated by the doctors who have come to Manpura, but Nazir would never allow her to be treated by a male. He is proud to keep his wife in purdah, away from the attention of strangers, including medical workers.

Nazir does his best to console her, bringing relief goods given by the HELP volunteers: matches to start a fire and rice to cook. Every day he sits patiently, waiting his turn in line to get more supplies. Yesterday they gave him a blanket from the big bales dropped from the sky. He wraps it around himself while she continues to shiver in the night, but she does not protest. Her mother told her to think first of her husband's needs. She knows how to be an obedient wife, always submissive. She has never asked for help from anyone. Her life has centered around her husband and family, and she depends on Nazir. But Nazir is worried. He cannot manage the myriad tasks of day-to-day work without her. He relies on her cooking his meager meals and keeping their living space clean and in order. He is already thinking that they must have more children, but he knows that unless she regains her health, she may be unable to bear more. So few women survived the cyclone. How will he find another one? When he tells her he will try to get another blanket for her, she is too dazed and ill even to thank him.

Fr. Timm says to Kaiser, "I'm concerned about the women who never appear because they are hidden away in their *baris*. I know they must need help. When we first came it was really impossible to involve women volunteers on the island because it was so harrowing. We were constantly encountering corpses before the burial details took care of them. That's why I told the Holy Cross Sisters who wanted to come right away to wait until things become a bit less difficult."

"Yes," Kaiser replies, "it's a tough job with few amenities. Where would they sleep? We don't mind communal quarters, but they will need some privacy. Clean water is still an issue as well."

"True," says Fr. Timm, "and dysentery has affected all of us."

"I can't imagine the men cooperating with them, either. They certainly won't give them any authority to make decisions," Kaiser adds.

"But perhaps we need to rethink this now, because the women undoubtedly have needs that our male volunteers cannot attend to," says Fr. Timm.

By the end of December, Kaiser is open to the sisters volunteering in the field. He can only imagine assigning them jobs traditionally offered to women, but fortunately ends his comments by leaving the options open, saying it is up to them to decide what they will do. He discovers they have much to offer beyond office tasks.

The Holy Cross sisters are most welcome. We were starved for volunteers and I was getting worried. Though the sisters are of limited usefulness in the field, they will be most helpful in taking care of the small things like filing and general secretarial work. They will also visit the homes but there are precious little practical things they can do without materials and a clear idea of what they can do best for the women. I have left it entirely to them to decide what to do (Zaman, December 31, 1970).

The first team arrives by boat from Chittagong: Sisters Lillian, Francis Bernard and Patricia, along with a young woman staying with them, Zuju, who donates her holiday to volunteer for cyclone relief work. Sister Lillian and Zuju stay together at the primary school for three weeks to carry out distribution of medicines and rice rations. They walk great distances across the islands to reach women who are in purdah and cannot come to a distribution point.

Sr. Lillian recalls, "We were sorry that the women had to wait and wait for food, and in the end actually receive very little rice, especially when we saw stockpiles of food hoarded in the chairman's house." She also remembers: "Doctors came from other islands by boat to take medicines meant for the people of Manpura. They even offered them to me. I would have none of it. I reported their theft" (Sister Lillian, conversation with author, January 21, 2013).

Other Holy Cross Sisters to go were Marian Teresa, Barbara Jeanne and Leonara, who were assigned to North Camp and helped in the planning and distribution of items, conducting surveys and doing whatever else was assigned them. These teams were followed by more volunteers over the ensuing months, making the intrepid sisters the core of the effort to reach secluded women survivors. The needs of Nazir's wife and many others like her could at last be met. Sister Joseph Mary recalls:

> Fr. Timm arranged for two medical teams of women to go to Manpura. In January, I, Sister Joseph Mary, accompanied Sister Mary Cecilia, SMRA,* a very experienced nurse, and we were stationed in Middle Camp. Sister Perpetua, also a Holy Cross Sister, accompanied Doctor Mrs. Azariah and they were stationed in South Camp. We lived in tents that had been previously set up.
>
> Our two teams dealt with the women in each of these areas. Many of them were injured in the cyclone and had serious wounds to be attended along with female and other problems. These women were never permitted to the leave their *baris* and were very happy to have medical help going right to their homes. The men, too, were happy for the medical assistance given to the women. Men who heard about our female teams came from distances, too far for the teams to go to visit, just to tell about the needs of their women, describing as well as they could, their illnesses to ask advice and medicine (Sister Mary Joseph, email message to author via Fr. Timm, July 23, 2012).

The sisters, trained and committed to healing, as well as familiar with the language and culture of Bengal, make an important contribution to the relief work by taking care of the medical needs of isolated women.

---

* Servi Mariae Reginae Apostolorum—Association of Mary, Queen of Apostles

Weaving a basket

An anecdote from Fr. Timm illustrates another aspect of the sisters' plucky resourcefulness:

It appears that the Russian pilots are particularly open to the charms of nuns. Sister Marian Teresa . . . when a Russian helicopter drops her off in Patuakhali on her way to the island from Dacca, discovers that Manpura is still a two-day's journey away. She plays on the pilot's heartstrings, telling him all the trials and tribulations she has gone through to help the victims of the cyclone. He succumbs and flies her and the doctor with her, straight to Sakuchia where they are coming to do medical work . . . When it came time to return, Sr. Marian again charmed the Russians and flew with them back to Dacca, where they took her to the gate of the airport and hired a motor rickshaw to take her to Holy Cross College. I told Sr. Marian later that it was good the Russians didn't have permits to leave the airport grounds, or she might have ended up on a sightseeing tour of Moscow (Timm 1995, pp. 147–48).

Russian helicopter landing on field cleared by HELP volunteers. (*photo courtesy of Richard Guerrant*)

Milkmaids

After dinner one night in December, in Aysen's beautifully decorated home embellished with Persian carpets and Turkish heirloom silver, we are enjoying chocolate mousse, imported cheeses and liqueurs served in crystal glasses. The conversation circles back, as it always does these days, to our work on Manpura.

I bring up a problem that has been a growing concern: "We're worried about the women who are isolated in their *baris*. The only way they can be reached is through their husbands, who are out all day struggling to rebuild their lives."

"Yes," Peggy says, "we have plenty of male volunteers, but they are useless in this situation, because the women are not allowed to show their face in public."

I add, "We've had problems with men who take relief blankets only for themselves when they say it is for their wife, leaving her shivering in these cold nights. The Sisters are coming as volunteers to the island to talk directly to women about problems they might be having with their children's health, their own health, and whether enough relief supplies have actually reached them." I see excitement in Aysen's eyes.

"I want to go," she says. "I'd really like to set foot on this little island that we hear so much about but never see. I'd like to help the women if I can."

I'm not surprised at Aysen's response. She always looks elegant, and has a beautifully appointed home that is the social center of our lives, but she also is perfectly at ease in the markets and crowded streets of Dacca, fluent in Bengali and curious about everything. Most of all, she loves adventure.

"It won't be comfortable living there," I warn her. "It's rough. The food is very simple. You won't have privacy or clean water. Are you sure you want to take it on?"

"Yes, yes, I really do. It's going to be very exciting. I'm going to see if Sandy Schweppe will go with me. She's heard so much about it from Walter. I think she'd like to see it for herself," Aysen enthuses. She recalls their experience:

Candy told me that women on the island were not getting enough help and needed women volunteers to help them. Sandy Schweppe and I decided to go. We flew to Chittagong by German relief helicopter and went to HELP office to meet her. She arranged a boat to take us to the island. We had no idea what we would be doing. We slowly and most silently sailed to the island as there was nothing to make noise, no birds, no dogs or cows, etc., except hugely ballooned dead bodies slowly passing by our boat. This is almost a month after the cyclone. When we arrived on Manpura we met Kaiser and Father Timm. They gave us a tent and few utensils to cook. People were everywhere. No privacy and no place to defecate so we used a tin can, but at night we used latrines while we guarded each other for privacy. Next day we were handing out blankets and I don't remember what else. Some Bengalis thought we were nurses and came to us for their wounds but we knew nothing about how to treat them. Father Timm told us to give them tetracycline to fight infections. Finally it was decided that I distribute milk for women and children and find out if there were births after the cyclone. I walked like a milkmaid for hours house to house and delivered milk to mothers. The women had great dignity and were very courteous and grateful. One day in our tent we saw the first ant crawling out from the earth and you should see how happy we were as life was coming back to the island. Wounded were the families who tried to hug the trees so they would not be swept by the force of water when the tide was pulling away after the storm surge, but many families watched their children taken away by the water, their cows, dogs, everything. When Father Timm, Kaiser, Sandy and I would sit down to talk, Kaiser would say if it was in his power he would built a house for every villager and present them with a key. What a lovely dream. . . . We were there a week? Ten days? Finally, we planned to go back to Dacca to our husbands, and to take a shower as it was

Christmas next day, so a Russian relief helicopter brought us back to Dacca.

Another adventurous volunteer is Sue King, the daughter of Jane and David King, the British Council representative. She makes a number of trips to Manpura to help. Kaiser writes about himself, Sue and their speedboat driver being stranded at sea after dark on the way to the island:

A few weeks later, I was returning from a trip to a district town in a speedboat when it got entangled in fishing net. By the time the speedboat driver managed to free the boat, a good hour had passed, the tide had turned and it got very dark suddenly. We had got turned around so much that we had no idea if we were heading out to the sea or inland. If we were heading in the wrong direction, we would run out of fuel in the middle of nowhere in the middle of the night and the sea had not been very kind to people not too long ago. Also, the daughter of the British Council representative was with us. What had started as a productive and pleasant trip was in ominous straits. We managed to discern a sandbar at some distance and decided to stay there until daybreak. We had bought a big fish from a fishing boat and we had half a can of orange juice. The speedboat driver got a fire going, cleaned the fish with the cut-off top of the one-liter can, and adding a little salt water, cooked the fish. It was the finest campfire I ever huddled around and the fresh fish seasoned with salty water and sweet orange juice was the most delicious seafood I ever ate. We lay down in the boat, shivering under two blankets for the three of us and before long, were lulled to sleep by the lapping of the water. I was suddenly startled awake by what sounded like the distant thunder of a tidal wave. But it was a wave of geese flying directly over us, their silvery wings glistening in the glow of the rising sun. There were hundreds and hundreds of birds and I felt privileged to see this unforgettable sight, lying in a boat in the company of a pretty young woman (Zaman 2013).

Aysen and Sandy with Russian pilots and villager
hired as a loader, December 1971
(*photo courtesy of Aysen and Pat Talmon*)

CHAPTER 15
Follow the Star

Having left Manpura on December 6, Jon returns the day before Christmas, unaware of how eventful his visit will be. This is his original account:

Rescue in the Delta

Sunken Country Boat

The sound of the amphibian rushes into my consciousness and grows louder until I see the speck emerge from the murky sky to the northwest. I've returned to Manpura to inspect the progress of home building and winter gardens, and won't be picked up till the following day. The stench is gone, the air still and fragrant with newly turned earth, the plaintive notes of a bamboo flute float out of the village Kauartek, and I am enjoying the peace and beauty that makes a poet of each Bengali.

The plane skids across the water with a deafening whine and seems close to sinking as it settles and comes to a halt. The pilot lifts the cabin roof and scrambles out onto the wing to yell at me. "There's a large country boat sunk in the river with about twenty men clinging to the bamboo cabin top. They're only a couple of miles off shore directly northwest of here."

"My outboard's running on only one cylinder. I've got five gallons of gas and my boat could sink with a dozen men in it," I reply. "Can you go land there and keep people afloat till I arrive? It'll be pitch black in fifteen minutes and I'll never find it without your beacon light."

236

"Impossible. I shouldn't even have come back here after dropping you. With the flight all the way down to Patuakali I'll just make Dacca on the fuel I've got."

"What about Chittagong? Can't you go there tonight and refuel?" I suggest.

"Sorry. Just no way. Relief Commissioner has to be back in Dacca. I'll fly out straight for the wreck—just go straight northwest. You'll find them. Good luck." He ducks back inside, putting the hatch down, and within a minute the lumbering old Goose is airborne again. Like he has said, he disappears into the haze towards the northwest. Big help!

Overloaded country boats

Running on One Cylinder

My battered khaki shorts and old jersey don't have a compass pocket and the open fiberglass landing skiff is so stripped it doesn't even have a single board for a seat. The forty-horse Johnson has been running on one cylinder, if at all, for a couple of weeks and I'd tried to fix it when I arrived that very afternoon without the slightest success. It still drinks gas like a high-speed engine but makes about seven knots flat out. Still, faster than paddling.

I walk the half mile to our cluster of colorful Sears, Roebuck donated tents and grab two flashlights, complete with faded batteries. Our petrol drum is bone dry, leaving me with one full tank in the boat, and the prospect of a refill if I want to take the time to run up the coast to North Camp, our major depot, located in the surviving school building. Light is fading fast, along with my recollection of where exactly northwest is, so I trot back to the skiff. The mud path is still warm under my bare feet but the air cools fast in December and I wish I had a sweater.

As I fear, the boat has been pulled far into the protected creek we use as a mooring place, and now it is low tide so I have to muscle it out through mud over my knees. I leap in as the skiff hits the river current and pull a half dozen times till the engine catches. Pointing in a direction somewhere between north and west I gallop off at a walk.

Battling Fog and Tide

An estuary is a strange body of water, especially to a boy raised on the edge of Narragansett Bay, where tides occur predictably and regularly at six-hour intervals. The massive discharge of the Ganges-Brahmaputra-Meghna delta, fourth-largest in the world, carries its suspended load of silt collected from as far away as Tibet and Kashmir hundreds of miles into the Bay of Bengal, which in turn, with its shallow basin, carries its tidal movements far north into the lower reaches of the rivers. The resultant interplay of salt and fresh water is highly variable and very confusing. The tide may rise while the current is still going out, and when both tide and current are ebbing, the resultant speed toward the sea of a floating object, like my little skiff, is astounding. My slow progress against the current can only be gauged by the painfully slow backward movement of the palm trees on the shore.

As if to relieve me of the problem of this troublesome awareness, night rapidly closes in and obliterates all but the stars overhead. The river is warm at night, holding heat from its long meandering across the face of the subcontinent. It breaths vapor into the air, which soon condenses in the cool evening to make a thin, long fogbank lying over the water, only a few meters thick. Into this accumulating mist the great square of Pegasus, the only constellation I can recognize in the northwest December sky, is swallowed. I pick some unknown twinkly gem higher up and continue on. I begin to think I'd covered the "couple of miles" mentioned by my pilot friend, when suddenly the engine leaps up, roaring with the propeller out of water, and I catapult forward to fetch up on the rising deck in the blunt bow. I pick myself up and step out into ankle-deep water, cursing pilot, Neptune and those fools who are somewhere out there clinging to a country boat. Why couldn't they have sunk on the *char* I just struck? Then they could get out and walk. I yell. No answer. Guess I'm not there yet. I put my back to the skiff and, with a multitude of groans, supplications and defamations, float her. It seems like a mile of splashing through endless shallows before the propeller has clearance and I am under power again.

I strain my eyes, peering ahead. How far can I see? Beyond the bow of the boat is blackness. Somewhere in that void is a sunken hulk with a collection of waterlogged souls clinging to a frail woven bamboo structure, waiting for the tide to rise. My God, yes, the tide was dead low when I pushed off. I wonder whether the hull is grounded, or just awash. Probably on the bottom since the green wood used in building these tubs is heavier than water. Anyhow, they load them to the gunwale with bricks, sand, rocks or other cargo of questionable value to the uninitiated eye, and when the river starts seeping in over the rail, they add six inches of freeboard by packing handfuls of mud, forming a bulwark along the gunwale. More like the moat walls on a kid's fortress at a Sunday beach outing than a structural extension of a cargo vessel, but they all seem to do it to get that last little bit of freight aboard. Their only concession to safety is the addition of a banana-tree stalk lashed to each side of the load at water level, in hopes that the buoyancy of the honeycombed stem will carry them through any rough weather that the river dishes out. I'd been running about the rivers of Bengal in a whaler at twenty-five knots for over two years and still swallowed hard as I passed fleets of these country boats, expecting to see them plunge straight to the river bottom in my wake. The boatmen just smiled, waved and went back to smoking their stubby ganga pipes.

Into the Abyss

The beam of the flashlight is swallowed in the night somewhere between the bow and infinity. I just can't tell where. I flick it off again and feel that moment of panic when newly plunged into absolute darkness: you wonder if you just suddenly went blind. The stars come back slowly, just the brightest at first, until, after an hour-long minute, I can see my chosen beacon, but well off to port. How could I get so far off course in one minute? An outboard is a devil to steer blind. The torsion of the prop is constantly throwing you to starboard. Under sail, the tug of the tiller, the sound of the leech flutter, and the breeze, however soft across your face, all quietly inform the receptive helmsman of a change in course. The roar and speed of an outboard serve to dull your senses in a meaningless racket and a self-generated wind always from dead ahead. I yank the boat back on course and wonder for a fleeting moment why this, more than any other direction, deserves to be considered "on course."

The brightest thing on earth is my luminous watch dial. I've been on the river half an hour. Perhaps three miles off shore, I wonder if I could have passed the sunken vessel. The engine dies with a twist of the handle. Slowly, the slapping on the flat bottom dies away. Silence. No sound of water moving. No voices. Silence perfectly meshes with the darkness.

Whistling in the Dark

Cupping my hands, I yell. Silence. Again, louder. Silence.

Wait, could that be a voice? I strain all senses, hands extending my ears. Silence . . . I think. My left ear begins a high-pitched ring. Can you strain an ear like you do your back? Damned imagination. There is fuel for about three hours running, with only me aboard. Half of that if loaded. I decide to go on in ten-minute intervals, stopping to yell. Manpura lies behind me, but where I can only guess. Almost twenty miles from north to south, it will be a pretty easy target heading east, I reassure myself.

Like a sputtering drunk, the engine's one working cylinder sets us back on our game of blind man's bluff. I wonder if Parker Brothers will be interested in this one as a party game. Race on into blackness and smash flat out into a drifting log, or eventually the shore some twelve miles away. Go too slow and the tide rises to snatch your goal away. Know the currents or you'll spend the night on a mucky char or, worse yet, awake to a sunrise ten miles out to sea with an empty gas tank to float home on. My confidence wanes as I count out the seconds. Must be time for next stop. Three minutes gone, the bright hands reveal. Could my watch have stopped? At eight minutes I can't wait any longer. Like Columbus' crew poised at the very edge of the earth, I have to halt, to grope once more in the silence before the inevitable plunge into the abyss. I am scared. No response to my yell. I place my thumb and index finger carefully against the top of my tongue, fill my lungs like Mark Spitz before the hundred-yard freestyle, and exhale with all my might. A piercing whistle cuts the still air. I push it out in a circle at least two miles across, searching for a sign of life. As I wait expectantly for a reply, I grin in recollection of the long summer hours spent perched on a tractor seat plowing or mowing, fingers in my mouth, trying to perfect this audible display of young manhood. Many a crooked row of corn was sown while nurturing that shrill note. Indeed, the only notoriety I ever gained on the college football field was from the grandstands, where I could clear a space around me of three bleacher rows with the deafening force of my shrill whistle.

Hearing Voices

Reluctantly, I pull at the engine rope and start off again. Three innings later, eyes sore from peering into interminable darkness, I stop for the last time. The fuel tank is half empty and my courage gone. Before the ripples from the wake die away, a faint chorus of voices drifts out of the mist far ahead. In a moment it comes again, barely audible but distinct. A shudder of excitement and relief passes through me as I jerk the engine to a start. Now I stop every two minutes, each time to hear the increasingly distinct reply to my yells until suddenly, above the sound of the engine the voices are behind and to my left. I'd passed within fifteen yards of the wreck without seeing a thing.

A vast flush of relief courses through my taut frame and I suddenly feel safe. It is distinctly a feeling of personal safety and not in the least related to any "higher mission" of rescuing or saving others. I can now head back to Manpura. Why is it that comfort in shared adversity is so universal?

As my weak light plays across the woven bamboo cabin, human forms seem to materialize motionless, out of the mist, in endless procession. "Al-lah, Al-lah, Al-lah!" they cry and laugh, obviously far more relieved than I. Twenty-two in all, clinging to the top and tattered edges of a tiny ephemeral island. The only sign of the sunken hull is the stern post, rising five feet above the river, still twelve feet above the keel. Shaped like one of Xerxes' fighting ships at the battle of Salamis, the bow of a Dacca country boat arches low over the water while the stern rises, reaching for the heavens in a graceful arch. Atop a sturdy hull is perched a bit of woven mat, more protection from the sun than anything else. As I slowly approach, two men push off from the wreck and frantically splash toward me. I gun the engine in reverse.

"Look, you idiots," I shout in Bengali, "if you all try to clamber aboard here at once none of us will get ashore. Who's in charge there?"

Taking Charge

After some heated babbling, one reasonably calm voice shouts back. There are indeed twenty-two men: four boatmen and eighteen workers comprising two tube-well-drilling teams. Both teams were headed for Manpura with 400 feet of two-inch steel pipe. They'd decided to share one boat and pocket the travel allowance for a second craft. More than half of them cannot swim.

"You organize yourself into two equal groups. I don't give a damn how you decide, but I can only take half of you at once. When I come alongside you come on board one at a time and sit flat on the bottom. If anyone pushes I'll shove off directly and go straight home without anyone of you." I mean what I say as I inch in. They decide to send the oldest and non-swimmers, and as the first few climb aboard they clamber aft to touch my feet.

"'Knock it off! You'll sink us. You might drown yet, so save all that till we're ashore," I order.

A scuffle with insane screaming and splashing breaks out on the flimsy cabin top. Arms grope for the panicked man as he flings himself at our skiff. The engine, already idling in reverse, churns backward at full throttle, and I douse the flashlight. He strikes the side of the boat and goes down, but a moment later my light finds him struggling to regain his perch on the bamboo.

"Okay, he'll be the last one to go," I yell.

"Because he can swim he was chosen to stay," explains an old man crouching at my feet, "but he's been raving the last few hours. If we leave him he'll drive the rest crazy or drown them all."

"It's up to you," I shout over to the leader, "but a repeat of that and I'm going home."

"We'd better send him. He'll be okay if he thinks he'll be saved," they decide after some heated discourse.

243

He comes aboard sobbing and docile, sitting exactly where told. As he carefully lowers his weight into the boat, we ship a gallon or so over the rail. He is the twelfth person.

"Next trip," I tell him, before he can lower himself to a crouch. Surprisingly, he scrambles back onto the wreck as ordered.

"Now, we're about five miles off Manpura," I explain, "and it will take me up to two hours to get back here. I will be back. For no reason should you leave this hulk. Here's a flashlight. It's very weak and won't last long. You are not to turn it on until I shine my light this way. You'll hear me coming for a long way, but save the light until you see mine. It's the only way to find you again. Understand?"

"The tide is rising fast. It will cover the cabin before two hours," comes the concern.

"Stand up, then. It won't rise above your chin. Keep the light dry. *Salaam aleikum*."

Orion as Guide

With the painful slowness of a steam locomotive pulling out of a station followed by three-score boxcars of moaning cattle, our overburdened craft plows through the still water, dragging a wake like Tugboat Annie. Slowly the stars light again as my eyes adapt. I find the friendly figure of Orion standing over the southeast sky, his sword dangling directly over Manpura, or so I imagine. Standing in the stern, peering across a dozen heads crammed into space designed for one-third that number, I feel like a platoon commander at Normandy. The question is not what will happen when we hit the beach, but rather, will we hit the beach? Our own bow wave threatens to rear up and inundate us in a paroxysm of self-annihilation, but the skiff manages to keep its blunt nose centimeters above the black river. Though we take water over the quarter rails, hands are busy scooping out each drop that climbs aboard. Shifting my weight to one side as I straddle the fuel tank, a few gallons splash noisily aboard. Not a centimeter freeboard to spare. If only the river will remain calm. The island can be no more than five miles distant; one hour at the outside. It is so dark we might run smack into the bank without ever seeing it, but that is no real problem in any case.

It seems we should have hit the shore by now. Heading just south of east we will come on the island somewhere near North Camp, situated two miles from the northern tip of Manpura. There really is no way we can miss it, stretched out for almost twenty miles like the backbone of the river. "Stop worrying," I tell myself. "Just wait till you have to find that sunken vessel again. Going east is a sure thing."

Canopus Winks

I have stars to steer by, and I hold fast to my course for close to an hour. Orion is etched in such lovely detail that I am sure I can see the swarming clouds of stars forming the great nebula of the hunter's sword. Below that is Sirius with its tremulous intensity, a testimonial to its Greek title shared only with the sun. My eye traces downward towards the nonexistent horizon to Canopus, the shining rudder of Jason's colossal ship, the Argo. Not visible north of the tropics, Canopus had been a discovery for me when I'd first come to Bengal. I do not resist the temptation to romanticize over its ancient namesake, the navigator at the siege of Troy, and my own use of its convenient position low in the southeast sky for my direction, this chill night on the Ganges Delta. But suddenly it is gone, and then back, and then gone again for a longer time. It doesn't fade, but rather is abruptly extinguished and switched on again. With none of the occulting characteristic of fog or a cloud, it has to have been eclipsed by a ship. I stop the engine and yell. No answer. No sign of life.

The star is clear and bright now, but it has surely been obscured by a moving object to the south. It can't be Manpura, or we'd have hit the shore, unless somehow we are far off course and passed it to the north heading on out to sea. Clearly impossible . . . then again, we are well overdue our landfall, and my stomach is in knots again. I start the engine, thanking its one faithful cylinder, and turn cautiously south. It must have been a vessel, I think, as we creep along. Just as I decide to swing back on course, Canopus disappears. No, it has to be the island with its tall palms snatching at our star. Minutes later, the bottom scrapes shore and the now-ebullient passengers spill out of the skiff onto the slipping bank.

No pilgrims newly arrived at Mecca ever treated the earth with more reverence or pleasure. They have not an inkling of how nearly we'd come to passing by this northern tip of Manpura and on out into the Bay of Bengal. The tide indeed is flooding and the river has changed course, flowing north toward its source. The curious game of hide and seek played by Canopus among the lofty palms saved the day. Canopus the navigator. Standing on the dark low bank, I dread the thought of another trip into the black river. Just a compass would be an immense help.

A Highway of Light

The matted rice straw feels warm under my water-logged feet. "Fire. Of course—a fire! Quick! Everyone gather all the straw you can, and heap it here." I sacrifice a cup of precious petrol to offset the dew and Manpura's first navigational beacon springs into flames. "Everything depends on that fire," I tell my erstwhile crew. "You must keep it at least five meters high."

I feel strangely confident with a quarter tank of petrol and a whispering engine as I push off alone; the conflagration over my shoulder will be visible for miles. Throttle wide open and twenty minutes out, the flames slip out of view, leaving only a glowing rim on the horizon behind me. I try the flashlight straight ahead, then sweep it in an arc. No reply. Could they have gone down? Perhaps the light failed. A faint sound of voices far to port. I see the light flashing insistently. The damned current set me far to the north again. They guide me in like a plane on a homing beacon. But for the light I'd have run them down. The water is up to

246

their chests and the quiet current pulls insistently at them. They'd managed to upend a couple of their long steel pipes and plant them in the river bottom, affording some support. The tide is still rising. So many lucky breaks had brought me back in time. Now, if the petrol will hold . . .

We steer straight down the highway of light cast by the bonfire to an exhausted and chilly landing. By then, villagers have been attracted to the shore and relief blankets are loaned to twenty-two wet and happy men. Zafrullah Choudhury agrees to accompany me to the creek near North Camp while another villager guides the bedraggled band along the shore route. A quarter mile from the inlet, the petrol tank goes bone dry. We pole the rest of the way.

"Gee, where you been, man?" Kaiser complains as I step into the circle of lantern light. "We expected you all day, but finally we couldn't wait—special dinner can't keep forever."

"I brought some guests to celebrate the big day, so stoke up the fire. There's twenty-two of them. Some Christmas!"

What a Christmas present!—twenty-five grateful souls. And I will never look at Canopus again without winking back at her.

Grinning at Canopus

On the southernmost island, Sakuchia, unaware of the drama of Jon's rescue at sea off the north shore, Catholic sisters and other volunteers have their own adventure. Fr. Timm recounts:

> Christmas found me in Sakuchia, the southernmost island. In the afternoon I was joined for a Christmas celebration by Fr. Banas, Russ Brown, a VSO [Volunteer Service Overseas] at Notre Dame College, Sisters Leonora, Barbara Jean and Marian Teresa and a British volunteer named Sue [King]. They had to return to their base on Manpura before nightfall. Fr. Banas and I co-celebrated Mass in the HELP tent and for Christmas dinner we had tomato soup and Franco-American tinned spaghetti which we had been saving up for the occasion.
>
> The party stayed on a little too late, for by late afternoon it was full ebb tide and we had to tow their motorboat through the mud in the small creek which led to our camp about a mile from the big river on the Bhola side. When we assembled on the river shore another problem developed. The mud was so deep that it came above the knees. Sr. Leonora consented to be carried out to the boat by Russ and myself but the others bravely ploughed their own way through the mud.
>
> That was the end of my Christmas adventures, but not of theirs. The motorboat got caught on a *char* in the river and by the time they got it free it was too dark to find Manpura. They anchored on an uninhabited island in the middle of the river and spent the night shivering in the boat, singing Christmas carols and waiting for the dawn (Timm 1995, p. 148).

Songs of Bengali Boatmen

The river has no bank, no shore
Therefore, which bank shall I leave,
to which shall I go?
From whom shall I know?
The clouds array themselves against me;
the lightning paints in golden flashes.
The river speeds swollen with rain.
In the lightning I see for a moment a golden picture
but never see it again.

A cloud gathers in the west
And there is a noise there like a roaring lion.
The rope securing the steering oar of my boat breaks!
And the boat goes reeling,
Oh boatman!
Be on guard as you row in high wind and storms,
Sharks and crocodiles are our neighbors!

Anonymous

CHAPTER 16
A More Permanent Organization

Pulling Figures from the Air

"HELP is the best organized and most effective volunteer group working in the cyclone area," the German consul general, Mr. Enders, assures the representatives of three German donor organizations who descend on Dacca on December 10. The consul refers them to Steve Baldwin, director of the Ford Foundation. When they meet Steve on the following morning, he details HELP's Manpura Plan.

"The initial relief phase of the plan is complete," he tells them. "The surviving population will now be supported through Food for Work Programs, and long-term development assistance provided through self-help cooperatives modeled after the Comilla Institute. So far the work has been paid for by the generous donations of European residents in Pakistan, of wealthy Pakistanis and by USAID."

"How has the government reacted to HELP?" the Germans ask. "Does the government object to a small area like the three islands around Manpura getting more support than the other affected areas?"

Steve said the government did not object, and gave them three reasons:

1. The government was interested in a pioneering project,
2. was glad about any help coming from outside and,
3. will most likely not raise objections because very many Pakistanis continue to be actively involved in the project (Bread for the World, *Report on a Trip to Pakistan*, December 1970, p. 8).

Encouraged by their conversation with Steve, the donors decide to speak with other HELP activists. That same afternoon, they hold a discussion with Jon and Lincoln Chen, who tell them about the work done by HELP. The donors are clearly impressed with what they learn in these two meetings, and inform a government official, Mr. Amisuzzaman, when they meet with him in the evening, of their intention to support HELP exclusively. "Mr Amisuzzaman was not pleased," they note in their report. He had expected their donations to be channeled through the government (Bread for the World 1970, p. 9).

Aware that interest in disasters is fleeting and will disappear as soon as a new crisis strikes another part of the world, we grab the moment. On December 11, immediately after being informed that the Germans have expressed interest in supporting HELP, Jon and Lincoln get together with "Abed, the quintessential cost accountant. [They start] pulling figures from the air and making up a project proposal practically overnight" (Zaman 2013). Drawing Viquar into their deliberations, they draft an estimate for the costs of long-term development, including local administrators to take over the work. Our most proactive volunteer group remains small, and many will soon move on to different assignments, but we are optimistic about engaging more participants, and particularly other local professionals.

The first step in making a long-term plan of our financial needs is to scratch out a list of our current funding sources, how much HELP has in the bank, and how much is in the pipeline in the form of promises: (Rs. 10 = US $2).

1. Rs. 180,000 ($9000) in bank of which 85,000 ($4250) represents private donations and 95,000 ($4750) is from AID. They owe us (2 to 1 matching agreement) another 90,000 ($4500).
  Count on in bank = Rs. 270,000 ($13,500)
2. German Church Group committed Rs. 600,000 ($30,000) to pay agricultural part of the 2-month Manpura Plan

3. War on Want are thinking of donating 4,000 Br. Pounds (From note in file on HELP's financial position prior to meeting with Bread for the World).

Always conscious of the valuable first-hand knowledge of the field coordinators, we send a helicopter to Manpura to fetch Kaiser in order to have his input in writing a detailed two-month funding proposal for rehabilitation. He writes:

> Going from Manpura to Dacca was no easy task. One afternoon, a large Pakistan Army helicopter landed in front of the school,of the few surviving buildings and now our operational headquarters.be important people from the government on an inspection tour, I thought contemptuously. One of the village boys came running to my room and said the pilot wanted to talk to me. The pilot told me that he had instructions to pick up the field coordinator of "HELP" and take him to Dacca. Our group is well-connected, I thought with a sense of pride. I quicklya few things and boarded the chopper. I remember falling asleep on the plush sofaJane King's house in Dhaka in the middle ofmeetingAbed and Jon.hadn't realized how totally exhausted I was (Zaman 2013).

The others work late into the night to come up with a reasonable budget to fund the Manpura Plan.

While Kaiser hops from Manpura to Dacca in a Pakistani helicopter, the German donors board their own country's helicopter to Manpura on December 12 to visit one of the three HELP camps to determine for themselves how well we operate on the ground. After a brief and positive visit, they are further encouraged to support our effort when the German military attaché reinforces what they have been hearing from others: that HELP is doing good work and will probably be allowed to continue their activities because so many Pakistanis are involved in it (Bread for the World 1970, pp. 9–10).

Dr. Gundert of Bread for the World on Manpura, 1971
(*Rainer Kruse, photographer; photo courtesy of Bread for the World*)

Our Heads Spin

Armed with what we fear may be considered an overly ambitious plan for 1.8 million rupees (about $383,000), Viquar and I meet Dr. Gundert and his colleagues at the Intercontinental Hotel after they return in the afternoon from Manpura. Their report notes: "Mrs. Rohde, prime mover behind the HELP initiative, came, together with some Pakistani fellow colleagues, to inform us intensively about the work to be done and to give us a chance to talk to them. It was interesting to see with what enthusiasm Mrs. Rohde, but also the Pakistanis, were engaged in their work" (Bread for the World 1970, p. 10).

Viquar recalls noticing how eager they were to make substantial donations to the relief effort, and how keen to avoid the corruption often present in larger organizations and in government.

The two men listen to our plan carefully. "They reported

that a comprehensive Manpura Plan is being worked out at the moment and handed over a document with details about their requirements for the next two months: 1.8 million Rupees (1.38 Million DM by the standard exchange rate, DM 900,000 by the tourist rate)"* We think our request must have overshot the mark, because Dr. Gundert's brow wrinkles and he looks terribly concerned. With a very serious face he informs us in his German accent, "Zat is too bad, because I vant to give you one million marks and my colleague here, he has another three million." Our heads spin with excitement at having what seems like a staggering amount of funds offered for HELP's long-term work.

> We were assured to receive detailed receipts/documentation for all the funds given to and spent by HELP. The HELP representatives very much welcomed the idea of sending Mr. Schneider to Pakistan as our representative for about one year in order to monitor their activities and report on their work.
> We have promised HELP—provided KED sanctions 3 million DM—assistance over that amount in a series of installments on the basis of detailed receipts/documentation on their part. As soon as the government (of Pakistan) should prevent the work of HELP or HELP stop their activities for other reasons, our support will also stop (Bread for the World 1970, p. 10).

Their report ends with a positive endorsement of HELP: "We are convinced that the money provided by KED and the money possibly coming from 'Bread for the World' can only be spent in an effective way through HELP, an organization that has already proved its worth" (Bread for the World 1970, p. 11).

Ongoing Bread for the World funds will sustain HELP ac-

---

* "German and British funds face problem of converting," December 17 *Morning News* article quotes the Red Cross Secretary General's cable to President Yahya: "Further aid would be seriously jeopardized if world public opinion knew that authorities didn't even give relief funds at least the same rate as that of tourist."

tivities on Manpura for the next four years. Hiring of more permanent staff, including an executive director, begins, with a working budget of 1,800,000 rupees (about $383,000) through the end of January 1971.

> Today makes four weeks since Candy's idea and our first commitment of $100 to relief to be delivered by ourselves. The remarkable fact is that we've not solicited any big money. The organizations are searching us out. It is a huge problem to grow like this, because we rely on only a few of us to administer the operation (Jon Rohde, letter to his parents, December 14, 1970).

"An Ethereal Experience"

No helicopter flies Kaiser back to Manpura as it had a few days ago to Dacca, but he finds the journey beautiful.

> I returned to the island on my own, first traveling to Chittagong, then taking the public launch to Hatiya and finally getting on a cargo boat to Manpura. Six men rowed the boat loaded with reconstruction materials for us. It was hard work. As it got dark, I watched with fascination the phosphorescent ripples of the oars in the water. There was no land and not a single boat in sight. The sky was resplendent with stars and the silence of the night was chopped by the rhythm of the oars. It was an ethereal experience (Zaman 2013).

When a young man arrives from London in December, his experience is rapturous in a very different way from Kaiser's. We think he will be as excited as we are about being involved in helping to rehabilitate the cyclone victims. After a couple of weeks with us in Dacca, he travels to Manpura and is assigned to work with Fr. Timm on Sakuchia. He lasts about two days before leaving the island to accompany some of the other volunteers to a festival in the Chittagong Hill Tracts, and then catches a flight back to Dacca. Jon asks him why he didn't go back to the island.

"Nothing to do there," he says. A child of the spaced-out sixties, he laconically learns to play the bamboo flute, *ganja* smoke filling his room, while Totomiah carries his meals to him on a tray. Not everyone is excited about taking up the challenge of HELP's work.

Registration of HELP: December 20, 1970

I explain our current situation in a letter home, dated late in December:

> This is sincerely the first moment I have had since the work we've started of relief operations after the Nov. 12 cyclone, and assuredly the very first moment of my being alone (only Miah in the kitchen). In a very short while the house will fill up again—in fact, here comes a car. Basically, the news is that we have been unbelievably and excitingly successful in our relief operation for Manpura . . .
>
> We are still operating on a nineteen-hour day, but are in the process of solidifying an organizational structure on a permanent basis. For the kind of rehabilitation work we are in the process of doing, we need to make so many contacts (this has been one of our most fortunate successes so far—we have had experts from everywhere come to the island and have good reports and analyses to act on), and the details of the operation are so massive, plus the handling of funds, that we need a more permanent organization.

With Bread for the World's promise of major funds, HELP moves into a new dimension. We feel more assured our plans for rehabilitation and development on Manpura stand a chance of being realized. Substantial monies also create more formal responsibilities. It is now imperative to register HELP under the Societies Registration Act of 1860 to legally "engage in charitable purposes and social welfare activities strictly on non-profit basis" (the first objective of the "Memorandum of Society"). Viquar Choudhury, in his capacity as barrister, and with his characteristic open-hearted pro bono attitude, accepts responsibility for writing the articles under which we will operate. He swiftly undertakes the registration of HELP as a "Society with Rules and Regulations." This document will give HELP legal status as an international charitable organization. At the December 20 HELP meeting in Dacca, Viquar summarizes the objectives and gives careful attention to the rules.

The first members of the governing body are F. H. Abed, Martha Chen, Viquar Choudhury, Rafiqul Hussain* and Cornelia Rohde. Besides these five, Sultana (Runi) Choudhury and Dr. Jon Rohde are listed in the memorandum as "desirous of forming a Society with the above objects."

Allocating funds to rent an office in Chittagong is one of the first actions the board takes. Lynn Bickley recalls: "A permanent staff was assembled and I was asked to be the Chittagong coordinator" (email message to author, March 4, 2013). At last Abed is able to have his personal space back. We can better relate to his desire to normalize his life now that we are running HELP's operations in our home in Dacca. "Right now we are using the downstairs room as headquarters. . . . It has become an office with blackboards, maps, files, chalkboard, typewriters, desks and humming with activity all the time" (author's letter to her parents, December 27, 1970). Meals and refreshments are on twenty-four-hour demand. It is Totomiah's turn to expect any number of people for meals. Long hours are crammed with planning, procurement and strategizing. Spare bedrooms are occupied nearly every night, because we often invite those who come to consult with us to stay over when our discussions stretch into late hours. I write: "We can't keep this up indefinitely, I'm even getting hives." Once HELP is formalized into a charitable society, the pressure on our personal space is diminished by the establish-

---

* Rafiqul Hussain is a capable fifth-year architecture student who volunteers for HELP in his spare time. His studies keep him from attending meetings, and he is finally voted off the board in April 1971.

ment of the Dacca office at One Elephant Road, Magh Bazaar. The stress diminishes and, as Lynn recollects about the change of pace in Chittagong, "work settled down to just 12 intense but rewarding hours a day" (email message to author, March 4, 2013).Only one month after the cyclone, we are running a generously funded development organization.

CHAPTER 17
On-the-Spot Management

Long-Term Field Coordinators

Five hectic weeks have passed since we landed on Manpura. By January 1, most of the original field volunteers have returned to Dacca to resume full-time jobs. Kaiser writes in his memoir:

> There was an urgent need to have a permanent field coordinator to implement the vastly expanded long-term rehabilitation program. It's one thing to have professionals of high caliber volunteer for a week or two to work in a rural area that didn't have running water, flush toilets, electricity, roads or, for that matter, anything that moved on wheels other than a few bullock carts. It's quite another thing to expect anyone to give up his comfortable life in the city to work for any length of time on an island that had lost everything.

Some who have proven they can handle the challenges of volunteering on Manpura away from their "comfortable life," and would like to return for a longer period of service, are prevented from making this commitment because of responsibilities to family or binding work contracts that do not allow extended periods of leave. HELP is fortunate to have two proven field coordinators step forward who do not have dependent families and who manage to juggle their other obligations. Both have already given several weeks of their time to HELP's field activities, so they are experienced with the situation on the ground.

First to commit is Fr. Timm, a renowned nematologist and Catholic priest educated at Notre Dame College in Indiana. He was probably happiest when he collected two hundred species of nematodes from an ice hole on a scientific expedition to Antarctica. Now he says he often spots a new one by looking out his window at a banana leaf. One he discovers is named for him: *Timmia parva*. He served as a teacher at Notre Dame College in Dacca before being appointed principal, and had been in the country for nearly twenty years when he landed on Manpura at the age of forty-two. He is inured to physical discomfort, unruffled when up to his knees in mud or sleeping on the floor of a broken building. He doesn't allow problems to wear him down, preferring to confront them head on or to move around them to tackle goals he can accomplish. "Why should the 'little people' always come last?" is a question he often asks. Although he listens carefully before he gives an opinion, he is never afraid to give it. He loves poetry and has an endless supply of jokes up his sleeve. Notre Dame College releases Fr. Timm from his duties as principal, at least until the college year begins again in June, allowing him to devote himself full-time on Manpura.

Fr. Timm up to his knees in mud
(*photo courtesy of Bread for the World*)

HELP's other field coordinator, Kaiser Zaman, like many of us, is twenty-seven when he begins volunteering for HELP. A Bengali born in Karachi, he is more familiar with Urdu than his mother tongue. Losing an arm in a rice-milling accident when he was eight years old never slowed him down. After earning an MBA, he accepted the position of personnel officer for Pakistan Shell Oil in Chittagong. Before becoming involved with HELP, he could often be found comfortably engaged in political discussions with friends at their after-hours social club. A logical thinker with a good sense of humor, he is a competent organizer and enjoys engaging with people and looking at every side of a question. Yet he is also a romantic who loves to be out under the stars. He arranges a month of paid leave for January, and persuades Pakistan Shell to compensate him for February as well, so he can take up the challenge of Manpura.

These two dedicated persons devote themselves to carrying out HELP's program. Close contact with them in the field is critical for a smooth-running operation. Both Fr. Timm and Kaiser regularly send detailed reports to the mainland, maintaining strong links between the field and supply centers in both Chittagong and Dacca. Kaiser, the quintessential personnel manager, includes vivid details in his reports about the volunteer dynamics and organization in the field.

Kaiser's Organizing Voice

```
Fieldcord's Report to Helpcentre, Dec. 12, 1970
by Kaiser Zaman

Hi, Gang!

Here I go again! only that I don't know when
this report will reach you. You want reports and
I write them. This clears my conscience (now,
don't raise your eyebrows).
```

Personnel:

I am glad to hear about the students that are coming. I agree that they will be most useful in specific jobs, since we aren't doing much direct distribution.

As for the MBA boys, I am a little doubtful as to how effective they can be as camp boss. What we need are mature people like Frs. Timm and Banas.

If Ali agrees to be with us for some time, he would need an assistant. Would the MBA boys be ready to take orders from people like him? Of course, I will be around ensuring the smooth working relationships. A mature man will have more weight and can be more effective in implementation and supervision.

Organization:

People of varied backgrounds are working here. Their inadequate knowledge regarding organization, record and file keeping, stores, maintenance and handling, etc., has resulted in each one keeping his own kind of records. A newcomer, unable to make sense out of it, starts all over again. This is where the MBAs could do a job—building up a uniform organization, preparing operating procedures. I don't want to sound pompous, but the fact remains that the current state of record keeping is unsatisfactory. We have made some progress. We have just completed an inventory of goods in hand and have got a rough idea of goods issued. If you could give us a statement of non-consumables supplied so far, we could make reconciliation and get a clearer picture. I feel so ashamed making such a lot of demands. Please ignore those which you think are not worth the effort.

With lots of love from all in Helpland,

Kaiser

Voice of Timm, Our Poet Priest*

Father Richard Timm, Field Coordinator of HELP

Stormy weather last night. I could sleep only half the night because of the rain and wind. "Sound of vernal showers on the twinkling grass." I guess I'm a hopeless romantic because I like Shelley and the sound of rain at night.

> "Delightfully the bright wind boisterous
> Ropes, wrestles, beats earth bare
> of yester tempest's creases."

How appropriate here and now. That's not "Ode to the West Wind," in case you were wondering.

---

* George Curlin remembers: "Manpura was my introduction to Father Timm, my tent mate in South Manpura. It took me a couple of days to realize who he was, and it was a conversation watching some bugs or worms or something in the mud that prompted him to mention the genus and species of whatever it was, when I put two and two together. His fame as an entomologist who was the principal at Notre Dame College was legendary. But by then I knew him as simply a wonderful, caring, hardworking incredibly decent human being."

Another personal note from Fr. Timm about a young admirer shows his soft spot for children:

January 28, 1971

"Hello" to all

To the Little Girl with the Big Heart (Candy, who else?).

Remember the cute little boy from Bhola who stayed overnight at HELP Chittagong and went with me to Hatiya? He came out to the steamer at Hatiya and greeted me and insisted on carrying my bag.

Time to stop,
Dick

"There was a small boy who was orphaned by the cyclone. His cheerfulness and resourcefulness were an inspiration to all. I was to encounter him many times on my trips to Hatiya and was always full of curiosity about what we were doing" (Timm 1995, p. 138).

Orphaned by
the cyclone

CHAPTER 18
Unused to Working
for the Common Good

Desperate Migrants

Nazir cannot remember a time when his stomach did not ache from hunger, when it did not gnaw and feel hollow as a gourd. There is no work for him in the landowner's fields, because he is the youngest of six brothers.

"If I only had some land," he sighs. He thinks of Abdul, his neighbor, who decided to leave the village because he heard there was new land open for settlers on the islands farther west; land built up slowly from silt carried down the big rivers running through the Gangetic plain.

"If I can only have enough to cultivate for myself, then maybe I can find a wife," he thinks.

He knows Abdul did not return home. "It must be working for him," Nazir thinks, his stomach twisting sharply. "I'm going to give it a try."

Jon describes survival on the *char* islands:

Families fight wars over those low *chars*, for as soon as a mud bank lolls its long back above the murky river, someone builds a sleeping platform of bamboo and palm leaves and moves onto the precarious perch. He plants a few stalks of rice and guards his new possession with the obstinacy of a man dreaming of ever-expanding paddy fields in the midst of a land where generations of subdivision have left only postage stamp farms. Three feet above the waters this pioneer sits out the blazing sun awaiting the inevitable cyclones that sweep up the Bay of Bengal, or the desperate farmer coming silently in his dugout at night looking for his lost fields that the river has quietly, insidiously consumed over the past decade, and finally, in the last storm even his home has been snatched away — a grim game of survival.

Toehold on a new life

Only the most desperate, rugged individuals shift to newly formed *chars*. Like Nazir, they are often the landless unemployed who have migrated to the islands fleeing dead-end lives. Escaping from destitution, they grasp the opportunity to subsist rather than starve. Having abandoned the familiarity of their mainland extended family, they no longer are part of the settled pattern of many generations living in the same village.

When Nazir arrives on Manpura, he finds only isolated households, with little sense of community. Neighbors are often viewed with suspicion. People take their affairs in their own hands, focusing on the welfare of their nuclear families. Working together for the common good is an uncommon idea on Manpura. Social fragmentation, along with competing ideas among the experts about how to create a viable system of cooperatives, compounds the problem of encouraging them to band together to develop or work toward the benefit of everyone.

Kaiser observes:

```
    Nearly out of decent typing paper, getting a
back ache from squatting on relief blankets,
hunting and pecking away at Jon Rohde's type-
writer:
    The new co-op guys don't agree with the way
the old ones set up co-ops. Result: revamping of
the whole show. The co-ops still remain a mere
channel of distribution, except that there is
little left for distribution. There was a co-op
managers meeting in North yesterday. Good turn-
out — more than 150 but some only members. Fr.
Banas, co-op workers and I spoke, mostly exhort-
ing them on self-help, rice seed storing and
cluster housing. Full agreement but little tan-
gible result. Local people have many problems,
so we mustn't push them too far too fast.
```

Managing Fairness: Manpura Plan, Phase Two

With the process of rebuilding and providing food supplies and clothing well underway by the new year, HELP presses ahead with the development program envisioned in the Manpura Plan, Phase Two. Taking ideas from the trainers at Comilla, Rangunia, Noakhali and Feni, HELP attempts to strengthen the formation of farmers', tradesmen's and fishermen's cooperatives. The plan

267

is for groups to share the use of goods procured by HELP, such as plows, cows, boats, nets, tools or building materials. At this point, foodstuffs bought by HELP are handed over to the relief officer of the civil administration for distribution. The evolving policy is to no longer give any HELP goods for free.

Kaiser explains:

Assistance from HELP, whether in the form or goods or otherwise, will not be given free. It will be given in exchange for services, because that is the only thing the people of Manpura can give in return. The services [mostly work] will be used for development work of Manpura only, [and include] road building, irrigation canal digging, building schools and mosques etc. It is important to instill in the people a sense of self help and hard work for the common good (Zaman, "Operating Instructions," January 1, 1971).

Villager adding another *hat* (foot and a half) to the one he is standing on to make a mud-walled building

268

Manpurans, used to relying on themselves, are already practicing self-help, but because their lives are a constant fierce competition for scarce resources, they find it difficult to recognize any benefit in cooperating with each other. Asking them to work for the development of the island seems an impossible burden to add to their daily battle for survival.

HELP organizers find it difficult to motivate them to form associations to work for everyone's benefit. Most become members only because they want to gain favor with HELP in order to receive loans or materials they need. They risk being left out of the queue unless they join.

Existing models of co-op organization shape the government's policy of encouraging every member of society to join and to adhere to a set of rules and regulations. Kaiser explains the rules to the organizers:

Co-operative societies in entire Manpura should have a uniform pattern. It should be ensured the office bearers are elected by majority consensus and the formation is in conformity with the legal requirements.

The richer elements on Manpura, like the Choudhurys, quickly see the advantage of taking charge by becoming elected officers of the newly forming groups. They figure they will be first in line for loans, and will be able to choose who else will be favored. They are able to lead the meetings and administer the societies by handling the paperwork involved, an impossible barrier for an illiterate person. For instance, an uneducated member would not be able to participate in this directive of Kaiser's:

Each co-operative will maintain at least two registers initially. One for recording the minutes of meetings and the other as Goods Received

and Loaned Register. The minute book should be
signed by all attending members. . . . The cooperative workers will then collate the lists of
requirements of all Cooperatives and prepare a
list, a consolidated statement of needs (Zaman,
memo to field staff, January 1, 1971).

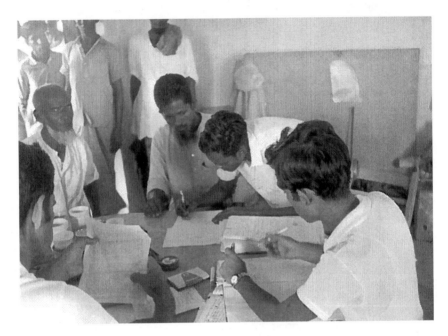

Signing up for cooperatives

HELP's promotion of the government's policy of inclusive-
ness ensures that members of co-ops consist of both the exploiter
and the exploited. Sharecroppers who are already in debt or be-
holden for labor to the wealthier leaders allow the large landowners to dominate, but have little confidence they will work for
the best interest of everyone in the group. Circumventing the
power structure on the island by having an educated rural-
development team help small landowners and the landless form
their own societies is not promoted. This is because HELP is at-

tempting to cooperate with civil authorities. The impoverished, who have come to Manpura to find opportunities away from the social hierarchies in more densely settled areas, find they are still the marginalized underdogs. HELP does not find a way to circumvent the dysfunction.

In theory, the cyclone that placed everyone on the island in the same dire condition could have been a window of opportunity for HELP to introduce cooperatives that only focused on the marginalized people of Manpura. But in retrospect, HELP didn't understand the social structure well enough to challenge the government's co-op model. Instead, it becomes, as Fr. Timm wryly notes, "a highly idealized experiment in instant cooperation."

Field staff finds group problem-solving or joint participation nonexistent. The less-advantaged members are not willing to speak up about their concerns during cooperative meetings in the presence of HELP or the power bloc on the island. Landless cultivators and small farmers are not proportionately represented in the managing committees of the cooperatives. They do not dare to say anything against the leaders, and are too cowed to generate ideas themselves. HELP takes charge of most business because the members do not have enough information to make informed choices. For example, HELP fixes the value of rehabilitation materials to exchange for rice seed, or makes the decision to bring in containers and moisture-testing meters for rice storage. We also exhort them to clear out the polluted tanks next to their houses, to store their seeds for the next harvest, and to agree to consolidate their land for cluster housing to protect against future storms. By making it clear that HELP goods will only be distributed through the cooperatives, the numbers of registered societies keep increasing, and the members turn up for meetings.

Throughout his time as field coordinator, Kaiser continues to give thought to a fair distribution policy and procedure, as his field note from March 17, 1971 indicates:

Policy:

Items of general benefit (roads, cyclone shelters) should be free.

Goods issued to individuals which do not produce an income (house) should be on long term loan basis (10 years).

Goods producing income (plows and cows) on loan repayable partly to the individual's saving account with his co-op and partly to the co-op's own account.

Flattening earth during road construction

Even though Kaiser is faced with overwhelming structural obstacles to promote community and to strengthen the co-ops, he remains optimistic. When he observes a group of young people resuming an initiative they had begun before the catastrophe, he begins to hope that a "principle of self-help is slowly crystallizing" among the Manpurans.

Self-help: House-building from material at hand

Local students who had their own social welfare society before cyclone keen to work again.
Will use them for census at North. Ali is using
a similar group in South. Wanted a place to have
office. I have promised to help when our building materials arrive. This morning they started
repairing [a] path. They are doing a good job
and are very much sold on it. They are doing
themselves proud and feeling so as well. It was
beautiful to see them work. Hope the others take
a lesson (Zaman, field note, December 31, 1970).

Cooperative earth work to build road on Manpura.
In return for work, goods are given through registered cooperatives.

Fishing Cooperatives

Early in January, Mobubal Alam, Jon and I are sitting together on
one of the long couches piled with bright pillows in our living
room, now the Dacca HELP center. We are talking to Brother
Flavian, who has served most of his life in the fishing communities.*

"Ze fishermen must get boats and nets! Ze *ilish* are running!
Ze zea will be zilver with fish!" he exclaims in his Belgian accent.
I imagine fish the same color as his thick shock of silver hair. His
eyes twinkling with excitement, he energetically gestures with
his hands as he describes schools of hilsa migrating from the wa-

---

* Brother Flavian of Diang (across the Karnafuli River from the Marine Academy Ghat).

ters of the delta upriver to spawn. "Ah, the *ilish*, the *ilish*!" he enthuses. "The sea jumps with light from their silver scales. Thousands and thousands of them surge in massive schools throughout the bay. The surface shines and sparkles. They run so thick, you can almost reach your hands out and scoop them into the boat." Bengalis call the delicious bony hilsa fish (*ilish mach*) "the darling of the waters," and the fishermen depend on the high demand for them for their living.* But with their boats swept away in the cyclone, they may miss the season's catch unless we can help them replace their boats and nets in time. Brother Flavian explains that a fisherman's share of the catch depends on who owns the boat. Due to seasonal variation in fish prices and the differing amounts of the catch, these poorest members of the Thana are caught in a vicious cycle of debt. By providing boats, HELP could break the cycle. We ask what material support the fishermen need from HELP. "Nets, equipment, and locally designed boats," he replies. Mobub offers to send co-op organizers to establish and prepare the papers to register societies of fishermen. It is easier to promote cooperatives among the fishermen than it is with farmers, because laborers already share the profits of their catch, and understand the way of working for everyone's benefit. We consider buying outboard motors so they can speed up the delivery of fresh fish to market, and discuss the feasibility of creating an ice plant with storage facilities to take advantage of seasonal price variations.

January 10, 1971 letter from the HELP Governing Body:

> Amongst the fishing communities, all the nets and boats were lost or badly damaged. [Nearly 46,000 of 77,000 fishermen in the area perished. Sixty-five percent of coastal fishing industry was destroyed.] Under the guidance of Brother Flavian, a man who spent twenty-five years with fishing cooperatives, HELP supplied nets, buoys, weights, ropes,

---

* *Hilsa*, or *ilish*, as it is commonly called in Bengal, is a symbol of Bengali identity. When the East Bengal football team wins, a dinner featuring *hilsa* is a tradition for celebrating fans.

anchors, timber, bolts, and tar. Already, one group is again laying its nets bringing much needed fish to the Manpura bazaars. The keels for five new boats of local design will be laid this week in Flavian's co-op yard near Chittagong using carpenters from Manpura. When complete, they will be provided, like most of our goods, as a loan to the co-op group with repayment over years reverting to the Central Co-op providing capital for new projects.

Sawing planks to make boats

Because of HELP's commitment to the fishing community, Akbar Kabir, the newly hired coordinator for HELP, could report on February 25: "Of the five fishing boats under contract (with the Chittagong Fishermen's Cooperative), three are nearly complete and the timber for two has been ordered. Fifteen more boats will be constructed; two fiberglass boats have been donated for experimental purposes."

Kaiser determines in his January 6 report that fishing and agricultural cooperatives should not be the exclusive focus:

```
Assistant Register of Coops have orders to
register only farmers and fishermen. They need
orders for registering others: traders, labor-
ers, bankers, bullock cart drivers. Explore pos-
sibility of giving loans through Coop Bank. They
will do the administrative work of loan realiza-
tion. Essential for capital formation. HELP
can't possibly administer loan realization.
```

By June 30, 1971, HELP reported that five fishing boats of local design were completed and given to five groups of Manpura fishermen, but the two eighteen-foot fiberglass boats we had expected to be donated by a foreign agency to test their suitability for local fishing were not received.

The June HELP report also indicates reservations about building an ice plant to keep the fish fresh:

Mr. Richard C. Kimball, a Consultant of East Pakistan Small Industries Corporation, undertook a visit to Manpura to prepare a report on small and cottage industries possibilities, including feasibility of ice plant and storage facilities. The report could not be submitted, as Mr. Kimball was evacuated [due to civil strife]. From discussions it appeared that the total catch of Manpura fishermen might not justify such a project.

Traditional *nauka* fishing boat

Fishing boat under construction

Treacherous Mud Bars and Fierce Tides

Since there were few housing materials available nearby, HELP arranged with Bro. Flavian . . . to send two fishery launches full of CI sheets to Manpura. Bro. Flavian warned the *majhee* [head boatman] not to travel at night because of the many treacherous mud bars in the area between Hatiya and Manpura. The boats arrived at Hatiya just before sunset. The *majhee* could see Manpura in the distance, so he decided to make a run for it. The next morning at 6 a.m. one of the crew, clinging to a plank and utterly exhausted, was cast up on the western shore of Manpura. The launches had almost made it but got caught on a mud bar north of Manpura and were ripped apart by the fierce outgoing tide. About a month later we heard that another crew member had survived also. He somehow made it all the way to Ramgati. The Governing Body of HELP, after much delay and objection, at the prodding of Dr. Rohde, who offered to raise the money, finally agreed to compensate Brother Flavian for half the value of the boats. Of course there was no insurance coverage (Timm 1995, p. 152).

Power Tillers vs. Cattle Tillers

Nazir is desperate. He knows he must plant whatever little seed he has succeeded in scavenging after the storm. He worries that relief supplies will soon be exhausted. He fears that the money he hopes to earn hiring out his labor in the Choudhurys' fields will not buy enough food to last him through the season, so he will need to supplement from his own small plot. After years, he managed to save enough to buy a bullock, only to see his animal disappear into the surging waters during the storm. He can still hear his terrified bellows and see his crazed eyes as the water sucked him into its rage. Nazir knows if his field is to be tilled, it can only be by his own backbreaking effort. His only choice is to pull the old wooden plow himself. At least he was able to salvage his plow because HELP brought pumps to clean out his tank after the storm. Standing in his field, Nazir wonders, "Will I ever have enough money to purchase another bullock?"

Because of the total loss of livestock, HELP considers importing power tillers to be shared among the cooperatives. Fr. Timm's February 1 field report notes two major drawbacks:

"High water levels in the rainy season" would make it impossible to use them, and there is a lack of "reliable repair options in case of breakdown."

His next report shows that the obstacles he brought up are real:

Three power tillers sent by government. Villagers say tillers can't operate in rainy season due to high water level—ranging from 2 feet and above. (13½ foot tide yesterday. Water up in all fields but no more in dug-out tanks than in fields.) Suggest expert survey before bulk order. However a few would be handy right now.

Oxfam at Char Kalmi has offered to repair our speed boat engines. If a power tiller goes bust mebbe we can send it down to them.

Idle power tiller

Kaiser's March 17 field note follows up on the idea of doing a careful survey prior to any decision about making any large order of tillers.

Please assess the reaction of the farmers to the idea of introducing hand driven power tillers as a year round substitute of plough animals. If encouraging response is forthcoming, HELP might consider importing large number of tillers from Japan and employ a Japanese engineer to train local people in repair and maintenance. Please obtain statistics of cultivable land in each co-operative, number of work animals (specify bullocks or buffaloes) previously in each cooperative, amount of land one pair of bullocks or buffaloes can plough in a day, how many hours can the two kinds of animals work in a day, height of water in the field at the time of ploughing in rainy season, etc. Since purchase of power tillers will involve huge sums of money, it is essential to gather reliable information of all aspects of ploughing and work capacity of animals.

The alternative is to purchase cattle from auctions and ship them to Manpura. Timm notes a year later that draft animals had become very scarce and expensive, and suggests that power tillers should be reconsidered.

In Bertan Gomes' "Final Report on Manpura Project," dated November 10, 1975, he mentions that ten power tillers were given through the cooperatives to all classes of farmers. But he also reports that the power tillers are idle, except one that is used to run a rice mill. They cannot be used for plowing in the rainy season, when the water in the fields is too high for them to operate.

Replace cows or bring in power tillers?
(Rainer Kruse, photographer; photo courtesy of Bread for the World)

CHAPTER 19
Grappling with the Cluster Housing Plan

Nazir, Abdul and Amin walk along one of the well-trodden paths between the fields after hearing Kaiser talk about the plan to build cluster housing.

Nazir asks, "Why is HELP asking us to give up our land? Will we be given fair payment for it?"

Abdul replies, "We'll be safer from cyclones if we live in the center of the island. They've promised us *pukka* housing so strong that the wind and water won't carry it away, but land is needed to build the houses on."

Nazir says firmly, "I won't give away any of my land, and I don't want my family to live next door to strangers."

"But you will be given a good house, and it will be maintained using cooperative funds," Abdul tells him. "That means you won't have to worry about keeping it repaired."

"Well, it might be all right for you, because you're a teacher, so you don't need your land. But I must have my land to grow rice," Nazir says.

"I've heard they will build the houses from a new kind of brick," Abdul says. "They call it Cinvaram, and it's supposed to be very strong."

Amin, brow furrowing, asks, "What about me? I don't own any land. I work on land owned by others. Will I be given a house under the new scheme?"

"We'd better go talk to Kaiser again, and find out more about what HELP has in mind," Nazir says.

Amin thinks, "I know who will get the good housing. It will be someone like the Upazila chairman, not a poor person like me."

The idea of building cluster housing is to introduce better protection for the population than sprinting for the tallest palm tree during the frequent cyclonic storms. Elevated centralized housing is proposed, but there are many hurdles to overcome before relocating the population to artificially raised ground in the center of the island. Persuading people to exchange their precious land to create an elevated space for safer homes becomes a major challenge. Kaiser's report shows how hard the field staff struggles to gain support for the concept and to figure out how to implement it. He feels a bit like the blind leading the blind. It may be a good idea, but how do we do it? Kaiser wisely suggests consultation, flexibility and, above all, sound planning:

```
Cluster housing:
Large number of problems of property exchange.
Landless people, planning, survey, etc. One
group ready to try but don't know how to go
about it. Neither do I. Could you send a CARE
expert to advise on multifarious aspect of mass
movement and relocation? Quick action required
before people lose their enthusiasm which will
be difficult to revive (Zaman, Fieldcord report,
December 31, 1970).
```

To help planners understand the difficulties of implementation, Kaiser, in his next report, takes the point of view of the islanders concerning the cooperative work necessary to undertake cluster housing:

Kaiser in persuasive mode

Tank filling and other self-help work are all very good but when one has no savings, no money and government food supply is inadequate, how can we work in something which is not productive right now.

Right now we prefer a sack of coal to a ton of gold in future. We haven't the manpower or resources left to have huge tanks filled up, ground leveled out and trees cut. Trees! Please let them stand. There are so few anyway. But if some have to go, well —

But where do we get the earth from, even if we were able to fill up a few pits? Filling one means digging another and we better not do that until plans are *pukka*.

We would like to retain as much of our old pattern of life as possible but sure, we agree to accommodate our brothers for a fair exchange and move a little and squeeze a little. But please respect the graves of our dead which are within our *bari* limits. The new scheme must circumvent that.

Of course, we would work for free if we had any means to sustain our families. Okay, give us the sustenance or barely enough for our sustenance and other minimal needs. Don't give the usual rate — the irreducible minimum at least, though.

We are illiterate and therefore can't give you a plan as to how things are and how they can be remodeled. Could you send a surveyor? At least one who has some experience as draftsman?* We will try to make a model of any plan for permanent housing with the bamboos we get so that we can see the problems and you can solve them before permanent housing comes up.

We realize that this opportunity of HELP won't be there forever and we must make the most of it.

But how about timber pillars instead of rcc [reinforced concrete]. Timber, wouldn't it be cheaper and last longer? Of course, it's for your engineers to look into. Just a thought, that's all.

As for making the bamboo houses, we will do it ourselves, but if you want us to do that on cluster pattern, then earth filling, clearing, etc. will need money. We haven't got any. And then not to forget — What's the permanent cluster pattern? We don't know that yet (Zaman, Fieldcord report, January 21, 1971).

To overcome resistance, HELP promises to build costly, sturdier houses, and proposes a mutual exchange of land among members of the cooperatives. It is a difficult process and has limited success. Those few who do express interest in living in houses clustered in a village pattern are eager to take advantage of HELP's willingness to provide materials. They are excited

---

* Deboo Chakma, a volunteer from the Chittagong Hill Tracts, has practical skills as a draftsman.

about having *pukka* CARE Cinvaram houses instead of the flimsier bamboo structures they lost in the storm.

Kaiser writes to the cooperatives' field organizers:

If a number of families form a "para" and have a population of over 500, we will consider construction of Cinvaram houses for each family. Cinvaram house is made of unburnt brick made of earth, cement and sand. CARE experts have promised to help us in this respect.

As soon as a cluster of houses is complete, we will try to build a *pukka* two-storied building in the center which may be used as school, mosque, or bazaar and as a cyclone and flood shelter.

The members should mutually arrange property exchange, and delimit a specific area where a Cinvaram pilot project can start. The members, and especially those living near the riverbank, should be encouraged to move to a central area near the road.

CARE Cinvaram block houses under construction on mainland

Am having extensive discussions with Ward #2. Many problems. Lot of earthwork will be required for filling up lot of useless tanks . . .

I think if #2 is to be used as a model, we must solve their genuine difficulty of their inability to provide much free labor . . .

My overall impression is that a rigid plan will not be workable everywhere. We must have a large range of alternatives and each much room for alteration to meet local needs and peculiarities of each location. The basic idea may be the same.

We have a few groups ready to live in clusters but we need engineers, designers, surveyors to do the actual designing in consultation with each group . . . We will face little difficulty in implementing any plan which is sound and oriented toward the specific needs/situation in Manpura. After all, the people have faith and hope in us.

Earth works to fill tanks
for cluster housing

<u>Plan so far</u>. List of 132 families in Ward 2 already submitted to Field Cord. Others will submit soonest. Dying to get going. "Either Cinvaram in, or Kaiser out." Exchange of *bari*-land nearer the river with paddy-land on site being organized by themselves.

Requirements West Side: 26 *baris* with average 7 families in each. Total area 13,600 square yards approx. for housing, plus more for one cow shed per family, one common yard per *bari*, tanks, nurseries for paddy and vegetable plots, one *kutchery* [kitchen] or public meeting room outside purdah area per *bari*.

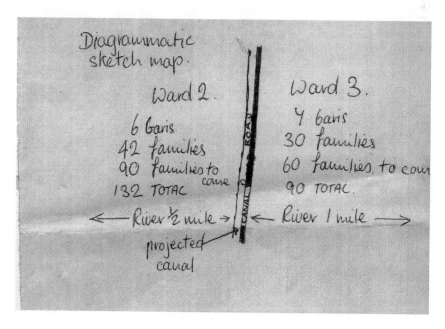

Present condition of site

Wooden rice husker on veranda of traditional house, pounding log and hole for rice on right, operated by foot (left) raising and lowering beam

Fr. Timm explains why most were opposed to the cluster village concept: "They had been living in strict purdah for generations, with few *baris* located close to each other. In a cluster village (which Manpura people perversely insisted on calling 'colony') houses would be side-by-side, as in a city, with little room between them" (Timm 1995, p. 151).

Shifting to multiple families living next to each other would require the population to make major upheavals in their established settlement pattern, because "the village grouping of families common in rural Bangladesh did not exist on Manpura, which instead had a scattered settlement pattern. The distance between houses was several hundred yards, with a majority of inhabitants consisting of nuclear families headed by young men who had migrated to settle on Manpura, away from their extended family" (*Manpura: A Socio-Economic Survey*, 1973, p. 16).

Before being halted because of resistance from the islanders, "HELP originally planned to construct three cluster villages in North, South, and Sakuchia . . . but decided to build only one 'colony', in the North, and cyclone shelters in the other locations. This was a measure of economy as well, since our funds could not cover three villages with *pukka* housing. The number of houses in the one village was also reduced from 200 to 100" (Timm 1995, p. 151).

Bertin Gomes, Administrator, CORR (seconded to HELP), in his November 10, 1975 closing report, describes how the plan evolved:

Though the cluster village scheme was thought to be a good one, the plan itself was defective, as there was no provision for kitchens, latrines, and maintenance work. As a result, there [were a] lot of murmurings among the people who gave away their cultivable lands for the construction of the cluster village.

Soon people came to me with their demands (which had been promised to them). I carefully studied the plan and started working accordingly. People soon found that it was useless to come to me, as I would not work according to their demand.

Then they started taking away our construction materials from our godown and working site. We complained to the police but it was crying in the wilderness, as the police would not stand against the influential landowners.

Very recently when our cement and paints were robbed by tying up our night guards, I filed a case against a number of people among which there was a leader, the copy of which I sent to all district heads up to ministerial level. It worked very well; a group of ten police personnel came at about 4 a.m. in the morning and caught the full gang and took them to the Thana Headquarters. We are at peace now.

Some landowners refused to take the houses and took payment for their land. I think it is better to give the houses to the landless and poor people of Manpura rather than giving to the big landowners who would undoubtedly exploit the poor ones. 38 houses have been allotted to the landowners and the remaining 62 to the landless. The outlook of the cluster village with a cyclone shelter right at the centre is splendid. But because 50% of the earth of the cluster village was washed away due to excessive rain in '74 and in the absence of turfing work, the inside part looks quite damaged.*

---

* People who moved into cluster housing are still complaining, forty-five years after the cyclone, about the lack of provision for maintenance. The expectation is that help will come from outside, rather than responsibility for repairs falling on them (January 2013 conversation with Al Haq Nazir Ahmed Miah, recipient of one of the hundred cluster houses).

CHAPTER 20
HELP on the Brink of War

Tough Going for Timm

Dear Linc, [Lincoln Chen]

It is so hot today that I am sweating in my T-shirt in the south office tent. Just think what it will be in a month. I'm glad I have my polar sunglasses. Can't you get the Russians to donate some of those electric fans which run on human feces? I'm sure we can keep up the supply of fuel.

My fever and dysentery were almost licked this morning, so I walked up to Kauertek to test my legs. Mr. Islam, the Relief Officer, was so happy to see me. He had waited for a long time to meet me and was sorry he hadn't been able to come. We could have had him eating out of our hands, but he has chest pains and has to go tomorrow with Aminur Rahman to Bhola and said he may not return. When I told him that I was the only foreigner here, he said: "Oh, aren't you a Pakistani?" If worse comes to worse, you can always take out Pakistani citizenship papers for me.

I thought my fever was gone and just now I took my temperature with a thermometer which Javed sent up from Kauertek. It reads at one hundred one and one-half. Either the thermometer is wrong or I had one hundred five yesterday.

This morning I went to look at the broken pump. It had run four hours when the spark plug broke in half. I've heard a lot of things going broke by themselves in this country but that one takes the cake. . . . I'm afraid we got a lemon. Guess who got the pump? Ward member nine of course. . . . I hope that Shahid was not pressured into favoritism. The member's secretary is a sly oily character. I'll send the pump to Chittagong for brazing.

In addition to what I ordered Sunday, there are an awful lot of essentials completely depleted, I found out when I came here yesterday. Today I got a note from Victor [Gomes]* who had time to check and found the same for north. And there won't be any boat until the 13th! The cook tells me the rice here is Rs. 45 per maund, but the price turned out to be only Rs. 40.

I'm sending these requisitions both to Dacca and Chittagong by mail in the hope that they will reach in sufficient time to get rice here on the 13th. I need more amoebic medicine in about three days, so I hope I am not draining away by then. If we get petrol tomorrow I'll go out scouting for food and medicine.

I gave a man medicine five minutes ago and now there are ten more waiting.

Carry on at your end.
Dick (Excerpts from Fr. Timm's field notes, February 1, 1971)

Unwelcome Plagues

No animals survived the storm. This absence changes with a sudden plague of rats. Although wiped out in the tidal surge,

---

* "Victor was there four years after I left (Aug. 71). I think he came into the job of director spontaneously when Bro. Donald Schmitz left. Victor now runs a big surveying (of cargos) business, in which he is reputed for his honesty" (Timm, email message to author, May 2, 2012).

along with their natural predators, cats and mongooses, new rats hitch a ride to the island on boats. Fr. Timm notes:

> They multiplied with extraordinary rapidity and grew as big as guinea pigs. Every bari was invaded by rats. We declared a bounty of 10 paisa per rat. Every day boys would bring in head baskets full of dead rats, most of which were killed in their own bari. At HELP office we were not immune to the plague. We were sleeping on the floor in an upper classroom of the primary school but rats worked their way under the gap at the bottom of the door and ran over our bodies at night. We would all get up (Kurshed, Victor, Ahmed and myself), light the lamps, and chase the rats (Timm 1995, p. 161).

After unsuccessfully trying to stop them by putting a board under the door, Timm mixes broken glass with concrete, but the rats dig through the fresh concrete, extracting all the pieces of glass and placing them in a neat pile on the veranda. Only when he puts a large dead rat by the hole do they stay away.

The rat plague dies out in a few weeks, but flies are the next curse. Timm remarks, "Even our rice was black with flies as we ate." Fortunately, they stay about as long as the rats did, and then disappear.

```
FIELDCORD'S REPORT (Fr. Timm)
February 03, 1971
```

As you can make out from the typing . . . you're right . . . I am in north camp pecking away at 5 wpm on the old unfaithful.

Imagine my surprise at seeing Sue King ambling into camp. There is little to add except that volunteer deployment will change when the MBAs come in. Roger [Clark, UK VSO] came back from Char. Will try to send him or Rick [Rohde] to Chowkighat if we get plane to get some sacks (for seed storage). With the four people coming on today's boat we are quite well set as far as volunteers are concerned, for the time being. Will be seeing ADC [Assistant District Commissioner] with offer of labor for road building which we can place at his disposal. When we hand out rehab goods to co-ops we will extract written promise to do value's worth of earthwork in road building. Will face complications from well-to-do.

Plan will be: when a co-op does certain amount of work the government overseer will certify saying this co-op has done so many cubic feet of earth work. Will work out value of total work at pre-agreed rate and exchange goods in return. This way, the ADC will be on the velvet, for his road building grant will go a longer way. We will be on the velvet, for we will get something in return. The villagers will be on the velvet, for they will get more value for the amount of work they put in and get a better road in the bargain. How does that grab you?

Enclosed is the first ever use of my much vaunted materials requisition forms. Hope we can use it more.

Don't worry about government relations at field . . . though not chummy, not bad either. You people must be having a far tougher time than us. Our hearts are with you.

All the best to all the hard working people at HELPCENTRE.

Changing Attitudes

On February 3, Fr. Timm comments about the lack of interest in public works after the immediate needs of relief are met:

The DM [District Magistrate] says they are hard pressed to get people to work on the road and today a local man told him the people got everything so they don't want to work. Apparently they must have had a fairly easy life before. I saw two guys at the bank yesterday with checks for 30,000, so there is some money around.

The following month, on March 17, Kaiser expands on Timm's comment about how attitudes change when a crisis is over.

The Manpurans today are not the same as they were in the first few days after the fateful night. They are more assertive and critical now. The basic characteristics of the people — unwillingness to work on anything which does not carry immediate personal gain, lack of cooperative spirit, rivalry and expecting free gift of goods — are now surfacing.

The nature of our operations has also changed in so far as we distribute through Coops and not on Ward Basis any longer.

The absence of permanent field staff has created great difficulties. By the time a newcomer gets to know the people and has a feel of the place, he pulls out.

. . . Just as the Manpurans are now a different breed of cats so are our volunteers. Some of them have a negative attitude, openly critical of the local people, casting all kinds of aspersions, while they themselves are sensitive to criticism by some locals and are easily hurt when they hear stories of dissatisfaction. They expect the people to ask no questions, make no criticism and always show their gratitude. We can't expect them to behave as we want when we violate our own declared policy of equitable distribution. They also do not see that it's only a handful of people who are critical while the vast majority is appreciative of our efforts, even though they express it only every now and then. Even the critics cannot be totally condemned. We have done precious little for the well-to-do and the middle class as such. We can't expect a man who harvests 5000 *maunds* of paddy a season to come to us on bended knees when we give him a hundred bamboo sticks.

Open criticism of Manpurans must stop forth-with. Under no circumstances should field staff take sides in village politics. Field staff should show greater degree of perseverance and understanding.

Gratitude or expression thereof must not be expected as an obligation on the part of the people.

Don't Build Fancy

During the first week of March, HELP confidently continues with plans for development on Manpura, delegating responsi-bilities and consulting with knowledgeable people. In one such instance, Dan Dunham, an architect and innovative development guru who spent many years in Dacca before moving to Calcutta, meets with HELP and other advisors on March 7 to plan hous-ing.

Dan: Individual houses should be cheap and ex-pendable since it is not economical to build each house strong enough to withstand cyclones and tidal bore. Instead, each *bari* should have a "*kutchery ghar*" (kitchen room) 10 x 7 feet with rcc [reinforced concrete] slab roofing with 2 foot or 2½ foot parapet. No stairs but steel rods stuck into the side of the wall for cling-ing onto the roof in times of tidal surge. Walls may be of anything. The cost would be Rs. 2000 [$425] per unit.

Father Young: CORR [Catholic Organisation for Relief and Rehabilitation] is making 4 inch by 4 inch concrete pillars in Chittagong for use in Char Jabbar. Each house will need 10 pillars. 1500 houses are projected. Like Dan, he says walls can be of anything. Even if the walls are washed away, the frame will remain. The cost would be Rs. 1200 [$250] per unit without the roof. HELP may want to put up a few this year on an experimental basis. If so, the contractor can be contacted through CORR and delivery taken at Char Jabbar.

Dan: Given the communication problems and shortage of highly skilled people, don't go for fancy, complicated and sophisticated construction. Construct the simplest type of buildings.

WR Khan (Engineering Advisor): The per square meter cost of rcc roofing is slightly higher than CI sheet, but more durable.

In deciding between CINVARAM versus burnt bricks, everyone present felt that bricks can be burnt on Manpura. Cost will come to around Rs. 60,000. Jon said that Hafizullah can burn any number.

There was full agreement that community cyclone shelters will not be used in times of need unless people live very close to these. In other words, the best chance that people will come to cyclone shelters is when they live in a cluster village.

Mr. Khan will finalize layout of cluster village, design of individual houses, cyclone shelters and ancillary facilities and cost estimate of each cluster project (Zaman, notes taken at the meeting).

Timm informs Kaiser on March 16:

We got permission from CORR to take the materials for three of their houses from the Chittagong contractor immediately and send them to Manpura for our three camps. Father Labbe says that local *mistris* can put them up, since all the parts are there. . . . None of the local sand is suitable [to make Cinvaram blocks] according to the report we got yesterday. . . . We have to make up our minds definitely in a big hurry, since time is running out. We will build one CINVARAM house at each camp. We can get sand at Sonapur for shipping to Manpura for construction.

Preparation of sites is the big concern of the Field Coordinator. The North camp has a large *bhitti* [foundation] 20' by 20', which will be suitable for one of the houses. Earth will have to be raised for the other, since it doesn't seem that any stilt house will be designed in time for us to build. The location of the new South camp also has to be finalized. The site near the cluster housing seems to be impossible to me, because of transportation difficulties. I think our camp will have to be nearer the western coast. There is one site available just north of the present camp and if we can finalize that I think we had better move fast on it and make ready for the buildings.

Cattle market

Replacement of cattle is Fr. Timm's next focus. On March 13, he writes from Dacca, to Kaiser on Manpura:

We haven't been able to get you more money for cow purchase. There is supposed to be a release of money on Monday, so that I could bring a large bank draft down with me, or if we can get the money transferred to another bank in time, they can wire it to our account on Char Fasson.

On March 16 he writes again to say why he must delay coming back to Manpura:

Kaiser, I got in a car accident Sunday with the CORR car and since I am still stiff from bruises I am staying on until Sunday night. Two of the Fathers travelling with me are in the hospital with broken bones, so I can consider myself lucky. We were pulverized by a truck in a cloud of dust on the Dacca-Aricha road. He came over on our side and hit us, even though we were half way off the road from passing a previous truck which created the dust cloud. I hope you don't mind staying a little.

We are trying hard to get money by tomorrow so that we can send you some for water buffalo purchase on Sandwip. Also, we should send a team to Laksmipur, north of Ramgati, for cattle purchase. That is one of the big markets for the saline areas. Savar Dairy Farm seems to be pretty well shut down. I went there yesterday. I don't think we will be able to get anything from there for a long time. Carl Ryther thinks that the young calves can adapt to the saline areas all right. If possible, we will try to send a few with the tractor shipment to see how they fare.

The first cattle procurement for Manpura was set for March 26. Victor Gomes, camp assistant, who was to remain with HELP on Manpura for four years, Hafizullah Choudhury, the Red Cross Representative, and myself, left at dawn by speedboat for Hatiya, where we caught the Dacca–Chittagong steamer to go to Sandwip Island to buy cattle. While we were on our way word came from Chittagong radio that the Pakistan Army had gone berserk the night before and slaughtered 120,000 Bengalis on the streets of Dacca (Timm 1995, p. 155).

Returning to Manpura with cattle purchased by HELP
(*Rainer Kruse, photographer; photo courtesy of Bread for the World*)

Political Collapse

As Fr. Timm learns on his way to buy livestock, the political situation reached the point of explosion:

As tensions mounted, Mujib suggested he become prime minister of East Pakistan while Bhutto be made prime minister of West Pakistan. Mujib was adamant that the constitution be based on his six-point program. Yahya and Bhutto vehemently opposed Mujib's idea of a confederated Pakistan. It was Bhutto's plea for unity in Pakistan under his leadership that triggered mass civil disobedience in East Pakistan. Mujib called for a general strike until the government was given over to the "people's representatives." Tired of the interminable game of politics he was playing with the Bengali leader, Yahya decided to ignore Mujib's demands and on March 1 postponed indefinitely the convening of the National Assembly, which had been scheduled for March 3. March 1 was a portentous date for another reason: On that day Yahya named General Tikka Khan as East Pakistan's military governor. He bore the unfortunate moniker "Butcher of Baluchistan" for his suppression of Baluch separatists. The number of West Pakistani troops entering East Pakistan had increased sharply in the preceding weeks, climbing from a pre-crisis level of 25,000 to about 60,000, bringing the army close to a state of readiness. As tensions rose, however, Yahya continued desperate negotiations with Mujib, flying to Dacca in mid-March. Talks between Yahya and Mujib were joined by Bhutto but soon collapsed, and on March 23 Bengalis following Mujib's lead in defiantly celebrating "Resistance Day" in East Pakistan instead of the traditional all-Pakistan "Republic Day." Yahya decided to "solve" the problem of East Pakistan by repression. On the evening of March 25 he flew back to Islamabad. The military crackdown in East Pakistan, called Operation Searchlight, began that same night ("Emerging Discontent, 1966-70").

Zulfikar Ali Bhutto, Head of Pakistan People's Party based in West Pakistan. It won fewer votes than Awami League in national elections.

General Tikka Khan became East Pakistan's military governor on March 1, 1970.

CHAPTER 21
Another Lethal Storm Strikes

In Dacca, not long after midnight on March 25, we are jolted awake by heavy thumps rocking the earth, as if a giant in thick boots is clumping through the park next to us. We fling open our bedroom doors leading to the second floor balcony and rush out into a night glittering with stars. Tracer bullets arc across the sky, accompanied by the constant heavy spitting of machine guns. The skyline lights up with bursts of red fires from burning targets. The furious giant is in fact the rhythmic boom of tank guns. We can hear planes take off for bombing sorties, and shrink with shame and anger, knowing our country is the major supplier of arms for the Pakistan Army.*

The attack continues relentlessly throughout the night. The next day we see billows of black smoke rising from extensive fires, and hear the sounds of machine-gun fire and tank blasts. We learn by word of mouth that the army has imposed a curfew on the city, but when it is lifted for a couple of hours after the second day of the attacks, we get on our bicycles to ride from Gulshan to the cholera hospital. Word is that the police lines, the East Pakistan barracks and key installations such as the airport, radio stations and newspaper offices were the targets of the bombs. Telecommunications were cut at midnight.

---

* "For its savage crackdown on the Bengalis, the Pakistan Army used imported guns, automatic weapons, mortars, artillery, trucks, armored personnel carriers, tanks, airplanes, and ammunition. The officers in charge were men trained in the United States and Great Britain. Most of the ordnance and supplies came from the United States, acquired over the years through our lavish grants of military assistance and subsidied arms sales programs" (Sen. Frank Church, address to Congress, May 18, 1971).

We are horrified to hear, by "jungle telegraph," that the settlements of the poor in old Dacca and other parts of the city were set alight, and people gunned down as they fled their burning homes. When we approach the hospital we see blackened rubble where a small *bustee* (cluster of slum housing) had been located near the rail crossing. A terrified family, whom we know because of their work at the cholera hospital, rushes up to us. "We saw army men torch the houses in the *bustee* near us. The people had no choice but to run outside. The army shot them even though they were screaming for mercy. So many people were killed. We're afraid they will come back and kill us too."* We tell the terrified group they are welcome to come to our house for refuge and explain how to find it.

Eventually, our house fills with twenty-six people fleeing the violence. They squeeze into the large room with a garden veranda on the ground floor, and we assure them they are welcome to use the kitchen for cooking. We have helped Totomiah flee to his village with his savings sewn into his seams and cuffs, and I take the opportunity to learn how to cook flavorful curries from the refugees in a effort to make up for time not spent with Totomiah. Not only had I squandered the chance to learn this master cook's mouthwatering Bengali dishes, but also how to pluck a duck, and how to make his flagship coconut cream pie, which he served at the end of every dinner. When the families finish in the kitchen, they are unnaturally quiet in their room, not wanting to alert any informer to their presence.

On our bike ride to Viquar and Runi's house to find out more about the situation, an army vehicle passes us, packed with soldiers holding rifles. They pay no attention to us.

---

* We learn later that the home of Dr. Hendrick Hare, acting director of the cholera lab, has been looted, and that Dr. Doyle Evans of the CRL and his wife were robbed while driving in Gulshan. Three British nationals were backed up against a wall in old Dacca and threatened with death before release.

"The Awami League has been outlawed," Viquar tells us, "and Sheik Mujib has been arrested as a traitor. He's been charged with bringing the country to a state of disintegration."

Runi is tense. "We are very concerned about the sheik's ministers because we know the army is hunting them. We're trying to find safe havens for them. Will you hide our good friend, Rahman Sobhan, until he can escape over the border?"

"Of course we will, Runi," I assure her. "It will be an honor to have him with us."

We hide Rahman in one of our upstairs bedrooms, sending meals up, and give him our shortwave radio receiver so he can be in touch with international broadcasts.* When military appear at our gate wanting to search the house, Jon refuses to allow them entry, insisting they will be violating our diplomatic immunity, which will cause an international incident. We actually have no such immunity, but they believe his bluff and back off. We breathe a sigh of relief that our guests have not been discovered.

Many of our cholera lab colleagues shelter someone needing a hiding place until they can escape the clutches of the army.** Aysen and Pat Talmon give haven to Arshaduz Zaman, head of protocol, and his wife Vasfyie. The Curlins take in our mutual friend Bilayeth Hussain. In the morning, George, dressed in a lunghi, finds Bilayeth making coffee in the kitchen, wearing a well-tailored suit. As George reaches for the tea bags, he asks him which direction he plans to walk to get to the border, but Bilayeth surprises him by saying he plans to escape in his car.

---

* Rahman Sobhan was the Awami League's Economics Minister. He escaped to Calcutta by walking through the rice paddies, although once he thought he wouldn't make it when villagers threatened to kill him because they thought he looked like a West Pakistani. His fluent Bengali saved him.

** Awami League political leaders were not captured by the Pakistanis, and escaped to organize the Bangladeshi government in exile. Using their networks and popular support in Bangladesh, they effectively organized the insurgency and lobbied for international support (Wikipedia).

The next day during the two hours when curfew is relaxed, we hop in our VW Bug to find out how the city has been affected. Streams of terrified people with cloth bundles on their heads clog the roads, trying to escape, fearful that nightfall will bring fresh attacks by the army. Thousands are streaming toward the river crossings, where they hope to distance themselves from the onslaught. Soon our small car is packed with those who are struggling because they are old or infirm. As soon as we drop them at the ferry ghats, we go back to pick up more.

Pakistani soldiers on the move

Documenting Scenes of Slaughter

When we learn that foreign reporters staying at the Interconti-nental Hotel have been rounded up and deported, Jon and I de-cide it is imperative to document the army's crackdown. We plan to hand evidence of the results of military action to Consul Gen-eral Archer Blood, who has sent out word that any information will be welcome. Our vehicle uses very little petrol, so we hope there will still be enough left in the tank after the previous day's foray to ferry refugees to the ghats, as well as for me to drive Totomiah across the city to check on the safety of his daughter and her family. We find her burying her jewelry in a glass bottle in the yard of her compound.

We've heard the university was a target of the military. After four days of heavy curfew following the initial strikes, I say to Jon, "Let's see what we can find out."

"I'll grab the camera," he replies.

As soon as we reach the center of the residential campus, a lone man rushes up to our car. "It's horrible what they did!" is his frightened first greeting.

"What do you mean? Show us," we say.

He leads us to Jagganath Hall, the dormitory for male Hindu students. Tank treads have churned up the ground and massive holes are ripped into the sides of the building. Walking up the steps to the entrance we notice the walls are heavily pock-marked from countless rounds of gunfire. We walk through the eerily quiet dorm, speechless with shock at the bloody hand-prints on the walls, and the floor stained with pools of blood. There are red streaks as if wounded or dead bodies have been dragged across it. Although gore is spattered everywhere, the most awful sight to me is finding the bloody prints of a student's bare feet. Wounded, he must have run to find refuge in the bath-room, where the tracks suddenly come to an end.

"Hurry! Come outside before the soldiers come back. I want to show you where the bodies are," the man says.

We scramble down the front steps of the building to the front yard.

"Look there. See the fresh dirt?" His voice is shaking. "They forced me to drag the dead out here. I counted one hundred and three."

We can see new earth packed down over a large area in front of the dorm.

"They dug a huge hole right there, and dumped in all the students they had shot. They murdered them and tossed them in one on top of the other. You have to tell the world what they did."

"We will. We promise you that we will," we say with determination.

"They killed so many in Iqbal Hall too. And many professors have been shot. Just ask anyone in that building over there where the faculty live," he adds as he hurries away.

Stunned, but determined to try to document as much as we can, we head off to the faculty housing. We find a man darting between two buildings.

"Will you tell us what happened here?" we ask when we catch up to him.

"Soldiers came in the night through the halls where our flats are located," he says. "Any door that wasn't locked they shoved open and entered. We could hear our colleagues pleading with them, and their wives sobbing and begging, but what could we do? We were too terrified to go to help them."

"We want the truth of these atrocities to reach the world," we tell him. "Do you know who is missing or who was shot?"

We write down the names of the professors he tells us have disappeared.

"Hurry away now," he warns, "before an army patrol finds us."

We decide to walk over to Iqbal Hall before we leave. We are horrified to encounter the same scenario we had seen in Jagganath, but in Iqbal, many bodies have been left to rot where

310

they fell, as if they have been washed up in another cyclone, only this time the disaster is manmade. Sobered, we drive back to Gulshan on nearly deserted streets before the curfew descends. Our camera is full of disturbing photos and our minds filled with outrage.

Driven by anger at the wanton brutality of the crackdown, we feel compelled to continue photographing whatever we can before we are grounded for lack of petrol. We head for Shankhari Bazaar where we often marveled at how Hindu craftsmen cut traditional conch-shell bangles, bracing the shell with nimble feet as they sawed thin slices to be polished into delicate jewelry. Shops here are also famous for shining pink pearls, the pride of Bengal. I treasure my bracelet of pearls carefully chosen by Jon. We became acquainted with some of the people who live in the market's alleys when we attended celebrations of Hindu holidays such as Durga Puja. The narrow lanes, normally teeming with crowds of shoppers, are deserted.

"Doctor! Doctor!" a voice shouts as we walk along one of the main *galis* (alleys). A young man we recognize comes running up to us. "My father has been shot! You must help us. Come with me. He's in here."

We follow him through a narrow doorway down a dark hall to a small interior courtyard where one shaft of light falls on a man lying on his back groaning. We can see immediately that he's been recently shot in the gut because fresh blood is spreading across his kurta.

"He was sitting in his shop, and a soldier shot him when he didn't give him a pack of cigarettes fast enough," one of the sons explains. "Please, Doc, do something to help us, or he will die."

"When did this happen?" Jon asks.

"Just now," the young man says.

The soldiers must still be in the vicinity because we can hear the sound of gunfire. For the first time, we feel vulnerable. We also feel sick, knowing there is nothing we can do for this poor man; that, sadly, he is very close to death. This incident will not be the last time we feel helpless, but somehow the first time remains the most vivid. That scene has stayed with us ever since, as has our next encounter with the brutality of the Pakistan Army.

Ramna Kalibari in 1969, scene of massacre in 1971

Fleeing back to our VW when the firing intensifies in Shankhari Bazaar, we swing back along Racecourse Road and notice smoke rising from Ramna Kalibari, the thousand-year-old Hindu temple to Kali with its small surrounding village, situated in the middle of the Ramna Racecourse.* Swerving onto the grass surrounding the temple area, we drive across it to the village. We

* Ramna Kalibari was one of the most famous and ancient temples on the subcontinent. Established over a thousand years ago by devotees who came from the Himalayas, it occupied 2.25 acres on the south side of the park, where its large tower or *shikhara* was a prominent landmark. Sheik Mujipur Rahman chose this site for his address on March 7, 1971. On March 27, the Pakistan Army bulldozed it.

encounter a most grisly sight. There is not a single living soul. Bodies are draped over the low compound walls, where they have been mowed down while trying to escape. Their arms hang down grotesquely, and torsos are twisted in their final agony. Corpses of men, women and children litter the compound. Even cattle and dogs have been slaughtered. Black smoke billows into the sky from the village and its temple set ablaze. We realize this must have just happened. We hastily snap photos of the tragic scene around us. Ominously, we notice three Pakistan Army military jeeps filled with soldiers racing across the field, heading straight for us. Never are we so grateful to our VW for rising to the occasion as we floor the gas pedal and flee in the opposite direction across the open field, blending into congestion when we reach the streets.

Our photographs are a horrifying firsthand account of attacks on civilian and student targets, particularly Hindus. When we learn that Steve Baldwin has gained a seat out on one of the PIA planes ferrying troops from West Pakistan into Dacca, we talk to him about smuggling our film to the press so news about the atrocities will be broadcast internationally. In a search at the airport, the incriminatory film is confiscated. In Steve's words:

> From what we'd been able to observe so far in taking friends and family to the airport, the military there occasionally searched passengers' luggage but only rarely their hand-carried bags and briefcases. So I loaded up file compartments of my large black Samsonite briefcase with miscellaneous office files, and I sprinkled among them Jon's precious roll[s] of film, my January–March diary pages, and our preliminary list of Bengali notables that had been confirmed as dead ... As it happened the search couldn't have gone much worse. Leaving my actual body untouched, they went through all the luggage first, even unscrewing shoe trees, and then a young Pakistani Army intelligence officer began a measured reading of my files, page by page. I started blustering something along the lines of, "These are official Ford

Foundation files and you have no business looking at them!" but he quietly ignored this, only replying in a cold, sinister tone, "And is this Ford Foundation business?" holding up my diary entries for the preceding days before me and then, shortly thereafter, an actual hand printed Bangladesh flag I'd been reckless enough to include in the files. He confiscated everything he thought might be incriminating, *including the now exposed rolls of film* (Baldwin 2009, p. 232).

In a stroke of mistiming, Jon's parents had decided to visit us in late February, anxious to reconnect with Jon's estranged younger brother who had been with us since December, and to experience firsthand the place they had only imagined from our letters. The week before the crackdown, we manage to secure seats for their exit on a chartered Japan Airlines flight that will fly evacuees to Bangkok. After an unassisted landing at Tejgaon Airport, the plane sits on the tarmac with its engines running while the evacuees board. Tense moments continue when the plane's brakes freeze and it seems they will not be able to lift off until water is frantically poured on the wheels to loosen them sufficiently for takeoff. We are relieved not to have the responsibility for his parents' security weighing on us anymore.

Evacuation

There is rising concern in all the foreign consulates for the safety of their citizens. Twelve days after the army crackdown in Dacca, we are ordered to prepare for departure. "Washington insist[s] that the airlift of dependents from Dacca be officially characterized as a 'thin-out' rather than an 'evacuation' so as not to offend Yahya" (Christopher Van Hollen in A. M. A. Muhith 1996, p. 236). At first we think we might be able to negotiate remaining behind, but are told that evacuation is mandatory for all dependents of official U.S. personnel, along with official personnel who are deemed nonessential for the continued operation of the diplomatic post. Pat Talmon will continue to administer the lab, with Henry Mosley in charge. We struggle with the certainty that we are being forced to abandon our Bengali friends and the work we are doing in the cyclone area. When we refuse to go, the specter of court martial for not obeying orders is raised.

Nearly all foreigners are flown out of the country, including many HELP volunteers. Many go before tensions reach the breaking point of military crackdown. Americans are one of the last groups to depart. Germans are airlifted from March 9 through 11 on German Air Force 707s. On March 9, sixty Britons leave on a voluntary basis. Their plane circles Dacca Airport for forty minutes while the airport tower refuses to speak in English to help the pilot land. Full-scale evacuations begin on March 30 of World Bank and UN employees, Germans, Japanese and Yugoslavs. British, French, Australians and Soviets decide to evacuate all their dependents. When I ask Fr. Timm if he will be going, he tells me, "Oh no, this is the time when the people need me the most." HELP certainly needs him too, since nearly all the other major players are being forced to flee.

Jon packs up his small lab on the third floor of CRL. (We learn that the army searches it after we leave.) We hastily secure most of our personal belongings in tin trunks in the middle bedroom of our house in Gulshan. When the order is given that no pets will be allowed on the evacuation flight, streams of distraught dog and cat owners bring their animals for Jon to put down with sodium pentothal. We are told we can take one small carry-on. Over a period of several days, Jon's brother and I teach Shiva, our clever Burmese cat, to lie down in a cane hamper, hoping he will pass security inspection. We create a false bottom to conceal him by putting a piece of Styrofoam on top of him, followed by my large silver Burmese bowl and a few other valuables. To keep peace in the family, Jon drops his threat to put him down, drugging him just before the flight.

After the United States refuses Blood's request to evacuate by USAF aircraft to Bangkok, evacuation takes place on April 4–6 on PIA planes that disgorge troops being transferred from West

Pakistan in an operation called the "Great Fly-In." Tejgaon Airport is on war footing, with hundreds of soldiers arriving in battle dress. A U.S. consular officer facilitates our rapid movement through a gauntlet of military personnel attempting to check our bags. It takes ten hours to fly to Karachi via Sri Lanka instead of a three-hour direct flight across India, but the government has announced the closure of their airspace to all Pakistani planes. During the refueling stop in Colombo, we press to the exit door, anxious to deplane to spread the news of what we have witnessed. The army retains our passports and armed soldiers block the exit, forcing us to remain fuming on board.

When our cat regains consciousness on the next leg, Jon takes him into the toilet to reinject him. By that time, many other small pets have also woken up. Jon drapes the cat like a fur collar around his neck when we disembark in Karachi, where U.S. officials meet us on the tarmac. They begin to disparage us immediately, saying, "Calm down. You're exaggerating what is happening in the East Wing. You're totally misinformed." We are incredulous that they would discredit what we have witnessed. They make sure we are isolated from newsmen. Archer Blood explains what the U.S. embassy and the government of Pakistan were thinking at the time:

> The prospect of a tired and angry group of Americans being accessed by the press just after they had been witness to a 1970s type of ethnic cleansing was very worrisome to the Embassy and the Government of Pakistan. . . . Ambassador Farland sent messages to the Con Gen to tell everyone 'to exercise that discretion which is expected of USG [United States Government] employees. We will expect, as I know you do, that official personnel and their adult dependents in talking with press in safe haven will keep constantly in mind their positions as USG representatives in Pakistan with the constraint and obligations this position demands (Blood 2002, pp. 234–35).

Jon writes: "Candy convinced me to make a stand on the Karachi tarmac as we arrived, insisting that the American position describing the slaughter as 'an internal problem of Pakistan' was incorrect and unethical. We were whisked away from reporters, and told that we were emotionally involved and not reliable" (Jon Rohde, "Women in the Bangladesh Struggle," in A. M. A. Muhith 1996).

A consular wife tries to reassure me: "You'll be fine after a good steak dinner and a tranquilizer. Just remember, the West Wing will *never* let the East Wing go."

Furious, I tell her, "If they don't want to split, they sure have gone about it in the wrong way. It's too late now. You'll see what happens."

No one can make us ignore a massacre. Since his own government appears not to be interested in what we have witnessed, Jon heads straight for the Indian Consulate. He agrees to tell them our eyewitness account of the crackdown in return for giving his brother a visa to India. He will be better off there, where he can study the bamboo *bashi* (flute), than in Iran, which we learn is to be our final evacuation post. Over a two-hour briefing, Jon details the atrocities we have seen the Pakistan Army commit. Jon's brother is given the visa. The next day we are flown to Tehran on Pan Am. At takeoff, loud cheers erupt on the plane, with Bangladeshi flags of liberation rising out of every pocket in defiant waves of green and red.

Immediately upon arrival in Iran, we draft letters to our senators: Jon's from Rhode Island and mine from Ohio. Senator William Saxbe of Ohio reads it into the Congressional Record. His direct line rings. It's his son Bart. "Dad, I read that piece you put into the Record by Jon Rohde. You remember him, don't you? We were together in the same graduating classes at Amherst and Harvard. You can certainly respect whatever he says." I return immediately to the Northrups in Washington to organize lobbying Congress to support the liberation of Bangladesh. Saxbe's support launches our effort like a rocket.

Hon. William B. Saxbe
(*photograph by Henry Burroughs, courtesy of AP*)

RECENT EVENTS IN EAST PAKISTAN

Extract from Record of the U.S. Senate containing letter dated April 17, 1971 from Dr. Jon E. Rohde, a physician evacuated from East Pakistan, to Senator William B. Saxbe.

Mr. SAXBE. Mr. President, I recently received a letter from a physician who worked in East Pakistan under USAID. He gives a good account of the recent events in East Pakistan. As you know, I objected last year to the sale of $15,000,000 worth of military equipment to Pakistan because I feared the tragic consequences of this action. I have just co-sponsored Senate Concurrent Resolution 21 which urges the suspension of our military assistance to Pakistan until the conflict is resolved.

I ask unanimous consent to have printed in the RECORD the letter from Dr. John [sic] E. Rohde because I feel that Senators should have the benefit of his insight.

There being no objection, the letter was ordered to be printed in the RECORD as follows:

HUDSON, OHIO April 17, 1971

HON. WILLIAM B. SAXBE

NEW SENATE OFFICE BUILDING,
WASHINGTON, D.C.

[I have omitted the first part of Jon's letter because it details
the atrocities described in the preceding chapter. He continues by urging Congress to condemn Pakistan's military action:]

The reports of Consul Blood, available to you as a Con-
gressman, contain a more detailed and complete account of
the situation.* In addition, he has submitted concrete proposals for constructive moves our government can make.
While in no way suggesting that we interfere with Pakistan's internal affairs, he asserts, and we support him, that
the United States must not continue to condone the military
action with official silence. We also urge you to read the
Dacca official community's open cable to the State Department. It is for unlimited distribution and states the facts
about the situation in East Pakistan.

By not making a statement, the State Department appears to support the clearly immoral action of the West
Pakistani army, navy, and air force against the Bengali people.

We were evacuated by Pakistan's Commercial airline.
We were loaded on planes that had just disembarked full
loads of Pakistani troops and military supplies. American
AID dollars are providing support of military action. In
Teheran, due to [diplomatic] support of Pakistan, I was un-
able to wire you the information I am writing.

Fully recognizing the inability of our government to
oppose actively or intervene in this desperate oppression of

---

* Consul General Blood, after being removed from his post in Dacca by
the Nixon White House, later received the American Foreign Service Association's Herter Award, which is given for "intellectual courage and
creative dissent."

319

the Bengalis, I urge you to seek and support a condemnation by Congress and the President of the United States of the inhuman treatment being accorded the seventy-five million people of East Pakistan.

No political consideration can outweigh the importance of a humanitarian stand, reiterating the American belief in the value of individual lives and a democratic process of government. The action of President Yahya banning the democratically elected majority party, who had ninety-eight percent of the East Wing's electorate backing them, ought to arouse a country which prides itself on the democratic process.

We urge you to speak out actively against the tragic massacre of civilians in East Pakistan.

Sincerely yours,
JON E. ROHDE

After reading Jon's letter to Saxbe, Senator William Fulbright, chairman of the Senate Foreign Relations Committee, requests Jon to testify in a hearing he holds on June 10, 1971 concerning the war in East Pakistan. Jon has just been released from the Public Health Service and returns to the United States from "safe haven" in Teheran to address the committee.

Excerpt from testimony of Jon E. Rohde at U.S. Senate Foreign Relations Committee Hearing:

I am shocked to learn that Members of Congress have been denied factual information of the occurrences in East Pakistan over the past two and a half months from our own officials still in Dacca. This information is, of course, essential to any considered judgment with regard to the formulation of foreign policy in this crisis. I know that an extensive body of factual information continues to be sent daily from East Pakistan to the State Department. When I was still there I, along with many other Americans contributed to that data. Many of the sources who have continued to send information directly to me over the past two months have provided the same factual reporting to the American officials in Dacca and have been assured of its relay through proper channels to the State Department. During his testimony before the Senate Foreign Relations Committee on April 30, Deputy Assistant Secretary of State, Christopher Van Hollen admitted the existence of factual reports from Dacca, but refused to make them available to the members of that Committee, as Senate Report No. 92-105 clearly points out. It seems ironic, indeed, that while I have worked for the United States Government for 3 years as a cholera expert, I should be here giving you information that the State Department has, while a cholera epidemic rages amongst the refugees in India with no American physicians to help.

Perhaps it would be useful at this point to relay to you a sampling of the information currently available from East Pakistan. The Army says it is in control of the country. However, on May 17, the Rocket, the largest river steamer in the country was hijacked and scuttled; on May 31 the key ferry on the only road between Dacca and Chittagong was destroyed; on May 17 bombs exploded in the major banks and the main government office building of Dacca; and every night trucks are seen rolling into Dacca loaded with bodies of West Pakistani troops. Although the automatic weapons of the 60,000 men Army have made possible a superficial kind of control over the province, it appears that only the urban population is dominated (Foreign Asst. Leg., 232–39).

His testimony causes a furious Fulbright to announce: "I have learned more from one unknown doctor than I can get out of my own State Department." We learn President Nixon has used "executive privilege" to prevent Congress access to the initial "cable of dissent" from the U.S. Consulate in Dacca, as well

321

as to their continued reports concerning the situation in East Pakistan.* We begin a thorough canvassing of members of the Senate and the House to secure their support for Bangladesh. I start an index card file, noting the best way to gain their interest in our objectives, and the progress we make with every contact. Our goal: persuade Congress to cut off all military and economic aid to West Pakistan. Our credibility is fuelled by eyewitness information from Henry Mosley, Pat Talmon, Fr. Timm and other credible sources about continuing army activities in East Pakistan. They send detailed letters and photographs by diplomatic pouch to Henry's wife Bunny and to Jon in Iran. Some find it a bit strange that letters concerning army atrocities are being forwarded to women nicknamed Candy and Bunny. We succeed in persuading Democratic Senator Frank Church to cosponsor with Republican Senator Saxbe an amendment to cut off all aid to Pakistan. Our success is largely because of the keen interest and support of an avid ally of Bengalis, Tom Dine, an administrative assistant to Church.

One day in his office, Tom surprises me by saying, "Candy, if you want legislation, you will have to write it. Why are you looking at me like that? I don't have time to put it together myself. You can have this desk right here. Feel free to use it whenever you want."

We hadn't counted on having to write an amendment to the Foreign Assistance Act, but we have grown accustomed to getting up to speed on unfamiliar ground. Convinced the best way

---

* "Our government has failed to denounce the suppression of democracy. Our government has failed to denounce atrocities ... We have not chosen to intervene, even morally, on the grounds that the Awami conflict, in which unfortunately, the overworked term genocide is applicable, is purely an internal matter of a sovereign state ... We, as professional public servants, express our dissent with current policy and fervently hope that our true and lasting interest here can be defined and our policies be redirected." From American diplomats serving in Dacca, led by Consul General Archer Blood, April, 1971, Cable of Dissent, quoted verbatim in "Dissent from US Policy toward East Pakistan" in A. M. A. Muhith, ed., *American Response to the Bangladesh Liberation War*, p. 201.

to make an impact on the war is to cut off all U.S. assistance to Pakistan, we figure we'd better sit down and begin drafting the legislation needed to make it happen.

Our Congressional lobby effort now focuses on building enough votes to pass the Saxbe-Church Amendment, an effort accomplished with many other hardworking former colleagues and friends, that by October 1971, leads to a Congressional vote to suspend worldwide U.S. foreign assistance.

It is the first time the Act had ever been defeated. By then we are in Calcutta working in the refugee camps for Oxfam Canada and the International Rescue Committee. Jon hires Bengali refugee doctors to run small camp dispensaries, and I hire refugee teachers to instruct children in tent schools.*

Endangering Friends

Jon's testimony for Fulbright is broadcast into East Pakistan on Voice of America, making Abed, Viquar and Runi even more re-

---

* The law is still on the books in 1972:

28 PUBLIC LAW 92-226-FEB. 7, 1972

"(w) (1) All military, economic, or other assistance, all sales of Pakistan, defense articles and services (whether for cash or by credit, guaranty, suspension or any other means), all sales of agricultural commodities (whether for cash, credit, or by other means), and all licenses with respect to the transportation of arms, ammunitions, and implements of war (including technical data relating thereto) to the Government of Pakistan under this or any other law shall be suspended on the date of enactment of this subsection.

(2) The provisions of this subsection shall cease to apply when the Report to President reports to the Congress that the Government of Pakistan is cooperating fully in allowing the situation in East Pakistan to return to reasonable stability and that refugees from East Pakistan in India have been allowed, to the extent feasible, to return to their homes and to reclaim their lands and properties.

(3) Nothing in this section shall apply to the provision of food and other humanitarian assistance which is coordinated, distributed, or monitored under international auspices."

solved to flee to London because of the heightened danger of the army command recognizing their association with us.

In the first week of September, 1971, we receive a report from Viquar in London stating:

> HELP BANGLADESH ... has come into existence prompted by humanitarian motives to organize and mount relief operations in the famine-stricken areas of Bangladesh. ... We believe that the best way to avert disaster is to infiltrate food grains and other relief materials into Bangladesh from the Indian borders. ... When clearance is received HELP will begin operations in Tetulia, a liberated area in the Northwest of Bangladesh.

Jon writes to Viquar and Runi on September 8, 1971: "Your plans with regard to HELP Bangladesh are ambitious and necessary, and we feel quite confident you can do the job. To this end I have gone to OXFAM Canada and really pushed to get their support for your efforts." He continues with words of caution: "The name HELP Bangladesh is a double liability and will significantly harm your ability to raise money. Bangladesh is a political concept, like it or not, and in that regard many will not get behind that concept who would otherwise underwrite the movement of large amounts of food to starving people. Secondly, and perhaps more important, HELP is a name that is not really fair to use in view of the obvious danger that this creates for the excellent work still going on Manpura. It would be a grave mistake to adversely affect a working operation in the most needy area for the sake of a name. The Pakistan Government need only look at the composition of the organizers to suggest connection. The HELP name would clinch it."

Fr. Timm recalls:

> Jon Rohde promised to keep from involving the name of HELP so that our organization would maintain the guise of neutrality. A short time later in London, two of the founders

324

of HELP, FH Abed and Viquar Choudhury, founded a new organization to lobby for Bangladesh in England, which they named "HELP Bangladesh." We were all afraid that government would crack down on HELP in Dacca as the operative arm of "HELP Bangladesh" in London (Timm 1995, pp. 164–65).

Viquar sets up a headquarters for HELP Bangladesh in Calcutta in September, to provide humanitarian assistance in his home area of Sylhet, entering East Pakistan through the border from Meghalaya (now Shillong). By the time he completes a survey for his pilot project in Tetulia, he has changed the name of his operation to Famine Relief Committee. Fr. Timm is still worried about a possible threat to HELP: "At a Governing Body of HELP on September 20 (at which I was elected as Chairman), we agreed that at the next Annual General Meeting we would drop the names of Abed, Viquar and Mahbul Alam Chashi, the foreign secretary of the government-in-exile in Calcutta" (Timm 1995, pp. 164–65).

One month later we update Fr. Timm about Viquar's work: "Viquar has been working tirelessly here [in Calcutta] to get an operation off the ground and he has done a magnificent job of threading his way through the morass of conflicting interests and political power plays" (Jon Rohde, letter to Fr. Richard Timm, November 3, 1970).

For the three months we spend working in the refugee camps, we often meet him, until Jon and I leave in December when Bangladesh is liberated and the ten million refugees start to return home. Viquar crosses the border to Sylhet and en route hears that an area called Sullah has been devastated. Huge numbers were killed during the Pakistan army occupation and homes burnt down because the area was populated by a large minority Hindu community. Returning to Dacca, he begins to raise funds for the resettlement of refugees in Sullah. In early 1972, Abed comes from London to assist Viquar in the work he has established. They decide to enlarge its mandate to include broader development challenges, officially calling their organisation Bangladesh Rehabilitation Assistance Committee, which will eventually evolve into BRAC under Abed's dedicated leadership (Viquar Choudhury, email message to author, 23 October, 2014).

Salt Lake Camp, Calcutta 1971

I stand in mud, knees weak,
stomach heaving in wet heat.
Rows of tarpaulin shelters
stretch relentlessly around me.
Narrow paths seethe
with threadbare refugees;
ten million and rising.
I know more are moving along
the bunds of Bengal's *aman* fields,
meager bundles on their heads.
A child comes close to me.
Impish eyes dart above
the growing swell of life
inside my womb,
scan my face playfully.
Her small slim hand slips into mine.

Cornelia Rohde

CHAPTER 22
More Rough Water

War may not reach Manpura, but the disruption to life through-out the rest of East Pakistan puts many of HELP's activities on hold:

· Self-help motivator T. Ali has to return mid-March to his hometown to protect his family. (He returns to Manpura after liberation, where he remains, actively organizing co-ops for the next four years.)

· Women's motivators (Ali's wife and her sister) cannot begin their work of instruction in cutting and sewing, knitting, child-care and women's education.

· Services of three co-op workers provided for in the plan cannot be secured because of abnormal conditions. Fortunately, fif-teen local co-op leaders were trained by Carl Ryther at Feni Co-operative Institute in February 1971 before the war, and returned to begin work on Manpura.

· Cooperatives cannot get needed support and supervision be-cause of the absence of organizers. Therefore, purchase and stor-age of seed cannot proceed.

· Flights from Bangkok are cancelled, with the result that seven thousand ducklings are not shipped.

· The consignment of an improved variety of chicken, ordered from United States by Carl Ryther, cannot be sent. Ryther is evacuated in April.

· One tractor, purchased in February for testing and to familiarize the tractor drivers with it, is at the Faridpur Farm of the Christian Agriculture Center, where it remains when Carl Ryther is evacuated. (He did not return to Feni until September 1972.) The order for two more tractors is cancelled.

· Only half of the order for 500 of an improved type of plow is fulfilled by a firm in Dacca. However, 1,000 standard plows are authorized to be made locally to meet the needs of the cultivators.

· The availability of draft animals (bullocks and cows) close to Manpura is uncertain, so HELP is advised to buy these animals through Savar Farm. The German consultant who is to help with the purchase is evacuated in early March. Scouting the markets in Hatiya, Bhola and Noakhali District reveals it is actually possible to obtain cattle close to Manpura. However, banks in the outlying areas are shut down, so funds to purchase them cannot be released.

· Of three boats carrying 30,000 pieces of bamboo (out of an order of 217,000), two are never heard from, and one *mahjee* (helmsman) reports to Sudharam Police Station in Noakhali District that his boat has been robbed of its cargo on the way to Manpura. It is not possible to reorder because the bamboo market in Feni Subdivision is too remote to travel to in unsettled conditions in order to make enquiries.

· The launch carrying 3,700 of the 30,000 corner posts ordered for house building encounters bad weather and has to return to

Barisal, where the posts are put into a storehouse. When conditions further deteriorate, all action is suspended.

· The original plan is to supply corrugated iron sheets for roofing, but it is not possible to obtain the necessary quantity. From March onward it is not possible to arrange import of this item. People are left to use less-desirable, but locally available, roofing materials of thatch and palm leaves.

· Consultants are no longer on hand to advise on how to build various types of low-cost housing devised by CARE, UNDP and Lions International.

· Installation of two rice mills, as a beginning to the introduction of small industries, cannot be initiated.

· No systematic and sustained program of student collaboration for studying specific social welfare projects or participating in field programs as part of their social work curriculum requirement can be undertaken.

· In Chittagong, the office secretary leaves on April 2 and no replacement can be found due to the war. On April 5, the executive assistant, Lynn Bickley, is evacuated, along with most of the expatriate volunteer helpers. An accountant appointed on April 1 does not join, and a new one only begins six weeks later, on May 15. Kaiser Zaman leaves his position on May 20.* Contact with the Chittagong office is severed by conflict in March, and the office closes on June 30.

---

* Kaiser Zaman quits Pak Shell on March 1, and is in Bhola getting supplies for Manpura when the army cracks down in Dacca. He makes it back to his family with difficulty. When the military search their Dacca home shortly after the crackdown, he is made to kneel in the street and told not to move by a nervous young soldier with his finger on the trigger of his machine gun. Kaiser leaves the country in August (Zaman 2013).

· It is very difficult to maintain contact with the field due to the disturbances. HELP is able to continue because many loyal field personnel remain in their posts, and Fr. Timm continues to be in charge of field operations. Because only two suitable managers can be found to run the three camps, he has to carry the workload of one camp manager as well as the overall supervision of HELP's work on Manpura.

Adopting a forward-looking posture in spite of the war, HELP's proposal for the second phase of the Manpura Plan, from July 1, 1971 to June 30, 1972, offers detailed plans for multi-sectored development of Manpura. On the basis of HELP's optimism about the future, Bread for the World reiterates its decision to continue its financial support. Their ongoing backing is a victory over cynicism.

The closest the conflict ever gets to Manpura is the sight of an approaching warship. Timm writes: "The military tried to come again last week by gunboat, accompanying the relief rice boat from Barisal, but they turned back because of the rough waters." The captain changes course, leaving them fearful but unharmed. The sea, which has proved so cruel, protects the islanders this time.

Throughout the war, Fr. Timm remains committed to shielding the people of Manpura. In August 1971 he writes: "My anxiety for the people of Manpura restrains me from committing myself to another project that I couldn't pull out of if something happened on Manpura." He is particularly worried about attacks on Hindus, and continues: "Suresh Master told me he knows for sure that his name has been turned in to Bhola. I left a letter with him which I hope will help him if he is taken, and I asked the FC to phone me from Hatiya right away if anyone is taken so that I can scoot down to Bhola and confront the military. Some of our

Fathers have managed to get people off, since the higher officials are generally humane."*

Letters from the Steadfast Priest: June 1971–June 1974

Fr. Timm is becoming concerned about problems with the governing body and administration of HELP.

25 June 1971
I'm back from Manpura to get some more money for cattle and to get HELP back on a firm footing. Kabir has turned out to be a hopeless procrastinator without someone to push him, so I am reorganizing the Governing Body to draw up a program which we can stick to and force him to act. Pat [Talmon, CRL chief administrator] and I were elected to the G.B. [Governing Body] at the last meeting but we had only 9 members and were to get one signature later. Kabir's lawyer friend tells him the election was illegal and so he is trying to get up a new membership of his own selection with the approval of the two lifeless members of the G.B. who are left in Dacca.

03 Sept 1971
Bro. Donald Schmitz [a teacher] is going down to Manpura for a year as F.C. to take my place. Nabi [CRL administrator] is doing a great job of running the GB and putting the heat on Kabir.

Mr. Kabir has a job as E Pak representative for National Shipping Corp. He will be leaving as soon as he gets on their payroll.** Nabi got his 2 candidates into the Governing Body and we

---

* In January 2013, Dr. Malabika Sarkar, a BRAC professional, recollected that in 1971, when she was a young child, her family fled to Manpura from Noakhali and lived in one of the Sears-donated tents for the duration of the war, finding protection on Manpura along with other Hindu families.

** Akbar Kabir left in October, 1971, after eight months as HELP's first administrator.

put out Alam, Abed and V. Choudhury. I hear Lynn
thinks we forced Kaiser out. Pat can put you
straight on that. I hope that Feroze can carry
the ball; at least, he will listen to advice.
Two nights ago he had the HELP Toyota stolen by
the Mukti [Bahini] for a short time. In the
meantime, he reported it and this led to many
complications. Then yesterday the keys disappeared, so he left the car with me until he
could have the ignition changed. We'll have
enough stories for 10 books.

Why Should the "Little People" Always Come Last?

I tried a liberal experiment which will probably sour me on
Liberalism for life. Naturally, everyone joined the cooperatives—except the most influential person of the island, who
was a member of the Barisal District Board—since that was
the only way they could get government or NGO benefits.
We carried out huge organizational meetings at which regional groupings of men were worked out (there were no
women's cooperatives). In all, 75 cooperatives were formed.
Each cooperative was to hold an open meeting for election of
officers and for cattle distribution lottery. All had agreed
that the fairest way to distribute new cattle, since everyone
could not receive at once, was by lottery, in which all had an
equal chance. This was regarded as a religious solution,
since all are regarded as equal in Islam. After the open lottery each co-op was to submit to me a list of members in the
order in which their names had appeared in the lottery
(Timm 1995, pp. 151–55).

The Manager was to read out the data sheets
so that everyone could hear and agree or com-
plain. All members of the co-op would then sign
as witness. The results were astonishing and
were my first introduction to what I later
termed "the power structure of the village."

One co-op had all the Hindu names last on its list. Another had four of one of the biggest families on the island in the top four positions. I called all four in and asked them whether there had been a meeting and an open lottery.

"Oh, yes," they replied, "ask any of the members." Various members when asked privately, agreed. I then asked: "And all these rankings are due to mere chance and not to your own arrangement?" "Oh, yes," they replied, "this is the way it happened."

One [member] of the family used to come to our camp to play chess once in a while, so I turned my attention to him. "You are a chess player," I said. "You should know something about the laws of chance. Let's sit down and figure out the odds of your four names coming out 1, 2, 3 and 4."

I sat down and calculated, and the odds against their taking the first four places were one in 460,800 tries. Yet they insisted, so I told them I would give them one chance. I would put all the members' serial numbers in a tin and would have 1000 drawings. If their numbers came out in order only once in 1000 tries they would be excused. Otherwise, they would be put on the banned list and would receive no further help.

I began drawing and in one trial, quite unexpectedly, two of the brothers' numbers came out successively. After 30 or 40 drawings the youngest brother, still a high school student, broke down. He admitted, "We made a mistake." I replied, "You did not make a mistake. You committed a fault." I put four of the Choudhury family brothers (Noman, Kanu, Shamsuddin and Mosnu) on the banned list and the word spread fast. Large landowners came from all parts of the island to beg me to remove the names from the list, but I was adamant. My sense of justice had been overly antagonized. Why should the "little people" always come last?

I hoped that all would learn the lesson that honesty pays and that no corruption would be tolerated. I succeeded so well that at the end of my six-month stay on Manpura the eldest brother paid me the greatest compliment on my work that anyone ever gave me. "Father Timm," he said, "you cannot imagine what it would have been like if you had not been here. I think that you have detected at least 50 per cent of the cheating" (Timm, field letter to Candy and Jon Rohde, August 10, 1972).

After banning the cheaters, the lottery took place and Fr. Timm wrote on August 10, 1971: "We got 16 lakhs into the cattle program just in time to make a real impact on the agriculture of Manpura. We gave out about 4000 cattle."

Cattle purchased by HELP
(*Rainer Kruse, photographer; photo courtesy of Bread for the World*)

However, Fr. Timm then faced other difficulties:

Kamal Choudhury made a contract with us to make 700 improved-style Manpura plows which would last 4-5 years, since the owner of the plow factory in Dacca was arrested by the military. The plows he turned out were outrageous, breaking right and left after less than a week of use, and yet he kept insisting that he be paid the full sum agreed on. I simply refused to do it but we haven't become enemies yet.

Hafizullah expected to get a loan from us of Rs. 5000 but according to our policy he was only due for Rs. 1500, so he didn't take anything because that was too small peanuts. He's still our friend, though and very helpful. I haven't caught him in a lie yet. Besides him, Suresh Master is the only one I would trust (Timm, field letter to Candy and Jon Rohde, August 10, 1972).

> When it came time to distribute agricultural loans, based on Tk. 200 per acre, an acute problem of memory arose. Men would come to the office and say: "Do you remember at the time of the survey when I told you that I had two acres of land? I forgot the exact amount. I actually own 20 acres." "Get out of here!" I would yell at them. It was a time of great tension (Timm 1995, pp. 151–55).

In spite of some farmers' memory failures, his August 10 letter reports: We had given agricultural loans to 63 people at north when I left. We are giving Rs. 500 loan for each 10 acres of land.

With the kind of manipulation and cheating the landowners were practicing to favor their own interests, I am surprised to come across the suggestion our new administrator, Akbar Kabir, made in mid-February, 1971. It shows an unfortunate disconnect between reality in the field and our own executives in the Dacca office:

Our primary societies have little provision for assisting large land-owning families who have suffered severely in the cyclone. It has been suggested that HELP give a grant of Rs. 25,000 in the first instance to the Bhola Central Cooperative Bank to advance loans to this group of Manpura farmers. Further grants will be conditional on field reports of such needs.

A letter from Fr. Timm to us on December 13, 1972 indicates HELP is not the only organization to face problems in the cyclone region:

I am sorry to see that you have put the $8000.00 into the OXFAM cyclone area projects, since they have just thrown in the sponge on these projects and have given them up as a bad job. With no experience or trustworthy person on their side to guide the project, they were taken for a ride. I am afraid that our HELP Governing Body members refused to profit by their experience, so I had Bread for the World send them a telegram limiting them to only one cluster village this year under threat of funds being cut off.

Independence Brings the Return of Mujib

Fighting forces an estimated 10 million, mostly Hindu Bengalis, to flee to India. By December 1971, India concludes they can no longer sustain the overwhelming population of refugees, and gives the order to invade East Pakistan in support of the East Pakistani people. The Pakistani army surrenders at Dacca and more than ninety thousand soldiers are taken prisoners of war. East Pakistan becomes the independent country of Bangladesh on December 16, 1971. Representatives of the Bangladeshi government and the Mukti Bahini were absent from the ceremony of surrender of the Pakistan Army to the Indian Army. Bangladeshis considered this ceremony insulting, and it did much to sour relations between Bangladesh and India.

At independence, Mujib was in jail in West Pakistan, where he had been taken after his arrest on March 25. He had been convicted of treason by a military court and sentenced to death. Yahya did not carry out the sentence, perhaps because of pleas made by many foreign governments. With the surrender of Pakistani forces in Dacca and the Indian proclamation of a ceasefire on the western front, Yahya relinquished power to a civilian government under Bhutto. The new government released Mujib, who flew to Dacca via London and New Delhi. On January 10, 1972, Mujib arrived in Dacca to a tumultuous welcome ("Emerging Discontent, 1966-70").

The exact number of people killed during the War of Liberation is unclear. Bangladesh says 3 million; independent researchers say it is up to five hundred thousand, the same number estimated killed by the cyclone.

Foreign aid agencies began to flood into Dacca to help rebuild the war-torn country.

Post-War Aid Effort Begins

In this communication, Fr. Timm points out how hard it is to make programs run efficiently while focusing on training local people to handle the management of them, especially without committed, energetic workers.

```
17 Jan. 1972
Some groups, particularly the Red Cross, are out
of their mind on bringing so many foreigners
into the country who don't know a blessed thing
```

about the place. RC is bringing in over 100 such idiots. In CORR we said we didn't want even Indians, except perhaps certain specialists, and then only when we couldn't get a Bengali. We won't buy anything that we can get or manufacture in the country. Perhaps in addition to my book on the politics of cattle distribution on Manpura Island I could write a book on the cultural aspects of relief in Bangladesh. It is difficult to establish the mean between efficiency and training of local people to take your place. I think the two can be combined, particularly by people like yourselves, who work 36 hours a day.

As Timm continues to inform us about HELP, his letters grow outraged about the crookedness he encounters. He paints a bleak picture of power plays on the island and manipulation of the reconstituted governing body, particularly by two administrators from CRL who were well thought of there and came to HELP with high recommendations: Feroze and Nabi. When Abed returns to Dacca after the war, in late January 1972, he sagely decides not to become embroiled in HELP politics and graft. He prefers to join the nascent development project his close friend Viquar has established in their home area of Sylhet.

08 Feb 1972
Viquar showed up with Abed at last Wednesday's meeting of the UN with the voluntary agencies. Viquar said that the Famine Relief Committee hadn't been able to do much in India but they hoped to set up a big project in Sunamganj, Sylhet District.

Abed confirms his and Viquar's plans in a letter to Jon and me on February 8, 1972:

Have met Nabi and Fr. Timm. Fr. Timm is working full time for CORR. Viquar and I decided

339

not to rejoin the board of HELP and formed BRAC
to work on the new projects. I think Nabi was
relieved to know that we did not intend to fight
for his power base.*

HELP Looks Corruption in the Face

Clearly, things are not going well on Manpura. Long-term stalwarts who have been with HELP since its inception lose their
dedicated spirit and quit in the face of the self-enriching behavior
of the two former CRL schemers who siphon off HELP funds.
Their actions mirror the corruption that has already become common practice in the Mujib regime ("Emerging Discontent, 1966-
70").

Fr. Timm informs us about the problems he faces:

25 Feb 1972
A press and info man from Bread for the World is
here and I am giving him a black picture. Fortunately, Brother Donald is back [from Manpura]
and he thinks that we should definitely call off
the building for this year. People can't agree
on a site for even one cluster village and there
are factions within the CORR personnel. T. Ali
is definitely quitting this time and Br. Donald
is ready to fire all Feroze's relatives (and I
am about ready to fire Feroze). Nabi, meanwhile,

---

* "A new organization has been set up in Dacca with the following as conven-
ers: Begum Sufia Kamal (poetess and social worker of great repute); S.R. Hussain (Coordinator of F.R.C. Calcutta); Akbar Kabir; Kazi Fazlur Rahman
(Burmah Eastern); Viquar and myself. The name of the organization is
'Bangladesh Rehabilitation Assistance Committee.' When we register as a charitable society on my return to Dacca the above will become the members of the
Governing Body.

"We have already selected three projects and a survey has been completed
in the 2 smaller ones and is continuing in the third and main project in Sunamganj Sub-division in Sylhet district. I shall be sending you details of each
within the next day or two. House building is the main worry at present. I am
going to Shillong in Assam tomorrow to see if bamboos and timber could be
imported to Bangladesh" (Abed, letter from Calcutta to Jon and Candy Rohde,
February 8, 1972).

340

is frantically politicking in his own inimitable style, trying to get us from telling anything pessimistic to the visitor. I would like to see them reduce to one camp (though Bro. [Donald] says it will make for big trouble) and lay stress on the medical program.

They were to send 5 power tillers for the *aus* [winter dry season] cultivation but have not yet procured them. CORR has recently purchased 300 within the country and many of them are already in operation. We are bringing in 50 Japanese operators and mechanics and going into power tillers in a big way in many of our [CORR] projects, since cows are not available or out of this world in price.

"People Go Bad"

Letter from Jon to Fr. Timm on July 2, 1972: "I feel rather bitter about the way HELP has gone, especially as I was instrumental in getting Feroze. I hope you are tough on them, and if need be, let the Germans know the full score. How is it that people go bad when they can do so much good?"

Fr. Timm to us on July 17, 1972:

Tomorrow, finally, is our crucial GB meeting of HELP. All the good men on the island have resigned already and a delegation from the island here now said that if Feroze sends back his henchmen they will be beat up. Nabi asked Feroze to resign but he refused to do so. Germany wants me to take the project under CORR or reorganize it, but I can see the legal squabble this would result in. The only hope as I see it is to impose strict regulations and restrictions, which I have drawn up, and when they are not carried out either to resign and fold up the project or to force the administration to resign out of incompetence.

A letter from Fr. Timm to us on April 8, 1973 indicates they have at last been able to break Nabi's control, after he had been cheating HELP for two years. Fear of becoming entangled in a legal battle slowed the effort to remove him, but when the illegal financial deals of Feroze are exposed, and Nabi is implicated, their resignations are finally secured.

Fr. Timm writes:

> I really felt sick about HELP for a while. Feroze went off twice to Bangkok and Singapore about cement and rods, staying almost 2 months, even though we had to pay a local agent the same amount as another agency which got cement more cheaply on the same shipment without ever leaving the country. I had Bread for the World demand an accounting from Feroze and he gave an evasive one after two months. Nabi is also implicated, since he went off for 14 days secretly. They played the black market somehow, though I don't know how. At least, they haven't given a bill to HELP yet and both say they are going to resign. We'll have to get in writing that they have no financial claims on HELP. A German is coming out to run things on the 10th, so I hope we can save the cyclone shelters and one village which is starting now. We broke Nabi's island clique, so they can't cheat down there anymore (our Field Coordinator rejects the second and third class bricks as they arrive. All are supposed to be first class). I just didn't have time to pursue the affairs of HELP more closely. Nabi is still trying to brazen it out in all innocence (I'm sure he wrote Feroze's defense); I'm afraid I'll push his face in some day if he keeps it up.

Timm describes Nabi's manipulation of tenders for construction:

Although many companies placed tenders for the construction on Manpura, only the Rollo Construction Company was asked to give a detailed bid. They got the contract. Mr. Falkenstorfer (Bread for the World) found out that their office is a hole in the wall, with one table and chair, so we suspected that it was a front for Nabi. Mr. F. had an independent estimate made which came out to nine lakhs lower than Rollo's. He put pressure on Rollo to lower the price and after they signed a paper promising to reduce the bill 2¼ lakhs they told Mr. F. they could have brought it down much further but that Nabi had siphoned so much of it off.

I don't feel all that bad, though, so don't get worried. I'm starting to feel like the Bengalis of Toni Hagan's contemplated book: *The Indestructible Bengali*.

The indestructible priest

CHAPTER 23
Coming Full Circle

Three years later, after the War of Liberation, Fr. Timm asked students from Dacca University to do a study of HELP's impact on Manpura. The issues with cooperatives, which Kaiser and Fr. Timm had raised in their field reports from the outset, remain unchanged, as the study indicates:

> About 80 per cent of the families had membership in these societies. To most members, cooperatives meant a mechanism of getting a loan and other material assistance. They had little knowledge and experience about the organizational structure and the problems of management (*Manpura: A Socio-Economic Survey*, p. 35).

The report goes on to note: "These societies did not evolve from the people, and they did not join these societies to work together." It confirms what HELP learned: "The people in Manpura were individualistic by nature and outlook. They were more inclined to handle their own affairs by their own efforts" (*Manpura: A Socio-Economic Survey*, p. 38). It also underscores our finding of the common man's vulnerability to vested interests and overreliance on HELP:

> Since the supervision of the cooperative societies was in the hands of HELP employees and since most of the funds came to HELP, there was a great deal of dependency among the people.
>
> Many respondents were amazed to learn that HELP might go away from Manpura. When the question was explained

to them [as to whether they would assume responsibility for decision-making], about 32 per cent of them could not answer. They were reluctant to say anything against the managers and directors.

Since Manpura has been included in the Government sponsored Integrated Rural Development Program, HELP will automatically be replaced by Government. The emphasis now should be changed from giving loans to individuals to the initiation of joint collective programs of building embankment, introducing irrigation, establishment of cooperative stores for agricultural equipment and supplies, etc. (*Manpura: A Socio-Economic Survey*, p. 39).

In making this recommendation, the investigators ignore the existence of extensive HELP-initiated public works and godowns for cooperatively owned agricultural equipment. Nor does the report attempt to tackle the basic issue of how to circumvent the stranglehold of the local power structure over the poorer elements in society. The report concluded, without giving any observational or concrete evidence, that "the cooperative system, despite its many bottlenecks, was observed to be a good institutional base for community development activities in the rural areas with distressed people in guiding the people's aspirations for cooperation, self-help, participation in community work and developing leadership and mobilizing people toward a goal"*

After several years of experimentation, BRAC discovered that cooperative approaches to delivering credit to poor people did not work unless they exclusively targeted the poorest sections of society. Success also depended on developing highly centralized control and service delivery structures.

When BRAC was not yet a twinkle in Abed's eye, HELP had centralized control and service delivery structures, but targeted

---

* During the period that HELP sought advice on cooperatives, the Comilla Academy's work was the principal model. After the war, it became apparent that the Comilla Cooperatives' central problem of fraud and weak controls "was possible not only because of individual dishonesty, but because the people were not made aware of their rights and were not in a position to voice their rights" (Wikipedia).

every person because it was government policy. This led to the cooperatives falling prey to "elite capture," making it hard to build member loyalty and create responsible leadership. As BRAC was to learn, in order to be effective, members must be from the same economic group, and ideally the organization must grow from grass roots level and be free of government influence.

A year later, Fr. Timm is still unconvinced:
I don't have much faith in the men's co-ops, but at least it is their own money they are squandering (letter to Jon and Candy Rohde July 18, 1974).

The following year, when HELP in fact does conclude its efforts on Manpura, Bertin Gomes in his final field report uses the word "non-cooperative" to describe the co-op societies.:

> The fate of the MTCCA [Manpura Thana Central Co-operative Association] is quite misty. Of course, it is not only the fault of the MTCCA but also the fault of the member societies, for the managers and directors of the primary societies are not only non-cooperative but are busy to fill up their own pockets. Let us hope that the Government will come forward to save the MTTCA from such a grave situation (Field Report, November 10, 1975).

Manpurans Remain Skeptical

After all HELP's efforts to build a hundred cluster houses and three cyclone shelters, the 1973 Dhaka University survey "indicates that the majority of the people were not convinced of their usefulness. Only 16 per cent of the respondents mentioned about the HELP built cyclone shelters."* They think that "in the

---

* "The Red Cross promoted 'killas' as a cyclone shelter. A huge heap of earth is put up in elliptical form and in a depression on top the people stayed during the storm. As I heard it, no one wanted to stay out in the storm and they put their cattle there. I heard of one instance where all the cattle drowned on top of the killa!" (Timm, email to author, October 13, 2012).

absence of access roads to them, it will be difficult, especially in the dark, to reach them. Most people said that they would stay at home as long as possible and then take shelter. The preferred means of shelter was climbing a tree. This was based on their experience of the 1970 calamity" (*Manpura: A Socio-Economic Survey*, p. 43).

Although fully aware of the tremendous loss of life in November 1970, most of them say they would protect their possessions. Weighing the chance of someone stealing their hard-won goods and chattels against the personal danger to themselves and their family, they balance the odds carefully. When a storm hits, the time lost making this difficult decision may mean that the only option left is to run for the closest palm tree.

Bertin Gomes's final report sheds more light on why Manpurans, even if they choose to flee to one of the three HELP cyclone shelters, might actually be forced to climb a palm tree instead: "The Manpura cyclone shelter has already been occupied by the Union Parishad Chairman rather forcibly and the Shakuchia cyclone shelter by the donor [of the land] himself."

December 6, 1973: The Water Rises Again

Amin's radio crackles. An urgent voice interrupts an advertisement for fertilizer: "*Warning!* Cyclonic storm approaching islands in Bay of Bengal from southwest. Winds are increasing in velocity and are currently 120 kilometers an hour. Prepare for evacuation of low-lying areas. Take your families with emergency supplies to your nearest cyclone shelter. Repeat. Dangerous storm warning in effect. High storm surge predicted."

Amin gives the news to Surendra, who lives nearby. Neither of their compounds is on the coast, so they are more protected from storm waters than many other islanders. They wonder if it is worth taking their families all the way to one of the three concrete shelters that HELP has constructed after the devastating 1970 cyclone. Surendra remembers the terrible toll that storm took, when more than half of the people on the island were killed, but says, "Let's wait to hear the next announcement. It may not be such a bad storm."

Nazir has just finished plowing his field with the cattle he obtained in the HELP-funded lottery. He often thinks what a good decision he made in coming to Manpura, even though he will never forget losing his wife and two young children in that killer storm. He feels blessed because the new wife he had arranged to have sent from Hatiya by her family, is about to deliver their third child. Abdul, his coastal neighbor, also feels a sense that life is treating him better. He has a Cinvaram house, constructed with HELP funds, and he and his wife now have a three-year-old son, who helps relieve the pain of the children they lost in the cyclone of 1970. They do not have a radio, but news travels fast on Manpura, and they hear that another bad storm is approaching. Nazir thinks, "I cannot leave my cattle. I must watch over them."

Abdul, also reluctant to leave, says to himself, "I know what happened to some of the people who went to the cyclone shelters when a storm warning was broadcast. The storm turned out not to be a bad one in spite of the warnings. Their tools and bedding were stolen, and they lost some of their livestock too. We must stay to protect our things."

Later that night, the wind begins to howl. Branches start to break and crash to the ground. Roof thatching is ripped off in gusts and hurtles through the air. Nazir grabs his wife, but she cries out that she is too heavy with child to run. He drags her to a palm tree and yells at her to climb, but she finds it impossible to move with any speed. To his horror, the water rises more rapidly than she is able to struggle up the tree. He can't leave her, swollen with child and terrified. The sea surges around their legs, threatening to pull them into its depths. She screams with her first birth pangs.

Abdul hears the rage of the cyclone coming and knows from experience that it is time to act. He shouts at his wife to grab their son and run for the nearest palm tree. He reasons that if a palm tree saved him before, it will save him again, so he heads, bent over double into the wind and pulls himself up the trunk as fast as he can. Tidal water heaves around them, rising swiftly.

The howling wind abates at last. Abdul feels as if he must be deaf because he cannot hear any sound. Stiffly he moves down the rough trunk of the palm tree, drops to the ground and looks around. Broken, tangled undergrowth, an occasional palm tree, shattered houses; everything has been destroyed or swept away by the storm. Dazed, he sees the flesh of his chest has been ripped bare, as if crows had picked at him like carrion. Is he the only person left on earth? Where is his family? His mind refuses to clear. It is still filled with the raging of the storm. Where is his wife? He had seen her clinging to the palm tree next to him, holding their son. He cannot bear the thought that they may be gone.

Surendra and Amin return from the cyclone shelter with their families after the storm dies. Surendra is distressed to learn that his chickens blew away in the heavy winds, and that his roof will need to be replaced, but he feels fortunate that everyone in his family is safe. Amin will also need to do extensive repairs to his house, but he will try to obtain a loan from his cooperative, and gives thanks that he has survived another cyclone.

A year later, in August 1974, Fr. Timm paints an image of prosperous Manpurans: "Half the numbers are cultivating the same amount of land and with rice prices tripled they are rolling in the clover (or rice)." His positive attitude remains irrepressible: "There are still problems galore (if there weren't, it wouldn't be Manpura), but I feel more 'above it all' now. . . . Projects seem most successful the farther away you are from them. Your name is still magic down here Jon; too bad you couldn't make it for this trip, since it promises to be a wonderful time."

Power Trumps Chance to Change

The power nexus of Manpura's largest landowning families quickly shifted back into its pre-cyclone pattern of manipulation and cheating. The traditional pecking order resumed once the dead were buried, food supplies regained and shelter rebuilt. Everything boiled down to power plays, at macro and micro levels: the power of the military, the power of the rich over the poor, the vulnerabilities among the poor, the power of cultural norms, the bureaucracy at every level, and the corruption of HELP's new administrators. It all meant the end of significant changes on Manpura. Although the initial good spirit and heartfelt initiative dissipated, the work begun was carried forward by the herculean efforts of Fr. Timm and the staying power of Bread for the World. Nevertheless, the effort was in place too short a time to establish any far-reaching changes in attitudes. Hearteningly, a nascent effort toward development was burgeoning in Sylhet because of Abed and Viquar's initiative; work that would encounter the same corruption and exploitative behavior inherent in rural systems, but through long-term efforts, learn ways to overcome it.

Abed in Sylhet in 1972 after liberation

EPILOGUE
Forty-two Years
After the 1970 Cyclone

Not long after dusk on January 20, 2013, five of us join the throngs boarding a small river steamer heading south down the Megna River from Dhaka (the name changed in 1982) to Manpura Island. Shepherding us through the crowds is Rosaline Costa, an intrepid human rights activist. She has worked for years with Fr. Timm, who strides alongside Jon and me, his indomitable spirit still radiant after more than sixty years in Bangladesh. Rosaline says he has long been promising her a trip to Manpura. She has taken on the task of logistics for our four-day journey. Sister Lillian, who was a volunteer with HELP for several weeks after the cyclone, is now eighty-two years old. She tells us with a light laugh that she is making a sentimental journey. As the boat swells with passengers and goods, I try to forget about reports of overloaded passenger boats capsizing in the river.

Would you like some of my *chat?*

Sadarghat

Steerage class on the *Tipu 5*

The *Tipu 5* launch leaves from the thronged Sadarghat only an hour behind schedule with a full load of 654 deck passengers and a handful of us in "cabins": tiny insect-infested cells illuminated by a swinging light bulb. A little activity with a scrub brush and some disinfectant would have made the space more agreeable. As the sun fades into the smog, and with the septic stink of the congested river in our nostrils, we dig into the chapattis, *dal* and pastries that Sister Lillian and Rosaline had packed in a cloth-wrapped tiffin-carrier. Fr. Timm, in deference to his ninety years, is given the only chair, while the four of us perch on the wooden platform that serves as a bed, curtains drawn to shield us from the eyes of curious passengers. Later we find plastic chairs to place on the upper deck next to the wheelhouse, where Jon has been practicing his faded Bengali with the skipper. We look for constellations as we chug down the inky river toward the delta with the ship's searchlight scanning the way ahead.

Jon and Candy on the captain's deck

Candy and Rosaline perched on the *Tipu*'s sleeping platform, laughing at one of Fr. Timm's jokes

Every hour or two, the *Tipu* lands with a series of loud crashes and jolts at another ghat, and yelling stevedores and jostling passengers shove in both directions at each brief stop. The bedlam makes sleep impossible. Peering into the morning fog, we pass fishing boats pulling nets even before the sun rises, and hurry to gather our things as we approach Manpura's *ghat*. Another crash landing and we disembark into the bustle of a typical crowded Bengali market. We enter the island's only car, sent for us by the Union Chairman, driving on an actual surfaced road two meters above fallow rice fields. The single concrete lane offers scant room to pass cycle rickshaws, an occasional motorcycle, and three-wheeled Tempos chugging with full loads of people, baskets piled high on the roofs. As we approach the center of the island, there are huge tanks, perhaps two hundred meters in diameter, substantial brick buildings and houses on stilts along the road. Most are constructed of concrete and have windows, and some have TV antennas. We even see a cell-phone tower. We stop in front of the Dak Bungalow, two stories high on concrete pilings, with electric wires drooping from its roof. We simply do not recognize the island!

When we left Manpura, the population was about thirteen thousand. Forty years later it supports seventy-nine thousand. The primary school where we had North Camp was swallowed by the river years ago. When Hafizullah Choudhury's house was wiped out by the river, his entire extended family shifted to Bhola, where it was reputed that the soil from their lands had been deposited. Jon is to discover on a long bike ride that the configuration we had encountered in 1970 of three separate *chars* (Manpura, Faizuddin and Sakuchia) has now been reshaped into one island as their channels filled in. Accustomed as the inhabitants are to the soil movement and erosion unique to river deltas, they simply resettle. Because of the rapid reconfiguration of the land, the need to shift homesteads can occur in only one generation. Adaptability remains a key qualification for anyone who wants to live in the delta, because of the river's powerful force. A boat-ride away, north of Manpura, a new island named Kolapari has formed out of soil eroded from old Manpura. It has twenty thousand inhabitants on fifteen thousand new acres. Another new *char* nearby, Nigam, has around twelve thousand acres of rich silt. Because families from the settled islands' large populations rapidly move onto these new islands, few migrants come from other parts of the country.

From the Bangladesh Civil Service (BCS) officer, we learn there are more than a dozen NGOs working on the island, most of them doing microcredit. None are involved with the cooperatives we had counted on to restore the economy and bring a measure of prosperity. Those had indeed collapsed. A positive development is that a total of twenty-two cyclone shelters can accommodate about twenty thousand people.

BRAC has two offices on the island, both high above the fields and capable of providing shelter to thousands of people in an emergency. Nearly all the schools are on concrete stilts, and their roofs can accommodate hundreds as well. A hospital is nearing completion. Out of the nine posts for doctors, two are filled. Half a dozen community health workers serve the island, but there is no family planning officer. The civil service officer tells us the cost of living is higher than on the mainland, because food, including eggs and vegetables, is brought in by boat. Electricity is generated for this central part of the island from six p.m. to midnight, Internet is available, though the connection is very slow, and newspapers arrive a day late.

Fishing is the primary occupation and major money earner for non-farmers. An ice plant enables the hundreds of fishermen to preserve their catch, sending huge, iced basket-loads dragged by a dozen men at a time onto the launch returning to Dhaka. Although many Hindu families have kitchen gardens, the remaining islanders do not. With no agricultural officer assigned to Manpura, there is little support for farmers, although we encounter many power tillers. We are surprised to hear that only one rice crop is cultivated. The fallow fields, so unusual in Bangladesh in this fertile *boro* season, are typical, the officer says, of a relief mentality that eschews work beyond what is absolutely essential. He emphasizes how habituated the islanders are to plentiful relief funds given after every cyclone, regardless of the extent of the damage. For example, after last October's cyclone (with no loss of life, but many collapsed houses and trees) the Red Cross donated thirty-six lakhs,* the Bangladesh government gave twenty-one lakhs and Save the Children and Muslim Aid donated foodstuffs. He thinks so much aid makes the islanders lazy. It appears the problem of relief syndrome that HELP encountered remains unchanged. We are impressed with the number of schools: thirty-seven primaries, thirteen high schools, including six *madrassas*, and three colleges, two of them for girls. We are whisked off to the nearby high school to be showered with marigold petals under banners proclaiming "Welcome Doctor Father Richard Team." Speeches are shouted through crack-

---

* One lakh equals 100,000 *takas*, or about $1,200 at the current exchange rate of 80 Tk to US$1.

ling speakers turned to painful volume. An engraved brass plaque is presented to Fr. Timm and tuberoses to each of us women before we are hurried off to the next school filled with young women, where further requests for more resources are couched in words of love and praise. Heralded as "an American expatriate, lover of Bangladesh, the founder, the dreamer, the great donor of education and many development activities of Manpura," Fr. Timm beams as he once again urges the next generation to study and work hard. The "Son of Proud Mother, Dreamer Great Man, Virtuous Great Founder and Harbinger of the Last Time" takes it all in and assures our hosts that their wish for our visit to be "excellent, successful and delightful" has already been fulfilled.

Honoring "Dreamer Great Man"

Surendra Chandra Das

Vivid Memories of HELP

In every gathering, we seek out the elderly, who recall vividly the night of the 1970 cyclone, their tragic loss of numerous family members and the difficult weeks that followed.

On our visit to Surendra Chandra Das's wooden home in a well-tended compound of the long-established Hindu settlement, the eighty-two-year-old former headmaster of the high school, and of Model School until 1989, relates:

"I lost twenty-two members of my family in the 1970 cyclone: my children, parents, sisters, brothers, my aunts and uncles. Only my wife and I were able to hold on to palm trees without being overcome by the twenty-foot surge of water. We had heard a warning of six* broadcasted, so we didn't expect the

---

* Cyclone warnings in Bengal are on a scale of one to ten, with ten being the most severe. Six is a moderate warning.

storm to be so bad. When we climbed down, there was nothing left. Our *bari* was gone, no tools, no kitchen implements, no food, rags for clothes, not even a match to start a fire. We scavenged in the mud to try to find something to eat.

"Over a week after that terrible night of the storm, I had just about given up, when out of the sky came a small airplane with a woman flying in it throwing out plastic sacks. We ran to see what they contained and found *dim* (egg), *khirai*, *muri* and *gur*. We ate and ate. We knew the plane would come back, because now they knew where we were."

When he is told that the woman who threw packets from that plane is sitting next to him, his fading eyes turn towards me and his face glows like a sunrise.

"We survived because of that food," he tells me warmly.

Moved by the sincerity of his comment, I think, "After all these years, how satisfying it is to know that those 'fast food' packets we assembled actually did the job they were meant to do."

He continues, "I feel lucky right up to now. If relief hadn't been distributed, we wouldn't exist."

Surendra is eternally grateful to Fr. Timm for protecting the Hindus against the army, and credits him for promoting harmonious relationships between the communities on the island; attitudes, we are told, that are still healthy today. Although nearly blind, he walks hand in hand with Fr. Timm wherever we go on our visit, acting as his devoted self-appointed guide and, most of all, his friend.

Al Haq Nazir Ahmed Miah

Al Haq Nazir Ahmed Miah, currently Upazila chairman, looks at us across his massive wooden desk and recalls that in 1970, when he was thirty-two years old, he was chairman of the union. "Ninety-eight percent of my ward was washed away in the storm. I did burial detail for weeks because there were so many victims. Foreign doctors treated our wounds from clinging to palm-tree bark, and we got relief supplies for more than six months. Our cows and buffaloes were replaced by HELP. I live in the HELP-built cluster village, but all the houses suffer from lack of maintenance. We were promised they would be taken care of, but no one helps us, so most of them are falling down and uninhabitable."

Abul Kashem

Abul Kashem, now sixty-eight, remembers how he rescued his wife who was stuck in the top of a palm. "When we climbed down I found a *dao* to cut open a coconut and *sego* palm heart from a fallen tree, which was all we had to eat. That's how we managed to survive until packets of cooked food were thrown out of a small low-flying plane." As he warms to his subject, his hands flutter in imitation of the motion of bundles of blankets and foodstuffs raining out of the belly of a cargo plane. "I volunteered for HELP. I know where Fr. Timm's camp was located. I remember T. Ali very well. He helped us for many years. We still use the rice-husking machine he invented. I also remember Habib being in charge of tents, although he did not give one to me." He rolls up his sleeves. "Look! These are my scars from clinging to the palm tree through the storm. The foreign doctors treated my wounds." He is delighted to learn that Jon was one of those doctors.

Purabi Bala Das with her son

Adorned in her gold jewelry, wrapped in a beautiful coral-and-turquoise paisley shawl, and proudly holding her bright-eyed young son in her arms, Purabi Bala Das, an office assistant at the Manpura Girls' Secondary School, comes forward to tell Fr. Timm the story she heard from her father, Janar Dorn Chandra Das, who died three years before.

"I had not yet been born when the cyclone hit. My father was only eighteen years old and not yet married. The police seized him when he came to one of HELP's camps on relief business, took him into custody, and told his family they had to pay 'protection' money. His family scraped together eight hundred takas, but the police demanded more. They managed to borrow another seven hundred takas. My father told me that when Fr. Timm learned about the extortion, he marched straightaway into police headquarters. He told the officer in charge he had a letter from a major general instructing everyone to help him in the relief work, and so they must release Janar immediately. They were scared that he meant Major General Tikka Khan, who was feared by everyone. We called him the 'Butcher of Bengal.' The police believed Father Timm, and released my father, who came back safely to his family."*

No wonder the speech-makers enthuse about Fr. Timm: "You will remain lively like bright star of the sky among the people."

Fortunately, while storms still buffet Manpura, there has been nothing approaching the scale of the 1970 cyclone. It is a fading memory for the few who lived through it and a part of history for most. As we drive to the ghat down avenues shaded by huge mango, jackfruit and neem trees, listening to the songs of wagtails and mynahs, we pass motorcycles and the occasional tractor; numerous tanks brimming with fish; goats, ducks and cattle in open fields; *pukka* houses on stilts and schools brimming with well-dressed kids; a crowded bazaar with medicine shops, tailors and motor repairmen; and craftsmen building a large boat. Fr. Timm tells us he would like to be buried on Manpura. I concentrate on keeping up with the pace he sets striding down the long jetty, heading for the *Tipu's* return voyage to Dhaka.

---

* Father Timm found that "almost everyone was afraid of someone higher than himself." He used it to advantage during the war, often confronting officials committing injustices with the threat of retribution from a higher authority.

The long jetty from the *Tipu* to the mudbank of Manpura

Rolling along Manpura's central highway

Pharmacy

Bathing ghat at a large tank

Here's a coin for a sweet

Hospital nearing completion

Vulnerable houses

Manpura ducks

Climbing a palm tree, this time to collect toddy

Walking to college wearing full *hijab*

Girls on the way to primary school

The path strewn with marigold petals to greet "Father
Richard Team"

BRAC office on Manpura built to withstand the storm surge of a cyclone

One of many homes raised on concrete pillars

Paved, elevated road down center of Manpura Island

Roadwork

Part of the fishing fleet

Working with nets
(note sandbagging to try to keep the shoreline from receding)

Fishing vessel with nets cast

Bringing some of the catch on board to sell

A team of men dragging a massive basket
of *hilsa* on board to be sold for a high
price in Dhaka

Heavy baskets filled with *hilsa* being offloaded in Dhaka

The Spirit of Help

What made HELP unique among field operations in the cyclone area? Believing that the tragedy was on a scale where every hand would be welcome, we moved straight into action, without wondering if we should or shouldn't because none of us were trained relief workers. It felt like a situation where common sense, an open mind and willingness were the attributes most required. Because little other relief effort was evident, we were willing to take a chance to try to help.

Being on the spot made it possible for us to move rapidly into action by seizing the moment, rather than wait for the government to get up to speed or assistance to come from outside. In such an urgent situation, it was useful that most of us were from privileged social and economic positions; we could afford to give both time and seed money to initiate a response, and we could tap the personal resources of like-minded friends and colleagues. Many people were willing to donate their time, and others were happy to have reliable people taking action—people who would make sure their contributions went directly for relief of the victims.

But there was more to it. We were youthful friends who trusted each other. Many of us were bonded in friendship even before the cyclone hit, so it felt natural to stay together in tough times, just as we had shared better times. Because we were all beginners, there was no sense of hierarchy. We recognized we were feeling our way together to solve problems, using one of our greatest strengths: flexibility. Not being soldiers or employees, we didn't have to take orders from anyone, but simply talked over plans among ourselves, with the islanders, and with people who had proven development skills, before deciding what action to take. Everyone participated, and all suggestions were valued and treated with respect. "Your idea is as good as mine" was the general sentiment. Because none of us had ever been involved in disaster relief, we had a high tolerance for learning from our inevitable mistakes, moving from naivety to strength. As can be expected in any situation, leaders rose among us; usually the ones who were most energetic, committed and organized. And the ones who chanced to dream big.

The largest part of the effort was planned, organized and motivated by women. Many of those who ran the operation from Dacca and Chittagong worked in tandem with their husbands, who initially carried out field operations. They were committed to the wellbeing of each other beyond their concern for the victims, but there was also a strong camaraderie among everyone, regardless of family connections. The warmth felt for one another seemed naturally to attract others who became willing volunteers, drawn by the positive spirit. We worked well together, often laughing at ourselves or at problems we faced; able not to take ourselves too seriously. Laughter often ricocheted around Abed's drawing room or surfaced in amusing anecdotes from the field. Humor gave us a sense of perspective and balance, and helped us leap over obstacles.

Those who volunteered were attracted to a hands-on, non-bureaucratic effort where they could make a personal contribution in a disaster of unprecedented scale. Once they became involved, they experienced the bonding of shared adversity, common in times of crisis. Preserved field notes show how well HELP volunteers related to one another, united by the strength of the cause. Remarkably, many who were attracted to working with HELP, while not part of the original intimate group of friends, signed their field messages with love because everyone felt included in the circle of caring.

Professional relief organizations send their employees wherever there is a disaster, and their families usually remain behind. They are committed to their work, but ultimately it is their job.

These professionals can be unfamiliar with and unaccustomed to the customs and challenges of the country, and have to rely on hired translators to communicate. Without local contacts, they often find it necessary to bring materials and skills from outside. We were fortunate to be locally based.

HELP's nature did change after we attracted substantial donations and became a registered voluntary organization. Although we were pleased to have funding for our ambitious plans for rehabilitation, it meant that the tenor of our work altered. With the need to pay employees, to be formalized as a charity, and to be responsible to a donor for massive sums of money, we began to move away from the informal spirit generated by our friendships and by voluntary service. In hiring outsiders as administrators, we were forced to put our trust in people we did not know intimately, sometimes to our disadvantage.

Although we did the best we could to find reliable feet to step into our shoes, when the core of HELP was evacuated or fled at the onset of war, it turned out that some of those feet belonged to corrupt and deceitful individuals, who destabilized our fledgling organization. After uncovering nearly half of the corruption on Manpura, Fr. Timm was then faced with the dishonesty of a pair of self-serving employees within HELP itself. Without his vigilance and fighting spirit, HELP would have collapsed. The other stalwarts instrumental in carrying out the ideals of HELP from April 1971 through 1975 included T. Ali from Noakhali *thana*, Victor Gomez, and Pastor Helmut Falkenstorfer of Bread for the World, who faithfully continued to fund the organization. I'm sure we all would like to think the islanders believed in the sincerity of our efforts, but we will never know the true outcome of our actions. Yet the unknowns are insignificant, because those of us who were involved carry the memory of the spirit of HELP inside us. Those of us who initiated HELP continued to be inspired by the unique experience we embraced. Becoming engaged in the desperate aftermath of that terrible storm was empowering, and helped many of us develop a sense of agency and a vision of the possible, taking our lives along roads we might not have traveled otherwise. We carry the knowledge that we responded with glad hearts in a time of great need, drawing on the unsuspected reserve of strength inside us that emerges when life puts us to the test, for it is "the compassion we impart to those who can give us nothing that is the true measure of who we are" (Anonymous).

"Dynamic Leadership"

This "charming" letter on the following page, from one of the many willing volunteers, can serve as capstone. It speaks volumes for the bonding that occurs when there is shared adversity.

F/4 Naval Avenue
Chittagong
3.12. 70

Dear DoctorJohn Rodey,

I reached Chittagong safe and sound. Thanks for
giving me the priority. The days I spent at Manpura with you
and my friends will remain memorable in my life. How proud
and honoured I was to serve the humanity under your dynamic
leadership. My eight days at Manpura has given me an opportunity
to learn how to tackle the situation speciality like this. I
can never forget you and your organisation. Had you not come
forward with your organisation in time, I am afraid the people
of Manpura would have died of starvation and disease. I, as an
humble citizen of Pakistan and a volunteer of your organisation
express my heartfelt gratitude to you and your organisation
for service to the distressed peolple. May God give you many
more years to live and serve the humanity.

I shall feel myself proud of serving under your
charming and dynamic leadership if you need my service, at any
time, to help the distressed people. Hope this will find you
in the best of health. Please convey my best regards to your
wife. With my best regards,

Sincerely yours,

(Shaukat Alley)

Address:- Shaukat Alley
F/4 Naval Avenue
Opp: Niaz Stadium
Chittagong (East Pakistan)

Raga Dhanashi
Caryapada 14, Dombipada

The river of life,
dark and deep, moves swiftly.
The two sides are muddy;
the middle is depthless.

Sailing through Autumn Fields

When monsoon rains
deluge the plains
of the broad Gangetic delta,
jali aman, deepwater rice,
rises with the floods,
lifts slender on long stalks
like tall grass on a prairie,
undulates as far as eye can see
refusing to be drowned.

Sails taut, we steer across the depths,
sweep through pliant waves of green
swaying ever to us,
ever away;
the only sound soft swish of reeds
bowing to the passage of our hull
before springing high again,
as if we'd never been there.

Cornelia Rohde

Where Are the Main
HELP Volunteers Today?

Al Sommer, MD
Dr. Sommer is Professor of Ophthalmology at the Johns Hopkins University School of Medicine and Dean Emeritus and professor of Epidemiology and International Health at the Johns Hopkins Bloomberg School of Public Health.
> Current residence: Baltimore, Maryland

Aysen Talmon
Aysen works as a freelance interior designer in Washington and Istanbul, and continues to entertain in both capitals with matchless flair.
> Current residences: Washington, D.C. and Istanbul

Cornelia (Candy) Rohde

After working independently as a curriculum developer and education-ist in Jogjakarta, Port-au-Prince and New Delhi, Candy devotes her time to writing poetry.

She spent five years in the 1990s developing Social Sciences teaching materials for BRAC's primary schools.

Current residences: Cape Town and Spanish Wells, Bahamas

Sir Fazle Hasan Abed

Abed directs BRAC, the largest NGO in the world, working in more than 69,000 villages, covering an estimated 110 million poor people in the field of income generation, health care, population control and primary education for children in Bangladesh, as well as in other parts of South Asia and Africa. Their main focus is on the empowerment of women, and helping the poor develop their capacity to manage and control their own development to achieve economic independence.

Current residence: Dhaka

George Curlin, MD

George retired from the National Institutes of Allergy and Infectious Disease, where he was deputy director. He still keeps a hand in with a vaccine project in India that is just coming to fruition.

Current residence: Annapolis, Maryland

Jon Rohde, MD

After a career in public health with the Rockefeller Foundation in Indonesia, Management Sciences for Health (MSH) in Haiti and in South Africa, and as Director of UNICEF in India, he now consults on health systems throughout Asia and Africa, and teaches at BRAC's James P. Grant School of Public Health.

Current residences: Cape Town and Spanish Wells, Bahamas

Kaiser Zaman

Kaiser was involved in humanitarian projects as the deputy or head of operations for various United Nations High Commission for Refugees (UNHCR) missions and nongovernmental organizations around the world. He writes and travels in his retirement. Kaiser worked with BRAC for two years in the late 1970s.

Current residence: Bangkok and Phuket, Thailand

Lincoln Chen, MD

Lincoln is the president of the China Medical Board. He currently serves as co-chair of the advisory committee to the François-Xavier Bagnoud Center on Health and Human Rights at Harvard University, while also serving on the board of the Social Science Research Council, the Institute of Metrics and Evaluation (University of Washington), the Public Health Foundation of India and the United Nations Fund for International Partnership. He has served as the chair of the board of BRAC USA.

Current residence: Brookline, Massachusetts

Lynn Bickley, MD

Lynn served on the faculty at the University of Rochester and Texas Tech University HSC School of Medicine, where she was professor and Associate Dean of Curriculum. She is currently the Acting Director of Women's Health Santa Fe, with a focus on primary care.

Current residence: Santa Fe, New Mexico

Martha (Marty) Chen

Marty lectures in Public Policy at the Harvard Kennedy School. Her areas of specialization are employment, poverty alleviation, informal economy and gender. She is also the international coordinator of the global research policy network, Women in Informal Employment: Globalising and Organising (WIEGO).

She worked with BRAC in the mid-1970s and currently serves on BRAC's Board of Directors.

Current residence: Brookline, Massachusetts

Margaret (Peggy) Curlin

Peggy established and served as President of the Centre for Development and Population Activities (CEPDA), working for twenty-five years with women throughout the world to better their lives and communities through family planning, maternal health, income generation and empowerment programs. Peggy passed away in 2005.

Suraiya (Putul) Hossain

After working in an architectural firm in London, Putul became a freelance interior designer in London, the Middle East and Bangladesh on both commercial and residential projects. Her current design focus is jewelry.

As a design consultant for BRAC, she was involved in the revival of Jamdani, Kantha and other product development and interior design projects.

Current residence: London

Richard Guerrant, MD

Dick's research is focused on the recognition, diagnosis, pathogenesis, impact and control of enteric infections and their consequences. He is Founding Director of the Center for Global Health at the University of Virginia School of Medicine, and is the Thomas H. Hunter Professor of International Medicine in the Division of Infectious Diseases and International Health. He is working to develop a network of Centers for Global Health at top institutions across the United States and abroad.

Current residence: Charlotte, Virginia

Father Richard W. Timm

Fr. Timm has continued to work in the fields of education, relief, development and human rights, focusing on tribal minorities and oppressed women and children. He is the founder of the Coordinating Council for Human Rights in Bangladesh (CCHRB). He also helped establish the Association of Development Agencies in Bangladesh (ADAB), a group of 130 private relief and development bodies.

Current residence: Dhaka

Runi (Sultana) Khan

Runi was a London banker before directing BIL Commerce Ltd. She is the founder and CEO of CulturePot Global, which brings together emerging and established artists to collaborate in a wide range of art forms. Productions feature artists from around the world, but with a distinct Bangladeshi flavor.

Current residence: London

Sandy Schweppe

Sandy is an artist, working in both pen-and-ink and oils. She has had solo and group exhibitions in Manchester, London, Berlin, St. Gallen (Switzerland), Osnabrück, and New Delhi. Her oil painting "Remember" was selected for the exhibition "Only Connect, The Essence of Life," a group show of fifty-four contemporary artists in New Delhi in 2002.

Current residence: Osnabrück, Germany

389

C. Stephen Baldwin

After a career with the Ford Foundation and Population Council, Steve cofounded a South Bronx charter school, and is currently chair of its board. He taught third grade there for three years, worked with a Head Start program and became a college counselor at the Automotive High School in Brooklyn on an AmeriCorps program assignment. Steve provides legal representation to UN staff members.

Current residences: New York City/ West Redding, Connecticut

T. Ali

T. Ali died within a few years of his return from Manpura, where he served for five years, and to this day is well remembered by the islanders for his dedication to their development, and particularly for his invention of a practical rice thresher.

Victor Gomez

Victor was HELP's Field Coordinator on Manpura for four years, from 1972 to 1975. He now runs a large cargo survey company in Bangladesh, and is known for his honesty (Timm, email message to author, May 2, 2012).

Viquar Choudhury

After practicing law internationally, Viquar established the Bangladesh Hospital Trust in 1997 to tackle neo-natal and maternal health challenges in inner-city Dhaka. Viquar is a founding member of BRAC.

Current residences: London, Dhaka

Walter Schweppe

Walter stayed with the Goethe Institute in various positions until his retirement in 2004, when he and Sandy moved back to his hometown. Stations along the road included Schwäbisch Hall, Germany, Dhaka, Calcutta, Trieste, Manchester, Berlin and New Delhi.

Current residence: Osnabrück, Germany

*There was youth in us then, a wild hope. It was during those long days that we were all merged into a unity, so that on another planet we shall recognize one another . . . "You also were there . . ."
That bad time blessed us and went away.*

—Isak Dinesen

About the Author

Raised in an Ohio apple orchard and educated in Massachusetts, Cornelia Rohde has lived since 1968 in Bangladesh, Indonesia, Haiti, India and South Africa. She and her husband Jon now live in Cape Town, South Africa, and in Spanish Wells in the Bahamas. They have two daughters. Cornelia's poems have appeared in various South African publications.

Glossary

achar – spicy condiment
aman – rice harvested in autumn
atta – wheat flour
aus – dry late-winter season
bari – home, family compound
bashi – bamboo flute
Baul – traditional folk singers of Bengal
bhai – brother
bharat natyam – Indian classical dance
bhitti – foundation for a building
boro – cold winter season
bustee – cluster of slum housing
chachi – aunt
Chakmas – ethnic group from Chittagong Hill Tracts
champak – frangipani
chapatti – unleavened bread
char – mud bank in a river
chashi – farmer
chat – Indian food or snack
cheera – crushed puffed rice
chingiri mach malai – shrimp curry
dekshi– large straight-sided aluminum pot
dal – lentils
dal puri – a puffed bread with lentils
dao – machete with curved end
dekki – rice pounder, husker
dhobi – washer man
dim – egg
Durga puja – Bengali Hindu festival
Eid – Muslim holy festival
fakir – mystic
gali – alley, small street

gamcha – small towel-like cloth
ghat – landing area
godown – warehouse
gulab jamun – sweet doughy balls
gur – unrefined sugar
hartal – strike
hilsa/ilish – a river fish, favorite of Bengalis
jalebis – pretzel-shaped sweet
jamdani – hand-loomed sari with traditional motifs
jhuming – slash-and-burn cultivation
jinn – spirit
kachi – sickle
khirai – a kind of cucumber
killa – raised earthen platform with a depression in the center
    (type of cyclone shelter)
kodal – short-handled hoe
kurta – long shirt with no collar
kutchery ghar – kitchen room
lakh– 100,000
mahjee – helmsman
maund – 80 pounds
mistri – skilled laborer
Mukti Bahini – Bangladeshi freedom fighters
muri – dried puffed rice
namaz – prayer
nauka – wooden boat
parishad – local elected government
petani bhai – farmer brother
pistash barfi – sweet with pistachio nuts
puja – Hindu ceremony
pukka – brick, solid
pukur – excavated pond
raga – melody in South Asian classical music
rajbari – home of the leader or raja
rashgulla – Bengali sweet made from milk

Rs. – rupee (in 1970, Rs. 5 = about $1)
rui – a large river fish
sego palm – edible palm
seer – about one kilogram
shutki mach – dried fish
sobji – vegetable
talagari – a two-wheeled wooden pushcart
tempo – three-wheeled motorcycle with passenger seats
thana – a county; also called *upazila*
tonga – horse cart
union – civil subdivision smaller than a *thana*
upazila – (Bengali), same as *thana* (British)
zamindar – landowner

References

Baldwin, Stephen C. *Shadows Over Sundials*. iUniverse, 2009.

Blood, Archer K. *The Cruel Birth of Bangladesh*. The University Press Limited, 2002.

Congressional Record, April 29, 1971. Extract from Record of the U.S. Senate containing letter dated April 17, 1971 from Dr. Jon E. Rohde, a physician evacuated from East Pakistan, to Senator William B. Saxbe.

de Borchgrave, Arnaud. "Pakistan: HELP for Manpura." *Newsweek*, January 4, 1971: 12.

"Emerging Discontent, 1966-70." Accessed September 20, 2013, http://countrystudies.us/bangladesh/16.htm.

Foreign Assistance Legislation, Fiscal Year 1972: Hearings before the Committee on Foreign Relations United States Senate: Ninety-second Congress, June 10, 11, and 14, 1971. Statement of Dr. Jon A. (sic) Rohde, U.S. Public Health Service. U.S. Government Printing Office, Washington, 1971: 232–39.

Greenhill, Basil. *Boats and Boatmen of East Pakistan*. David and Charles, Newton Abbot, UK, 1971.

Guerrant, Richard. "Brief Cholera Lab Memoir: July 1970–March 1971," *Smriti*, ed. Amal Mitra, 2012.

Gundert, Helmut. *Report on a Trip to Pakistan. (Bericht Uber Eine Reise Nach Pakistan)*. Bread for the World, December 12, 1970.

Jansen, Erik and Trygve Bolstad (photographer). *Sailing Against the Wind: Boats and Boatmen of Bangladesh*. The University Press, Ltd., Dhaka, 1992.

Kinvig, Noel. *Beyond the Cabbage Tree.* AuthorHouse, UK, 2009.

Manpura: A Socio-Economic Survey. Dacca University: Institute of Social Welfare and Research, 1973.

Morning News. December 17, 1970.

Moudud, Hasna Jasimuddin. *A Thousand Year Old Bengali Mystic Poetry.* University Press, Ltd., Dhaka, 1992.

Muhith, A. M. A., ed. American Response to the Bangladesh Liberation War. Bangladesh: University Press, 1996.

Rohde, Cornelia. *Poems Without Borders.* Tulsi House, Cape Town, 2011.

Rohde, Jon. "Women in the Bangladesh Struggle." In A. M. A. Muhith, ed., *American Response to Bangladesh Liberation War.* Bangladesh: University Press, 1996.

Schanberg, Sydney H. "After Pakistani Storm: Grief, Indifference." *New York Times,* December 30, 1970: 1–2.

Schweppe, Walter. *Sins of My Youth.* Impromptu, New Delhi, 2004.

Sommer, A., and W. H. Mosley. "East Bengal Cyclone of November, 1970: Epidemiological Approach to Disaster Assessment." *Lancet* 7759 (1972): 1029–36.

The Societies Registration Act of 1860: Memorandum of the Society and Rules and Regulations of "HELP". Associated Printers Ltd., Dacca-1, 1970.

Timm, R. W. *Forty Years in Bangladesh.* Caritas Bangladesh, 1995.

"Why Secret Trip?" *The Express,* January 29, 1971: 1–2.

Zaman, Kaiser. *Nine Lives of the Cat That Keeps Going and Going.* Unpublished manuscript, last modified September 2013.